The Political Economy of the Middle East

Series Editor

Ashraf Mishrif, Humanities Research Centre, Sultan Qaboos University, Al Khaud, Oman

This series explores the nature of Middle Eastern political regimes and their approaches to economic development. In light of the region's distinctive political, social and economic structures and the dramatic changes that took place in the wake of the Arab spring, this series puts forward a critical body of high-quality, research-based scholarship that reflects current political and economic transitions across the Middle East. It offers original research and new insights on the causes and consequences of the Arab uprisings; economic reforms and liberalization; political institutions and governance; regional and sub-regional integration arrangements; foreign trade and investment; political economy of energy, water and food security; finance and Islamic finance; and the politics of welfare, labor market and human development. Other themes of interest include the role of the private sector in economic development, economic diversification, entrepreneurship and innovation; state-business relationships; and the capacity of regimes and public institutions to lead the development process.

The book series is Scopus Indexed.

Ashraf Mishrif
Editor

Business Resilience and Market Adaptability

Pandemic Effects and Strategies for Recovery

palgrave
macmillan

Editor
Ashraf Mishrif
Humanities Research Centre
Sultan Qaboos University
Al Khoud, Oman

ISSN 2522-8854 ISSN 2522-8862 (electronic)
The Political Economy of the Middle East
ISBN 978-981-97-2961-6 ISBN 978-981-97-2962-3 (eBook)
https://doi.org/10.1007/978-981-97-2962-3

This Palgrave Macmillan imprint is published by the registered company Springer Nature Singapore Pte Ltd.
The registered company address is: 152 Beach Road, #21-01/04 Gateway East, Singapore 189721, Singapore

To my father and
the memory of my beloved mother

Acknowledgments

This book is the outcome of the papers presented at the international conference on the Impact of COVID-19 on the economy and society that took place at Sultan Qaboos University on 10–12 October 2022. Under the patronage of the Minister of Commerce, Industry and Investment Promotion, participation of senior officials from the World Trade Organization (WTO), United Nations Conference on Trade and Development (UNCTAD), and Oman Chamber of Commerce and Industry, this conference attracted over 100 scholars and researchers from 16 countries, with extensive participation from the government, the private sector, and the academic community.

The author and editor of this book would like to express his gratitude to Sultan Qaboos University for its generous financial and logistical support in organizing this conference. I am also grateful to the Oman Chamber of Commerce and Industry for their participation and continuous support to the OCCI Research Chair for Economic Studies. My thanks and appreciation go to all the authors who devoted their time and efforts to write their papers. My thanks also go to my research assistant Maryam Essa Al Maqbali for her excellent support during the preparation of this book. Without their tireless efforts, this book would not have been produced and come out in the market.

Special thanks to Palgrave Macmillan for their outstanding support during the publication of this book. My thanks also go to the three anonymous reviewers who provided rigorous comments and feedback that helped us to improve the quality of the manuscript.

The publication of this book comes at a critical junction in the global economy. So, I hope that our analysis will assist policymakers, academics, students, and other stakeholders to understand and respond appropriately to the economic effects of the pandemic for a better future.

Contents

Notes on Contributors

Fadi Abdelfattah is an associate professor and department head at the Modern College of Business and Science in Muscat, Oman. With a distinguished academic career, he has contributed extensively to indexed international journals and served on editorial and advisory boards. Dr. Abdelfattah's expertise spans consumer behavior, leadership, entrepreneurship, innovation, technology adoption, and healthcare management. He has a track record of securing multiple research grants, supervising postgraduate students, and serving as an examiner. Dr. Abdelfattah has taught a wide range of undergraduate and graduate courses and played pivotal roles in various committees and initiatives. Notably, he and his team have developed highly successful undergraduate and graduate programs, attracting a substantial student body of over 350 individuals.

Sufian Abdel-Gadir is Associate Professor of Economics at the Department of Public Law, Sultan Qaboos University. He headed the Quality Assurance and Academic Accreditation Unit (QAAA) at the College of Law from 2016 to 2021. Sufian was honored with the Best Teacher Award (2018–2019) and Best Academic Advisor (2020) at SQU College of Law and was recognized as a distinguished scholar by the Euro Journals in 2020. Dr. Sufian serves as a managing editor and sits on the editorial boards of several international journals. His research interests span sustainable development, energy economics, AI, development economics, international economics, private capital flows, institutions and growth, and political and economic freedoms. he holds a Ph.D. in Economics from AUTH, Greece, and an M.Sc. in Econometrics and Social Statistics from the University of Khartoum, Sudan.

Kawther Al Abri is an administrative professional with over 10 years experience in optimizing productivity, efficiency, and service quality in the administrative field. Excellent and highly dependable team player with a master's degree in business administration. She graduated in 2015 with a Master of Business Administration (M.B.A.) from the College of Economics and Political Sciences, SQU. She is currently serving Sultan Qaboos University as a Head of Department of university man administration. Her areas of interest are strategic Management, Leadership, Entrepreneurship, and Business Administration.

Zainab Al-Balushi is Assistant Professor in Logistics and Supply Chain Management, College of Economics and Political Science, Sultan Qaboos University. She was the head of the Quality Assurance and Academic Accreditation Unit and as Fellow in the Center of Excellence in Teaching and Learning. Zainab is a founding board member of the Oman Logistics Association, actively contributing to the formulation of Oman Logistics Strategy 2040. She is chairperson for Women in Transport and Logistics. She served as a reviewer for numerous journals including Supply Chain Management and International Journal of Physical Distribution & Logistics Management. Her research interests encompass regional supply chains, Supply Chain Uncertainty and Risk Management, 4IR and logistics, and Logistics Education.

Raya Al-Brwani is an ambitious Ph.D. candidate and instructor at A'sharqieah University, Ibra, Oman. She has strong management and communication skills with a background in research assistance. Recognized with honors for academic excellence, her research interest is in Entrepreneurship, Leadership, Management, and Marketing.

Idris Al-Hsani has a master's degree in supply chain and Operations Management from the College of Economics and Political Science at Sultan Qaboos University. He is currently serving as the Director of the Office of Undersecretary for Commerce and Industry at the Ministry of Commerce, Industry, and Investment Promotion. Idris has a distinguished professional background, having previously held the position of Director of Finance at the Public Authority for Investment Promotion and Export Development (Ithraa). His journey continued with a pivotal role as the Director of Investor Services at the same entity. Idris is also recognized for his insightful master's thesis titled "Navigating the New Normal: Unlocking Opportunities and Overcoming Challenges in the Logistics Sector Post-COVID-19: Case Studies from Oman." His academic and professional pursuits showcase a commitment to understanding and addressing the dynamic challenges in the logistics sector.

Khulood Al Abri is an administrative professional with over 9 years of experience in the administrative field. Excellent and highly dependable team player with a master's degree in library and information science. She graduated in 2019 from the College of Art, SQU. She is currently serving Sultan Qaboos University in the Coordination and Follow up department in the Vice Chancellor's office. Her area of interest is scientific research in the field of libraries, information, data, and big data. She has research papers presented at various scientific conferences.

Amira Al Kaabi is an administrative affairs researcher. Bachelor's degree of Management. She graduated in 2011 from the College of Economics and Political Sciences, SQU. She is currently serving Liwa Science and Innovation Center. Her area of interest is Leadership, Innovation, and scientific research. She aspires to reach an influential effective leadership level.

Marya Al Mamari is a learning resources specialist in the Ministry of Education. Excellent and highly dependable team player with a master's degree in library and information science. She graduated in 2019 from the College of Art, SQU. She is currently serving the Liwa Science and Innovation Center. Her areas of interest are creative Thinking, Innovation, and Information Literacy.

Wejdan Al-Subeihi is a research assistant at the Humanities Research Center, Sultan Qaboos University, Oman. She has a B.Sc. in logistics and Operation Management from Sultan Qaboos University.

Laila Al Sibani is a graphic designer at Sultan Qaboos University with 10 years of experience in designing visual identities, publications, and everything that relates to graphics. She obtained her master's degree in graphic design (innovation) from UOW Malaysia KDU University College in 2021. Laila has a very good knowledge of scientific research, which prepared her to participate in international conferences and publish her research papers in international peer-reviewed journals. In the last conference she participated in, she received the award for best scientific paper. She currently works at the Omani Studies Center at the university and looks forward to earning and giving more in her field and delving deeper into scientific research.

Jawaher Al Balushi is an experienced assistant lecturer with a demonstrated history of working in the higher education industry. Skilled in Entrepreneurship Education, she is a strong education professional with an M.Sc. focused on International Business from Coventry University. She is a Ph.D. student and researcher in entrepreneurship and entrepreneurial inclination. She is an entrepreneurship coach and trainer certified TOT by a recognized international organization. Not only that, but she has published many book chapters and papers in very important and recognized reviews.

Khalid Abed Dahleez is an associate professor and dean of the College of Business Administration at A'Sharqiyah University, Oman. Additionally, he holds the role of Director of Planning & Development. With over a decade of academic experience, Dr. Dahleez specializes in teaching M.B.A. and undergraduate courses spanning marketing to entrepreneurship. He has a robust research background, acting as a reviewer for various international journals and actively contributing to small business development and career advancement workshops. Dr. Dahleez also offers professional training in relationship marketing and project management.

Hisham Al Ghunaimi started his career in the banking sector in Oman, and worked in various multinational commercial and diplomatic organizations in finance, accounting, and HR sections. He worked as a faculty member for different higher education institutions where he taught financial and management courses and now is at A'Sharqiyah University in the college of business administration as an accounting and finance lecturer. He is certified by the International Academy of Financial Management as Master Financial Controller and Chartered Cost Controller. Furthermore, he is also a recognized quality management internal auditor and certified as an organizational Manager from the Leadership and Learning Organization Centre.

Ali Al Hatroshi is an M.B.A. graduate from A'Sharqiyah University, he is also an assessment expert in the Ministry of Education of Oman.

Hussam Al Halbusi is Assistant Professor in the Management Department at Ahmed Bin Mohammed Military College (ABMMC), Qatar. His research interests lie in Business Ethics, Information Systems, Entrepreneurship, and Innovation Technology Adoption. He has published extensively in reputable journals and actively serves on editorial boards. Committed to academic excellence, Dr. Al Halbusi continues to inspire students and contribute to advancing knowledge in his field.

Faten Hamad is currently an associate professor in the Information Studies Department, at Sultan Qaboos University, Oman, and the library and Information Science Department, University of Jordan, Jordan. She specializes in computer science and information science. She obtained her Ph.D. degree in information science from Aberystwyth University in 2013. Her research interests are big data and data analytics, smartness and AI applications, information systems implementations and management, sustainable development, organizational innovation, and organizational sustainability.

Maryam Al Maqbali works as a Dietitian at the Sultan Qaboos Comprehensive Care and Research Centre, Muscat, Oman. She previously worked as a research assistant in the Humanities Research Center. She has B.Sc. in Human Nutrition and Dietetics, from Sultan Qaboos University, Oman.

Khaled Medekhel is a professor at Echahid Hamma Lakhdar Université—El Oued, Algeria, specializing in business incubators and emerging institutions. He is one of the founders of Zedny Souf Center and was its director. Before that, he was an Assigned teaching professor at the International Islamic University Malaysia. He is now a member of the Sustainable Economic Institutions Business Management Laboratory at the Faculty of Economic Sciences at the Echahid Hamma Lakhdar Université—El Oued. He has participated in many national and international scientific forums.

Ashraf Mishrif is the founding director and research chair of the Oman Chamber of Commerce and Industry Research Chair for Economic Studies, Sultan Qaboos University, Sultanate of Oman. Prior to that he was Associate Professor at King's College London and taught at various universities including Qatar University, Ahmed bin Mohammed Military

College Qatar, Anglia Ruskin University, Cambridge, and the University of Greenwich, London, UK. He assumed several executive posts including Cultural Advisor for the Egyptian Embassy Cultural Bureau in London, Managing Director of the London-based consulting firm EU-Med International, and International Advisor and member of the Academic Board of Directors, Boston Business Management School, Singapore. Dr. Mishrif is an expert in economic development and the political economy of the Middle East, with a special focus on the Gulf region. He established and led several research clusters, and master's and doctoral programs in political economy, foreign direct investment, international trade, economic diversification, and Euro-Arab economic relations. He provides advisory services to international organizations and governments including UNCTAD (Geneva), UNIDO (Vienna), UK Trade and Investment (London), Islamic Development Bank (Saudi Arabia), and Social Fund for Development (Egypt), Chambers of Commerce, Authority of Development of SMEs, Authority of Industrial Estates, and Special Economic Zones (Oman). Dr Mishrif manages several strategic research projects and regional development programs, with a research budget of US$1.2 million and 32 research staff. He is Fellow of International Society for Development and Sustainability (Japan) and the Book Series Editor of Palgrave Macmillan Political Economy of the Middle East. He authored and edited several books, book chapters, and peer-reviewed papers, including two volumes on economic diversification (2018) and nationalization of the labor market in the GCC (2023).

Muskan Mustaqeem currently holds the position of Assistant Professor in the Department of Adult and Continuing Education and Extension at Jamia Millia Islamia, Central University, situated in New Delhi, India. She holds both an M.Phil and a Ph.D., both of which she completed from Centre for West Asian Studies at Jamia Millia Islamia. Her doctoral research is centered on the topic of Indian Labour Migration to the Gulf and Its Impact on Left-Behind Families. Furthermore, she has actively participated in various national and international conferences, where she has not only presented her research findings but has also contributed to scholarly discussions in her field. Her research portfolio encompasses a diverse range of subjects, including West Asian Politics, Labour Migration, Remittances, Families Left Behind, Diaspora Studies, Gender and Migration, as well as GCC relations.

Rasha Osman served as Assistant Professor of Political Science at the Department of Political Sciences within the College of Economics and Social Sciences. Additionally, she held the role of coordinator for the postgraduate program at the University of Juba, Sudan. With extensive teaching experience, Dr. Rasha is deeply involved in research and has published numerous papers in international peer-reviewed journals. She has Ph.D. in Political Sciences and another in Economics from AUTH, Greece, with an expected completion date in September 2024.

Behnaz Saboori is Associate Professor at Sultan Qaboos University's Department of Natural Resource Economics in Oman, and is a researcher in environmental economics, energy economics, tourism economics, food economics, climate change mitigation, and applied econometrics. Her rigorous scholarship has graced reputable peer-reviewed journals, including those indexed in SSCI and SCIE. She actively engages in the peer review process for reputable academic journals.

Ramzi Sallem is Assistant Professor in Management at A'Sharqiyah University. He is also a coach and expert in the field of entrepreneurship for more than 15 years that gave him significant experience in the development of entrepreneurial potential among the youth. His experience has been the major inspiration for his academic research. He has always been interested in studying the complexity of entrepreneurial phenomena given the cultural differences between the different regions, namely those that belong to the same nation. He is conducting continual research on how to change the inherited culture by designing different entrepreneurship training programs that aim to enhance entrepreneurial skills among the students of HE, especially in Arab countries.

Othmane Touat is Professor of Economics at Algiers 3 University in Algeria, holding a Ph.D. in Economic Analysis. With over 17 years of experience in both the banking sector and academia, Prof. Dr. Othmane Touat previously served as a banker at the Arab Bank Plc Algeria branch. His primary research focus encompasses international trade, international economics (with a specific emphasis on the Arab region), banking, and economic development. Dr. Touat plays a pivotal role as the head of a research team at Algiers 3 University, dedicated to exploring fintech and fostering digital transformation within the Algerian banking sector. His contributions extend beyond academia, as he is recognized as an author in Arab Gulf magazine, offering perspectives on economic trends.

Abdullah Al Yarubi is the head of the Information Technology Department at (AFMSS). In, (2020), he received a master of IT Administration from Middle East College. He has (15 years) of experience in the field. He is actively involved in developing the department services to meet the organization's goals. His areas of interest are Information Technology solutions, Technology Management, Strategic IT Planning, and Artificial Intelligence, Big Data, Electronic systems, and academic education.

Abbreviations

ASJP	Algerian Portal of Scientific Journals
AVE	Average Variance Extracted
COVID-19	Coronavirus Disease 2019
CR	Composite Reliability
CT	Contact Tracing
DUMV	Dummy Variable
ECT	Error Correction Term
EMR	Electronic Medical Records
FAO	Food and Agriculture Organization
FMOLS	Fully Modified Least Square
GCC	Gulf Cooperation Council
GDPPC	Real GDP Per Capita
GFSI	Global Food Security Index
HRD	Human Resource Development
ILO	International Labour Organization
IMF	International Monetary Fund
INF	Inflation Rate
MARS	Mobile Application Rating Scale
MENA	Middle East and North Africa
MoHERI	Ministry of Higher Education, Research, and Innovation
PLS	Partial Least Squares
POPG	Population Growth Rate
RT-PCR	Reverse Transcription-Polymerase Chain Reaction Test
SEM	Structural Equation Modeling
SME	Small and Medium Enterprises
UNCTAD	United Nations Conference on Trade and Development

UNICEF	United Nations International Children's Emergency Fund
WFH	Work From Home
WHO	World Health Organization
WTO	World Trade Organization

List of Figures

Chapter 9

Chapter 10

Chapter 11

Chapter 12

List of Tables

Chapter 6

Chapter 9

Chapter 10

Chapter 11

Chapter 12

CHAPTER 1

Pandemic Effects on Enterprises and Markets: An Overview

Ashraf Mishrif

1 Introduction

The COVID-19 impact of business and entrepreneurship started as early as December 2019, When China reported an outbreak of COVID-19 and March 2020, when the World Health Organization (WHO) declared the coronavirus a pandemic. This incident has had significant consequences and disruption in health, economy, education, and social life (Ciotti et al., 2020), with huge implications for the business sector at the local and international levels. The severity of the virus, which was highly contangoes and caused the death of over five million people and over 776 million infected cases, prompted governments around the world to introduce restrictions and containment measures to limit the spread of the virus and to prevent the healthcare system from being overwhelmed. These restrictions included lockdown, movement restrictions, social distancing,

A. Mishrif (✉)
Humanities Research Centre, Sultan Qaboos University, Al Khoud, Oman
e-mail: ashraf.mishrif@gmail.com

A. Mishrif (ed.), *Business Resilience and Market Adaptability*, The Political Economy of the Middle East,
https://doi.org/10.1007/978-981-97-2962-3_1

boarders' closure, and closure of factories, commercial centers and business activities that require public interactions such as local markets (Han et al., 2020).

Indeed, one cannot underestimate the human and financial loses and economic damage of the COVID-19 pandemic since the outbreak of the Spanish flu in 1917. The entire people on earth were badly affected by the pandemic that disrupted their lives, changed their patterns and lifestyle, and caused huge psychological, mental, and physical illnesses caused by the fear of infection and long period of immobility, isolation, and loneliness. The closure of businesses resulted in huge layoffs of hundreds of millions of workers globally, causing significant decline in income and deterioration in the social and economic conditions of their families. The pandemic disrupted the global markets, affecting both demand and supply and disrupting the global value chains. The lockdown and borders' closure in China and main industrialized nations delayed the supply of manufactured goods and spare parts, while preventing the export of agricultural products and raw materials from developing countries in a way that contributed to global food insecurity. The share size of public health crisis and its economic and business implications reaffirmed the concept of interdependence in the global economy.

Interestingly, the financial loses and economic damages caused by the pandemic crisis have been accompanied by unprecedented rise in innovation, creativity, and acceleration in digitalization across the business sector, with small and medium size enterprises (SMEs) leading the way. This chapter attempts to explain the resilience of enterprises to deal with the consequences of the pandemic and the extent to which markets effectively adapted to the changing circumstances and new business conditions in the post-pandemic era. More specifically the overarching focus is on the ability of enterprises to develop new business strategies to help them to survive the pandemic and remain competitive in the market, while adapting to the changing business environment and market conditions that evolved during and after the crisis. This chapter also serves as an introductory chapter for the book, where the flowing chapters provide in-depth analysis of some of the key issues discussed here.

2 The Resilience of Enterprises During the Pandemic

Academic literature and business reports indicate that SMEs play a crucial role in economic development. SMEs do not only create jobs and generate income, but they also contribute about 60% of global GDP, 40% of industrial production, and 35% of worldwide exports in developed and emerging countries. Undoubtedly, this performance of SMEs has declined during the pandemic for several reasons, not least because countries tightened their trade restrictions. The disruptions to the global supply chains have also reduced demands for goods and services, forcing many companies to downsize their operations and decrease spending and investment. This is evident in the case of China, where lockdown policy caused a severe impact of SMEs cash flow. The pandemic's restriction also affected entrepreneurs' ability of getting entrepreneurial funding. Many SMEs ended up restricting their commercial activity due to limited access to raw materials caused by supply chain disruption (Lestari et al., 2021).

Despite the pandemic's effect on SMEs performance, some SMEs performed well by absorbing the disruptive changes caused by the crisis and seizing the opportunities created by this challenge. They also showed resilience by adapting to pressure and responding to the changing conditions of the market (Fath et al., 2021). Zighan et al. (2022) also argued that many SMEs were able to stay resilience and innovate new strategies to stay productive and turn threats into opportunities. Some SMEs used digital tools such as Zoom and Google meet to achieve smooth remote working, others adopted online selling methods, and more innovative ones managed remote production processes by using automation. The resilience of firms was evident in their rapid response to the changes brought and capacity to stabilize firm's operation in the short term. Firms also showed adaptability to the challenging situation through innovation, learning, product improvement, and employee skills improvement, while strengthening their capacities to increase their chance of successfully emerging from the pandemic (Pongtanalert & Assarut, 2022). The positive mindset of company executives, competitive approach, innovative methods, flexibility, effective use of social networks, and strategic leadership traits proved essential skills in discovering new business opportunities during the pandemic. Meanwhile, companies were able to enhance their resilience through implementation, causation, transparency, collaboration, and communication with other internal and external stockholders (Pongtanalert & Assarut, 2022; Purnomo et al., 2021).

Moreover, business resilience has been achieved by companies through the surge in the use of electronic platforms during the pandemic. Most companies realized the importance of leveraging new abilities by using digital technology to change organizational strategies and operation. They considered digital technology as an important part in the firm's business innovations instead of a supporting function. They also realized that technology allows for a quick transformation of business models along with having varied capabilities that can rapidly enhance companies' growth and performance such as artificial intelligence, 5G, and 3D printing. The surge in the adoption of digital technology was rapid as any delay could lead to a bigger gap in the required changes in the business environment. As digital technology reached a maturity phase, firms were able to achieve organizational flexibility. Companies followed different methods toward digitalization, starting with accelerating digitalization, digitalizing sales function, and finding digital partner (Priyono et al., 2020) and ending with applying digital technology in all firms function to support the company's operation (Alrashed et al., 2022; World Health Organization, 2021).

Functionally, the digital transformation adoption was considered by many companies as the main mechanism to avoid short-term business collapse and to overcome the pandemic effects with resilience. Digitalization offered a broad range of value creation opportunities for business activities. For example, enterprise resource planning (ERP) and warehouse management systems were integrated by companies with business-to-customer (B2C) and business-to-business (B2B) e-commerce sites to handle orders automatically. Also, firms integrated their customer relationship management (CRM) platform with their ERP platform to support and boost sellers' productivity. Companies easily afforded most of these services because they are provided as cloud-based software, while increasingly adopting other digital technologies such as predictive analytics, the Internet of Things, smart manufacturing, robots, and blockchain. In their efforts to add value through the analysis of small and big data to improve customer service, many companies are currently creating smart versions of conventional items that gather and supply consumers with various data on for example health monitoring and fitness to offer new consumer value (Soto-Acosta, 2020).

Empirically, the huge surge of e-business and e-commerce platforms was a direct result of the pandemic that reduced consumer purchasing capacity due to lockdown, with most consumer turning away from traditional business and started making purchasing online (Dahbi & Benmoussa, 2019). The main advantages of e-commerce include cost reduction, increased sales and productivity, reduced time processing wide market reach, and high customer loyalty. E-commerce helped companies to expand their markets beyond national borders at low cost, locating suppliers, business partners, and customers across the globe more easily. This enabled some analysts to argue that the adoption of e-commerce was a key for survival business strategy during crisis (Lestari et al., 2021; Mishrif and Khan, 2023b; Priambodo et al., 2021).

Statistically, COVID-19 had a positive impact on the global e-commerce and e-business, which grew by 5% to reach 18% in 2020, over 19% in 2021, and is expected to reach 21.8% in 2024 (Touil, 2021). Global e-commerce sales increased significantly to approximately US$ 5.2 trillion in 2021, compared to US$4.2 trillion and US$3.54 trillion in 2020 and 2019, respectively. This growth enabled e-commerce companies such as Amazon and electronic mediation programs such as Google to increase their profits due to updating their communication feature with their consumers (Mdani & Seddaoui, 2022). In Germany, most companies shifted to e-business and used PayPal and other online payment methods that amounted to US$524 million sales, resulting in an increase in the use of e-commerce by 10% in 2020. According to UNCTAD, Latin America's Mercado Libre, achieved sales twice as many per day in 2020 compared to 2019 along with Africa Jumia platform, an e-commerce platform, that made an increase of 50% in transaction in the first half of 2020. Also, China's online retails share of sales increased from 19.4% in 2019 to over 24% in 2020. In the Sultanate of Oman, the Ministry of Commerce and Industry has established a department for e-commerce, with the aim of regulating and developing the industry and keeping up with advancements and contemporary techniques and systems for buying and selling through electronic channels. This indicates that the country has not only developed the legal and political structure that ensures safe and secure trading, but it also pooled together banks, companies, and consumers themselves (Alroya, 2022). In fact, this growth in e-commerce was not only attributed to the protectionist measures by consumers to avoid being infected during the pandemic (Koch et al., 2020), but it has also helped companies to survive during the crisis, to the extent that online shopping is considered as one of the fastest growing phenomenon, if not the new norm in business, in the post-pandemic era (Aryani et al., 2021).

3 Market Adaptability Through Innovation and Digitalization in Supply Chain

Although the pandemic caused huge disruption to the global markets, SMEs and corporations were able to adjust and respond to the changing circumstances brought about by the outbreak of COVID-19. As the market dynamics were rapidly changing, many companies were not only being adaptable to the external environment, but they were also internally embracing changes, promoting new ideas, and engaging in innovation. Successful companies were proactive and worked hard to develop new products, processes, and strategies that gave them a competitive advantage. While almost all companies were shocked by the unexpected reality of the pandemic, those operated in the logistics and supply chains system were better able to survive and thrive in the new environment. Meanwhile, their flexibility and adaptability enhanced creativity and innovation, enabling their employees to develop new skills, recognize, and exploit new opportunities that aroused during and after the pandemic. Thus, the logistics and supply chain sector were well equipped to develop and implement supply chain mitigation strategies, smart technologies, and innovative methods that were critical for its survival (Khan et al., 2022; Mishrif & Khan, 2023a).

Undoubtedly, technology and innovation played a crucial role in maintaining the performance of supply chain logistic sector. Mishrif and Khan (2023a) argue that the pursuit of survival forced companies to innovate and use digitization to overcome the negative effectives of the pandemic. They assessed the success and challenges faced by companies in digitization policy design, adoption, and implementation and their effects on operation, outputs, and customer base during the pandemic. They revealed a positive impact of digitization, and that the cost of technology prevented some companies from using emerging technology or implementing their digitization policy. Interestingly, they identified a shared opportunity for both supply chain companies and technology providers, where the former invest in technology infrastructure and add technology as an important component in their business models. The latter, in turn, would consider the costs of implementation and adoption issues of technology in the supply chain companies, a model that could result in technological sustainability at the time of economic crises.

Apparently, the pandemic was the main driving force of digitalization and automation in the manufacturing and supply chain sectors in the past four years. Many companies use digital supply chains to focus on the needs of the customer and enable chain members to get real-time information using emerging digital technologies such as Internet of Things, cloud computing, and big data analytics. Digital transformation was also essential in enhancing supply response time by reducing the time for access to needed information or transfer, as well as increasing supply chain visibility, connectivity, resistance, and resilience (Ngo, Nguyen, et al., 2023; Ngo, Pham, et al., 2023). In addition, digital twin utilization helped companies in achieving a smooth flow of goods and services during the pandemic, which minimized person-to-person contact and prevented the transition of the virus across borders (Batty, 2018; Unidas & Nations, 2022). The utilization of blockchain was useful in enabling companies to interact through virtual platform, effectively serving as COVID-19 containment measures and limiting human connections. Thus, blockchain technology facilitated direct supplier-customer transaction and offered a modern system for tracking assets and ensuring data accuracy. Also, blockchain provided protection for the supply chain process from cybercrime, tampering, and fraud (Muduli et al., 2022).

The experience of COVID-19 illustrated the need to adopt automation and robotics in business models in critical sectors such as manufacturing, logistics, and supply chains. While about 80% of warehouses globally had no automation process before the pandemic, most of these warehouses were under huge pressure during the pandemic to start applying automated technology that could replace the diminished workforce. As the number of staff on-site decreased, automated mobile robots, automated storage, aerial drones, and automated guided vehicles were programmed to carry out complicated tasks with almost zero human intervention. These tools proved useful in increasing efficiency and speeding up order handling and processing, while robotic automation provides a tangible return on investment, lowering the rate of returns and boosting customer satisfaction. Thus, automation helped logistics and supply chain companies to improve their efficiencies, achieve economies of scale, and flourish in the highly competitive marketplace (Karmakar, 2021; Partida, 2021). Mishrif and Khan (2023a) argued that logistics, transportation, and supply chain companies in Oman witnessed a significant improvement in operation and output due to digitalization and the use of technology in online payment (21%), online platform for business (16%), cloud services to work from home (13%), e-invoicing platform (13%), self-driving autonomous vehicles (13%), artificial intelligence based virtual assistants (7%), and sensor based tracking (8%).

4 Market Adaptability Through Innovation in the Food Sector

Food production and supply was another sector that showed resilience and innovativeness during the COVID-19 crisis. In fact, the pandemic caused a significant disruption to many activities of the livestock, fisheries, agriculture, and supply chain, negatively affecting food production, access, and food supply (Mardones et al., 2020). The pandemic also threatened and limited workers' mobility in harvesting, processing, transporting, and distributing agriculture commodities (Ingram, 2020). This worsened by boarder closure that limited migrant workers availability. As a result, the food production and supply industry has become more innovative and introduced technology to different aspects of food production and supply. More focus was placed on food production and processing automation, as well as replacing human labor with machines to minimize the risk of using labor who could be absent due to restrictions or illness.

The investment in automation in food production and processing would not only reduce the risk of disease transition and food contamination, but it could also reduce the cost of food production. The approach to the innovation in food product is to involve iterative cycles of developing the target genotype and production environment, which will use plant biotechnology with advanced genomics and gene editing as well as engineering a suitable environment that can be created inexpensively. This will allow for achieving sustainable food production regardless of pandemics and climate changes (Henry, 2020; Reardon & Swinnen, 2020). Other innovations and technologies used during the pandemic are advanced traceability systems, including the blockchain technology, modern biosecurity arrangements such as food safety culture promotion in food processing farms and facilities, biopesticides application in agriculture, and industry 4.0 technologies. Technological advancement in food technology is rapidly increasing to develop a traceable food system that is safe, more digital, and has a more secure supply chain. This industry has also begun to use different technologies such as AI, the internet of things, blockchain, and sensor technology that allow for food and commodities tracking from the farm to consumers, enhance food supply chain visibility, and reduce the time of food contamination tracking (Galanakis et al., 2021).

Moreover, the pandemic has changed the nature of the market, forcing companies to adapt to the changing environments. The most noticeable change was the sudden surge in the use of online food shopping as the lockdown limited people's movement and social interaction. Data shows that online food expenditure exceeded 50% of household food expenditure, these rates were even higher as the number of confirmed COVID-19 cases increased, and people who lived in large cities were more likely to buy food online (Gao et al., 2020). For example, online shopping in grocery has grown significantly in the Arab Gulf states. Online grocery in the Middle East and North Africa region grew by 33%. In KSA, over 50% of Saudis bought food and groceries online compared to 6% before the pandemic. In the UAE, food and grocery demand increased by 20–40% compared to 2019, which, in turn, increased the number of grocery and food online stores. According to Instashop statistics, online grocery shopping applications download increased by 70%, and daily order increased by 50% in March 2020. In Qatar, online grocery shopping increased by over 35%. All these changes are expected to be long lasting around the globe (Ben Hassen & Ei Bilali, 2022).

5 Pandemic Effects on Labor Market

The labor market was negatively affected by COVID-19, with many companies being forced to change their business strategies and shifting some of their operations to online activities. COVID-19 containment measures such as lockdown and social distance also forced many companies to layoff many of their workers, increasing job loss and unemployment rate around the globe (Blustein et al., 2020). According to the World Economic Forum (2021) the pandemic caused a loss of 114 million, a reduction in working hours that was estimated to be equivalent to 255 lost full-time jobs, and a loss in labor income worth US$ 3.7 trillion in 2020. Despite these losses, the pandemic accelerated innovation and the use of technology in the workplace by emphasizing the importance of adaptability in labor work.

On the positive side, the widespread effects of the pandemic created new conditions in the workplace that forced upon us remote work and flexible working hours. These effects also made it mandatory for companies to accelerate digital transformation, the use of telecommunication and telework to facilitate remote working in an unprecedented speed. These changes in the work patterns have given popularity to industry 4.0 concepts, approaches, and technologies as effective tools to minimize the disruption of the pandemic. One could also argue that the pandemic contributed to the creation of a new working culture and environment, where new business models and working methods were introduced, acquisition of new skills helped employees to make the most of contemporary information technology, cloud computing, internet of things, big data analytics, while changing corporate culture and behavior and altering employee expectations and roles. Employees got used to teleworking as a new pattern, where technological tools such as phones, email, online meeting were used to communicate with their coworkers and employers (Savić, 2020). These new work arrangements allowed many companies to consider hybrid working on a large scale in the post-pandemic period (Urbaniec et al., 2022).

What are the benefits of remote or hybrid work? Remote or hybrid work offers numerous benefits for employees, employers, and organizations. For employers, the main benefits include cost reduction, reduced office cost and requirements, increased staff retention, and increased employee productivity. For employees, the key benefits include saving money, increased job satisfaction, more flexibility, improved work-life balance, having family support, absence of workplace pressure, and reduced stress (Prasad, 2021; Savić, 2020). Empirical research shows that employees working remotely are happier and more productive compared to traditional workers (Blumberga & Pylinskaya, 2019). The study revealed that over 90% of remote workers were able to work more productively because they felt more comfortable and worked independently on their task. According to the study results, being under pressure to do a task can negatively affect their performance and remote work was linked to improved performance.

The above-mentioned benefits of remote working for both employers and employees were realized during the pandemic. For example, the percentage of full-time employees working remotely in Europe increased from 5.4% prior to the pandemic to more than 40% in 2020 (Grimm, 2021). According to the OECD (2021), about 47% of employees in the

UK and France worked remotely during the first lockdown in March 2020. In Australia, remote work rates were 1.5 times higher in December 2020 compared to March in the same year. Also, Japan experienced significant increase in telework rates from 10% in 2019 to 28% in May 2020a. These rates were significantly higher than in the Gulf Cooperation Council (GCC) countries, where almost 95% of governmental institutions relied on remote work in 2020. According to Al-Arabiya, the number of electronic information transmissions between government departments reached 143 million interactions in April 2020, an increase of almost 70% over the same month last year. This has given beneficiaries, including citizens, residents, and the business sector, access to more than 3600 different electronic services, while half a million government workers conduct more than 10 million minutes of meetings each day. These levels of interactions confirm that the COVID-19 pandemic has accelerated the use of technology in changing the nature of work that is expected to last in the post-pandemic period.

6 Aim and Structure of the Book

The aim of this book is to examine the resilience of the business sector during the COVID-19 pandemic and the extent to which enterprises and markets were able to adapt to the changing conditions brought about by the pandemic. The book explains how innovation, digitalization, and use of technology helped to minimize the negative effects of the pandemic on both enterprises and markets. It also aims at underlining the roles of flexibility and adaptability in mitigating the externalities caused by the outbreak of the pandemic in national and global markets. These core concepts are examined in real-time case studies, where authors conducted extensive analysis of empirical research in several economic and commercial sectors in many countries across the world. The role of entrepreneurial intention, creativity, innovation, and technology in company performance, survival, and development is illustrated. Most of the analysis focused on business sectors that are critical to economic and social development such as SMEs that is the backbone of the business sector in terms of investment and job creation, the logistics and supply chain that proved vital for providing factories, companies and manufacturing facilities with raw materials and spare parts, labor market, and the food security sector that is critical to jobs, health, human wellbeing, and social welfare.

The book is structured in thirteen chapters. It begins with an introductory chapter, where Ashraf Mishrif provides an overview on the impact of pandemic on the business and economic sectors and the extent to which enterprises and markets were able to adapt to the changing circumstances brought about by the pandemic. His analysis focuses on the core concepts of innovation, resilience, and adaptability that characterized most enterprises and markets during the pandemic. He argues that the new business characteristics that emerged and developed during the pandemic are highly likely to last in the post-pandemic period.

In Chapter 2, Khulood Al Abri, Marya Al Mamari, and Amira Al Kaabi examine the impact of COVID-19 on innovation and entrepreneurship, with specific reference to SMEs in Oman. They highlight the importance of innovation and entrepreneurship as vital sectors in establishing SMEs that play a major role in economic development in most developed economies. Their overarching focus is on the SMEs that are members in the Public Authorities of the Small and Medium Enterprises Development in Oman and how they companies were affected by the government decision and procedure to control COVID-19. While using secondary and primary data covering the period 2016–2022 to analyze the impact of the pandemic on SMEs, they identified three. They conclude that three areas of opportunities for these companies: technology support, financial and economy, and market.

In Chapter 3, Hisham Al Ghunaimi, Ramzi Sallem, Ali Al Hatroshi, and Jawaher Al Balushi investigate the impact of entrepreneurial alertness and innovativeness on SMEs' crisis management in Oman. They provide their analysis through an empirical case study of A 'Sharqiyah Governorate's entrepreneurs. A survey of 166 entrepreneurs reveals a significant relationship between the entrepreneurs' alertness and innovativeness during the pandemic. This research opens multiple horizons to delve into other topics to understand how to improve innovativeness and entrepreneurial alertness traits among entrepreneurs for better risk and crisis management, while drawing the attention of policymakers to prepare a future generation of entrepreneurs to be able to effectively respond to future crises.

In Chapter 4, Fadi Abdelfattah, Hussam Al Halbusi, Raya Al-Brwani, and Khalid Abed Dahleez evaluate opportunities in e-entrepreneurship through the role of self-perceived creativity. They argue that e-entrepreneurship is crucial for economic development, driving innovation and new business creation. The focus of this analysis is on investigating the mediating effect of self-perceived creativity on the relationship between opportunity evaluation decisions and entrepreneurship. Analysis of primary data of 305 Omani entrepreneurs using Partial Least Squares (PLS-SEM) reveal that self-perceived creativity and opportunity evaluation decisions have a significant direct impact on e-entrepreneurial intentions. Moreover, the opportunity evaluation decisions and e-entrepreneurial intentions are found to be mediated by self-perceived creativity. This chapter underscores the crucial role of creativity in shaping entrepreneurial aspirations, where the process of evaluating opportunities catalyzes enhancing e-entrepreneurial intentions.

In Chapter 5, Khaled Medekhel surveys previous studies published in the Algerian Portal of Scientific Journals ASJP between January 2020 and December 2022 to examine the impact of pandemic on e-commerce. While assessing the opportunities and challenges of e-commerce during the pandemic, he notices the multiplicity of areas in these studies on the impact of the pandemic on e-commerce, dealing with several sectors, countries, and regions. He ends by underlining the obstacles of e-commerce.

In Chapter 6, Kawther Al Abri, Laila Al Sibani, Abdullah Al Yarubi, and Faten Hamad explain the role of Tarassud Plus application in serving the government and society during the pandemic. They aim to explore the role of technology to control the spread of COVID-19 by investigating the technological services provided by the private sector in Oman. They present Emushrif Company as a case study of companies that supported the government to control COVID-19 using Tarassud mobile application. They reveal that 83.6% of the surveyed individuals expressed satisfaction with the technological services offered during the pandemic. They end by stressing the importance of society's preparedness, readiness, and willingness to engage with new technologies and electronic services provided by the government.

In Chapter 7, Touat Othmane critically examines the extensive disruptions in global supply chains and the challenges confronted the transport and logistics sectors during the pandemic. He explores the uncertainties surrounding the potential for sustainable recovery, set against the backdrop of evolving virus variants, persistent waves of infections, and heightened geopolitical complexities. The disruptions have induced substantial transformations in supply chain dynamics, consumption patterns, and demand trends, resulting in a notable surge in logistical bottlenecks, port congestion, delays, and a significant escalation in shipping rates and associated costs. These challenges serve as a catalyst for numerous opportunities within these sectors, encompassing digital transformation, climate change mitigation, environmental sustainability, and advancements in energy and food security. He concludes by stressing the necessity of formulating and implementing robust policies and strategies that steadfastly prioritize the future resilience of global supply chains, transportation networks, and logistics services.

In Chapter 8, Idris Al Hasani and Zainab Al Balushi examine the challenges and ramifications stemming from this unprecedented crisis within the logistics and supply chain sectors. They explain the disruptions precipitated by the pandemic, causing operational standstills, closures, and complicated logistical entanglements. They also investigate how adversities during and after the pandemic instigated inventive solutions, cultivating novel opportunities amid the chaos. They provide their analysis through two logistics and transportation firms in the Sultanate of Oman. The chapter also encompasses a comprehensive analysis spanning various transportation modes, including road, air, and maritime sectors, as well as interpreting the strategic responses of senior management to this unforeseen external upheaval.

In Chapter 9, Rasha Osman and Sufian Abdel-Gadir examine the effects of pandemic on food security and supply chain in the Middle East and North Africa region. They employ Johansen Cointegration tests using data collected from international reports of the World Bank and FAO covering the period 2012–2022 to identify long-term relationships among variables and fully modified least square (FMOLS) to measure their magnitude. The results stemming from the Johansen Cointegration tests unveil the existence of a long-term co-integrating relationship between variables and food security in MENA countries. FMOLS analysis underscores the adverse effect of COVID-19 on food security in these countries. The find that per capita income exhibits a positive and statistically significant correlation with the food security index. Equally, factors such as climate change, inflation rates, and agricultural land area exert a negative influence on food security within the MENA region. They underscore the imperative for MENA governments to reassess policies pertaining to food security, fostering adaptability to unforeseen crises and supply chain disruptions that may loom on the horizon.

In Chapter 10, Maryam Al Maqbali and Behnaz Saboori investigate the impact of the pandemic on food security in countries with different income levels. They surveyed 31 papers from Google Scholar and 20 papers from Scopus to present a bibliometric assessment of the effect of the pandemic on food security, food production, and supply chains. They find a strong association between the pandemic and food insecurity and that its impact can vary based on countries' income levels. In low- and middle-income countries, the pandemic impact on food security is mainly due to lockdown and movement restriction policies. In the high-income countries, the impact of the pandemic on food security is due to other factors such as stress and anxiety. They end by concluding that the pandemic and its related restrictions have adversely affected the quality of life of most people, in particular food security.

In Chapter 11, Muskan Mustaqeem assesses the impact of the pandemic on prospects of Indian workers in the GCC. She argues that the pandemic caused an economic recession, the closure of diverse businesses, restricted mobility leading to job losses, and salary reductions for expatriate workers. The gradual economic recovery raises concerns about the future employment prospects for Indian expatriates in the GCC, particularly for those in low-skilled occupations. She indicates a decline in new overseas migration from India to the GCC, influenced by factors such as the kafala system, structural adjustment policies, a slowdown in the construction sector due to oil price fluctuations, remittance taxation, and the impact of COVID-19. She also notes that many expatriates found themselves either compelled to work reduced hours or faced unemployment, resulting in diminished incomes. A sample survey of 133 expatriates from Bihar working in both public and private sectors in the GCC reveals significant disparities in the perceptions of COVID-19 management by the GCC government between low-skilled and skilled emigrants, impacting their anticipated future employment.

In Chapter 12, Ashraf Mishrif and Wejdan Al-Subeihi assess the implications of the pandemic for workforce in the Sultanate of Oman. They explain how the government and companies design new policies and regulations to manage the negative impact of COVID-19 on the employees as well as on the company's revenues. They aim to explore the changes in the workforce policies and analyze how the leave policies, incentives, working hours, health insurance, benefits, and training were affected during COVID-19. The data analysis reveals that the workforce policies were impacted by the pandemic and that there was a substantial decrease in the wage payment and reallocation of the working hours. Analysis also shows that leave was allowed unpaid, and the companies were less eager to finance training and international visits. The chapter helps policy makers to rethink crisis management strategies.

In Chapter 13, Ashraf Mishrif explains the ramifications of the pandemic on the business sector and the extent to which enterprises and markets responded to the changes brought about by the pandemic in the business environment. He argues that the pandemic experience was unprecedented in terms of pace and scope and that many enterprises could not withstand its harsh economic and financial consequences. He stresses that there are importance lessons that could be learnt from this experience and that both governments and enterprises are encouraged to prepare for the next crisis that could be even worse than the pandemic.

7 Conclusion

This chapter explained the impact of COVID-19 on enterprises and markets during the pandemic. It illustrated the negative effects of the pandemic on the business sector, with many companies being forced to close, downsize, postpone operations, lay off employees, and reduce working hours and employees' salaries to curtail financial losses. Despite these challenges, this chapter found a significant positive effect of the pandemic on enterprises and markets. Businesses did not only show resilience, innovation, and digitalization that enable them to survive and recover from the pandemic, but they also developed innovative working methods and corporate culture that brought prosperity and sustainability in the business sector. This chapter also found that a significant positive effect of the pandemic on the markets through flexibility and adaptability to the emerging changes in the global markets. Remarkable achievements were made in the logistics and supply chain sectors, the food sector, and the labor market, most of them managed not only to absorb the pandemic shock but also to utilize innovation, digitalization, and adaptability to develop effective means for recovery.

References

Alrashed, S., Min-Allah, N., Ali, I., & Mehmood, R. (2022). COVID-19 outbreak and the role of digital twin. *Multimedia Tools and Applications, 81*(19), 26857–26871.

Aryani, D. N., Nair, R. K., Hoo, D. X. Y., Hung, D. K. M., Lim, D. H. R., Chew, W. P., & Desai, A. (2021). A study on consumer behaviour: Transition from traditional shopping to online shopping during the Covid-19 pandemic. *International Journal of Applied Business and International Management (IJABIM), 6*(2), 81–95.

Batty, M. (2018). Digital twins. *Environment and Planning B: Urban Analytics and City Science, 45*(5), 817–820.

Ben Hassen, T., & El Bilali, H. (2022). Impacts of the COVID-19 pandemic on food security and food consumption: Preliminary insights from the Gulf Cooperation Council region. *Cogent Social Sciences, 8*(1), 2064608.

Blumberga, S., & Pylinskaya, T. (2019). Remote work advantages and disadvantages on the example in it organisation. In *International Conference NORDSCI*. Athens (Vol. 281).

Blustein, D. L., Duffy, R., Ferreira, J. A., Cohen-Scali, V., Cinamon, R. G., & Allan, B. A. (2020). Unemployment in the time of COVID-19: A research agenda. *Journal of Vocational Behavior, 119*, 103436.

Ciotti, M., Ciccozzi, M., Terrinoni, A., Jiang, W. C., Wang, C. B., & Bernardini, S. (2020). The COVID-19 pandemic. *Critical Reviews in Clinical Laboratory Sciences, 57*(6), 365–388.

Dahbi, S., & Benmoussa, C. (2019). What Hinders SMEs from Adopting E-commerce? A multiple case analysis. *Procedia Computer Science, 158*, 811–818.

Fath, B., Fiedler, A., Sinkovics, N., Sinkovics, R. R., & Sullivan-Taylor, B. (2021). International relationships and resilience of New Zealand SME exporters during COVID-19. *Critical Perspectives on International Business, 17*(2), 359–379.

Galanakis, C. M., Rizou, M., Aldawoud, T. M., Ucak, I., & Rowan, N. J. (2021). Innovations and technology disruptions in the food sector within the COVID-19 pandemic and post-lockdown era. *Trends in Food Science & Technology, 110*, 193–200.

Gao, X., Shi, X., Guo, H., & Liu, Y. (2020). To buy or not buy food online: The impact of the COVID-19 epidemic on the adoption of e-commerce in China. *PLoS ONE, 15*(8), e0237900.

Grimm, J. (2021). Securing the remote workforce in the new normal. *Computer Fraud & Security, 2021*(2), 8–11.

Han, E., Tan, M. M. J., Turk, E., Sridhar, D., Leung, G. M., Shibuya, K., ... & Legido-Quigley, H. (2020). Lessons learnt from easing COVID-19 restrictions: An analysis of countries and regions in Asia Pacific and Europe. *The Lancet, 396*(10261), 1525–1534.

Henry, R. (2020). Innovations in agriculture and food supply in response to the COVID-19 pandemic. *Molecular Plant, 13*(8), 1095–1097.

Ingram, J. (2020). Nutrition security is more than food security. *Nature Food, 1*(1), 2–2.
Karmakar, S (2021). Logistics automation helps businesses navigate the new normal. Maritiem gateway. https://www.maritimegateway.com/logistics-automation-helps-businesses-navigate-the-new-normal/
Khan, S. A. R., Waqas, M., Honggang, X., Ahmad, N., & Yu, Z. (2022). Adoption of innovative strategies to mitigate supply chain disruption: COVID-19 pandemic. *Operations Management Research, 15*(3–4), 1115–1133.
Koch, J., Frommeyer, B., & Schewe, G. (2020). Online shopping motives during the COVID-19 pandemic—Lessons from the crisis. *Sustainability, 12*(24), 10247.
Lestari, D., Siti, M., Wardhani, W., & Yudaruddin, R. (2021). The impact of COVID-19 pandemic on performance of small enterprises that are e-commerce adopters and non-adopters. *Problems and Perspectives in Management, 19*(3), 467.
Mardones, F. O., Rich, K. M., Boden, L. A., Moreno-Switt, A. I., Caipo, M. L., Zimin-Veselkoff, N., ... & Baltenweck, I. (2020). The COVID-19 pandemic and global food security. *Frontiers in Veterinary Science, 7*, 578508.
Mdani, H., & Seddaoui, N. (2022). The reality and contributions of E-Commerce in light of the Corona pandemic—International experiences. *Journal of Contemporary Economic Research, 5*(2), 10–13.
Mishrif, A., & Khan, A. (2023a). Examining the effects of COVID-19 on logistics and supply chain networks in Oman. *Journal of Emergency Management, 21*(7), 289–306.
Mishrif, A., & Khan, A. (2023b). Digitization policy design and implementation in the logistics and supply chain sector during the time of Covid-19. *Journal of International Logistics and Trade, 21*(3), 135–158.
Muduli, K., Raut, R., Narkhede, B. E., & Shee, H. (2022). Blockchain technology for enhancing supply chain performance and reducing the threats arising from the COVID-19 pandemic. *Sustainability, 14*(6), 3290.
Ngo, V. M., Nguyen, H. H., Pham, H. C., Nguyen, H. M., & Truong, P. V. D. (2023). Digital supply chain transformation: Effect of firm's knowledge creation capabilities under COVID-19 supply chain disruption risk. *Operations Management Research, 16*(2), 1003–1018.
Ngo, V. M., Pham, H. C., & Nguyen, H. H. (2023b). Drivers of digital supply chain transformation in SMEs and large enterprises—A case of COVID-19 disruption risk. *International Journal of Emerging Markets, 18*(6), 1355–1377.
OECD. (2021). Teleworking in the COVID-19 pandemic: Trends and prospects. https://www.oecd.org/coronavirus/policy-responses/teleworking-in-the-covid-19-pandemic-trends-and-prospects-72a416b6/

Partida, D (2021). *How commercial robotics will power the logistics industry in 2021.* Robotics tomorrow. https://www.roboticstomorrow.com/story/2021/02/how-commercial-robotics-will-power-the-logistics-industry-in-2021/16246/

Pongtanalert, K., & Assarut, N. (2022). Entrepreneur mindset, social capital and adaptive capacity for tourism SME resilience and transformation during the COVID-19 pandemic. *Sustainability, 14*(19), 12675.

Prasad, K. D. V. (2021). Remote Working Challenges and Opportunities during Covid-19 Pandemic. *Journal of Business Strategy, Finance and Management, 2*(1), 01–03.

Priambodo, I. T., Sasmoko, S., Abdinagoro, S. B., & Bandur, A. (2021). E-Commerce readiness of creative industry during the COVID-19 pandemic in Indonesia. *The Journal of Asian Finance, Economics and Business, 8*(3), 865–873.

Priyono, A., Moin, A., & Putri, V. N. A. O. (2020). Identifying digital transformation paths in the business model of SMEs during the COVID-19 pandemic. *Journal of Open Innovation: Technology, Market, and Complexity, 6*(4), 104.

Purnomo, B. R., Adiguna, R., Widodo, W., Suyatna, H., & Nusantoro, B. P. (2021). Entrepreneurial resilience during the Covid-19 pandemic: Navigating survival, continuity and growth. *Journal of Entrepreneurship in Emerging Economies, 13*(4), 497–524.

Reardon, T., & Swinnen, J. (2020). *COVID-19 and resilience innovations in food supply chains*. IFPRI book chapters, 132–136.

Savić, D. (2020). COVID-19 and work from home: Digital transformation of the workforce. *Grey Journal (TGJ), 16*(2), 101–104.

Soto-Acosta, P. (2020). COVID-19 pandemic: Shifting digital transformation to a high-speed gear. *Information Systems Management, 37*(4), 260–266.

Touil, Y. (2021). E-commerce gains in light of the corona pandemic—An overview of e-commerce in the country of Saudi Arabia during the pandemic. *Economic Researcher Review, 9*(02), 435–451.

Unidas, N., & Nations, U. (2022). *FAL Bulletin No. 393. Digitalization in ports: Application of digital twins to complex logistics*.

Urbaniec, M., Małkowska, A., & Włodarkiewicz-Klimek, H. (2022). The impact of technological developments on remote working: Insights from the polish managers' perspective. *Sustainability, 14*(1), 552.

World Economi Forum. (2021). *COVID-19 has caused a huge amount of lost working hours*. https://www.weforum.org/agenda/2021/02/covid-employment-global-job-loss/

World Health Organization. (2021). *How COVID-19 triggered the digital and e-commerce turning point*. https://unctad.org/news/how-covid-19-triggered-digital-and-e-commerce-turning-point

Zighan, S., Abualqumboz, M., Dwaikat, N., & Alkalha, Z. (2022). The role of entrepreneurial orientation in developing SMEs resilience capabilities throughout COVID-19. *The International Journal of Entrepreneurship and Innovation, 23*(4), 227–239.

PART I

The Impact of COVID-19 on Entrepreneurship

CHAPTER 2

Impact of COVID-19 on Innovation and Entrepreneurship: Small and Medium *Enterprises in Oman*

Khulood Al Abri, Marya Al Mamari, and Amira Al Kaabi

1 Introduction

Entrepreneurship is using resources and abilities to exploit opportunities and taking the adventure to implement an innovative idea (Mustafa, 2016). Innovation has been a significant element to achieve sustainability in entrepreneurship. Because it is based on problem solving which faces societies and transforms it into business (Askary, 2021).

Global pandemic of COVID-19 affected the whole world, and it caused large transformations that had not existed before. It caused many human and economic damages. Several Precaution procedures have been imposed, such as home quarantine, airport lockdown , and travel prohibition. This led to most educational institutions to be closed during the pandemic. On the other hand, the medical supplies and Food Sector

K. Al Abri (✉) · M. Al Mamari · A. Al Kaabi
Sultan Qaboos University, Seeb, Oman

A. Mishrif (ed.), *Business Resilience and Market Adaptability*, The Political Economy of the Middle East,
https://doi.org/10.1007/978-981-97-2962-3_2

demand have increased. Because people are afraid of its expiration and the Suspension of global supply operations (Barashidi, 2021).

The innovation and entrepreneurship sectors were not far from these effects, many institutions in this field have changed. The effects take two sides. On the one hand, it causes damage to economic activities and laying off employees. On the other hand, technology and digital economic activities have affected transformations positively. Also, new business opportunities have appeared to fill the gap in demand as delivery companies. In addition, online shopping has become the most popular new trend as International Statistics indicate that over the past few years (Barashidi, 2021).

The chapter aims to achieve three main objectives as follows:

Identifying the COVID-19 challenges those faced by the Small and Medium Enterprises in the Sultanate of Oman.
Identifying the COVID-19 opportunities were found at the Small and Medium Enterprises in the Sultanate of Oman.
Statistical analysis of entrepreneurship card members during the period (2016–2022).

Chapter questions

To achieve these objectives, the chapter will answer the following questions:

- What are the challenges that faced Small and Medium Enterprises in the Sultanate of Oman during COVID-19 period?
- What opportunities were found for Small and Medium Enterprises in the Sultanate of Oman during COVID-19 period?
- What is the statistical analysis of entrepreneurship card members during the period (2016–2022)?

Chapter Determinants

Place Determinants: Small and Medium Enterprises Development Authority in Oman

Subject Determinants: Identifying challenges that faced Small and Medium Enterprises in the Sultanate of Oman during COVID-19 period, opportunities were found for Small and Medium Enterprises and

Statistical analyses of entrepreneurship card members during the period (2016–2022).

Human Determinants: Administration of Small and Medium Enterprises Development Authority in North Al Batinah Region at Sultanate of Oman.

Time Determinants: COVID-19 Pandemic Period.

2 Literature Reviews

The impact of the Corona pandemic on entrepreneurship in small and medium enterprises:

The economic effects of the Corona pandemic have forced large enterprises in general and small and medium enterprises to innovate to survive. The repeated lockdown forced people to stay at home instead of running their business. Thus, their profits declined, and some enterprises have stopped working because of the low level of sales and the inability to pay the wages of their employees . However, some enterprises have tended to innovate and change working methods to survive and compensate for the loss. The study of Ismael, Sorguli, Aziz, et al. (2021) applied in Iraq indicated that the Corona pandemic has a clear impact on small and medium enterprises, the partial and full lockdown imposed by the government restricting access to markets. Therefore, it was difficult to export and import materials, which led to the stop of some businesses, and the data indicates a decrease in average productivity by 67%, Sales by 65%, jobs by 27%. SMEs make up more than 90% of existing companies worldwide, so they are called the backbone of the global economy Mirzaye, 2021. It is confirmed by the study of Al-Hajj and Othman (2022) that small and medium enterprises have a vital role in the manufacture of the country's economies, as they add value in strengthening local products and expanding their field. In the study of Al-Hajj and Othman (2022), which was applied to the Sultanate of Oman, the results indicated that most of the enterprises by 96% were affected, especially in the annual revenues. It is important to mention that most of the enterprises were small and medium enterprises which were the most affected, representing 81% of the total Omani enterprises.

2.1 Challenges and Opportunities Faced Entrepreneurs and Innovators in SMEs

The technological revolution is an important key considering the current competition. It has become one of the main indicators in the strategies of leadership and taking opportunities in the markets. Moreover, the sustainability and superiority of recent enterprises are based on the ability of their owners and employees to make the state of creativity sustainable. Digital transformation also contributes to the development of public and private enterprises, improving efficiency and reducing effort. In addition to providing investment opportunities for enterprises and the development of technologies and infrastructure (Shaban, 2021). The study reviews the opportunities that emerged during the Corona pandemic, which changed the traditional working methods for SMEs and the challenges they faced to survive the economic crisis.

On one hand, innovation in the business model of SMEs during crises is useful for recovery and growth, as these innovations, no matter how small, can be implemented quickly. Some factors such as time, financial pressures, and responsibility also play a key role in this. For instance, the experience of innovation in the restaurant that was affected during the pandemic, they changed the way of working in to delivering meals to homes, making discounts in case of ordering from the restaurant and changing the furniture of the restaurant In line with social distancing by placing them in the form of old Iranian houses. Thus, added value instead of closing the business or laying off employees. The same applies to some Iranian education institutes that changed the idea of face-to-face education to virtual classes. As a result, the institute continued its activity and did not face any decrease in the number of employees. Thus, created a culture of online education during the Coronavirus pandemic. In addition, some activities such as selling clothes were able to increase their income and volume of sales through their innovation in making content about their business in social media and offering products via the internet. Also, they conduct some competitions with various prizes on social media to gain more followers (Mirzaye, 2021). The results of the Al-Barashdi study (2021) confirmed that the Corona pandemic has accelerated the trends of entrepreneurship enterprises towards digitizing as well as increasing the number of new and innovative projects. Therefore, the existence of many opportunities for the growth of the digital entrepreneurship sector enhances business resilience. Thus, having a positive effect on economic growth. The Sultanate's stimulus policy has also been pursued through the establishment of the Entrepreneurship Award to encourage young entrepreneurs and provide incubators for digital projects. The results also indicate that Omani society is a young society. Young people in the age group 18–29 years constitute 27.6% of the total population. Fortunately, most of them have positive attitudes towards applying technology in their business. It is good to mention that 76.5% of Omani job seekers are young and can be directed to entrepreneurship.

On the other hand, the Corona pandemic has swept around the world, causing many crises. Thus, governments take some actions to limit its spread in the absence of a vaccine or effective treatment for Corona. Because of the length of time that the world has gone through since the end of 2019, this pandemic has changed the behaviors of consumers. Moreover, the pandemic contributed to the emergence of many challenges for entrepreneurs because the world has experienced changes. The Breish study (2021) classified the potential challenges of SMEs into seven challenges: (challenges related to human resources, operational processes, and the attendant disruption in operational processes). Thus, increased inventory costs and the costs of storing it, financial flows, supply chains and the associated difficulty of communicating with suppliers, health and safety, Cybersecurity, which is one of the hardest challenges. Because working from home was an opportunity for hackers, as home appliances are not as secure as work devices. The enterprises will not be able to supervise all employees and their devices.). The Gorzelany-Dziadkowiec study (2021) reported that a crisis over the Corona pandemic revealed major challenges faced by companies and supply chains in terms of working conditions and crisis preparedness. Consequently, the results indicate that services, transportation, and storage are the most affected, especially in the category of small enterprises.

Weaver (2022) and Al-Hajj and Othman (2022) study agree that financing and legal frameworks regulating economic borrowing are the most prominent challenges in the chart of small enterprises, as it showed that these enterprises did not have enough support from the government to overcome the financial crisis. Moreover, the lockdown affected workers' payments and wages, which threatened some of them to stop. Also, some enterprises changed their mechanism to sell by internet. However, some projects could not be marketed or sold electronically, so they stopped working completely.

Table 1 Sample coding

Position	*Code*
Assistant Director of Investment and Finance	A
Head of the Department of SMEs Development Authority	B
Entrepreneurship Specialist	C

3 Methodology and Data Collection Tools

The chapter followed the qualitative approach represented in semi-structured interviews, and the content analysis tool. Thus, Interviews were held with the administrators of the Small and Medium Enterprises Development Authority in North Al Batinah Region (three participants), and they included five general questions about the study's aims. These tools help to get deep to the COVID-19 challenges and opportunities in the Small and Medium Enterprises through the perspective of the authority. Moreover, we used a content analysis tool for the statistical reports of entrepreneurship card members as one of the digital transformation initiatives during Corona pandemic. It includes detailed and credible indicators about entrepreneurship card members which is available in website via the following URL: https://sme.gov.om/ar/media-center/publication/. These tools together will help to obtain accurate data and achieve more credibility of results.

Sample coding:

Table 1 shows sample coding.

4 Chapter Findings and Discussion

The purpose of this chapter is to identify the impact of COVID- 19 on innovation and entrepreneurship in SMEs Development Authority. The chapter will be divided into topics according to the study questions to recognize the opportunities of entrepreneurs and innovators in the pandemic period. Second, the challenges which have faced the entrepreneurs. Finally, the overall cumulative growth in the numbers of Entrepreneurship Card members (2016–end of 2021).

Results related to the first question about what are the opportunities of COVID-19 for the entrepreneurs in SMEs Development Authority?

The data were collected through interviews which provide a lot of valuable data about the opportunities for entrepreneurs in the Corona period. First, technology supports opportunities. Second, Financial opportunities by SMEs Development Authority. Finally, economy and market opportunities.

4.1 *First, Technology Support Opportunity*

Corona period taking the world forward in technology. As Sample A said because of closing and quarantine policy, technology has entered strongly and allowed the world to communicate without restrictions and conduct business easily, while all the ways were stopped. Thus, technology enhances entrepreneurs to launch online platforms to provide their services. What is more, technology indirectly helped entrepreneurs to market their products. Therefore, while entrepreneurs used to focus on providing products rather than concentrating on marketing as an essential tool to success in their business, technology enhances the access to customers easily. This finding is consistent with the study of (Mirzaya, 2021) which is inficiase some activities such as selling clothes were able to increase their income and volume of sales through their innovation in making content about their business in social media and offering products via the internet. Also, it has been proven by a study of (Shaban, 2021) which is referred to Digital Transformation contributes to the development of public and private enterprises by improving efficiency and reducing effort.

Sample B mentioned while, the Authority has been started up recently at that time in 2020 with essential services to support entrepreneurs in the small and medium enterprise, few of them have subscribed or are aware about the authority. Therefore, in that period when these enterprises got losses and debts, the Authority put its effort to present services online as a supporter or extender of these enterprises. Thus, entrepreneurs benefit from the services online like loan waiver and payment Postponement of the bank installment. Consequently, most enterprises have risen and recovered from the losses.

4.2 Second, Financial Opportunities by SMEs Development Authority

Sample B said, The Sultanate of Oman has realized the importance of entrepreneurship in small and medium enterprises for the economy, and the importance of promoting this economic sector in the pandemic crisis. Therefore, many government initiatives have been launched to stimulate this sector. This agreed with Al-Barashdi study (2021) which confirmed the Sultanate's stimulus policy has also been pursued through the establishment of the Entrepreneurship Award to encourage young entrepreneurs and provide incubators for digital projects. Also, the SMEs Development Authority Put its effort to enhance entrepreneurs in the Corona period.

As Sample A mentioned, the Authority provided financial support through eight ways. First, Banking facilities support. It was evident through Postponement of installment, interest/dividends, credit facilities and loan rescheduling. Second, tax facilities and exemptions like income tax reduction, income tax installment, loss departure, exemption from tourism, and municipal tax. Third, license fee exemptions. Fourth, Postponement of payment of monthly subscriptions in the Social Insurance System. Fifth, reduction licensing fees like environmental licensing fees. sixth, exemption from delay fines. Seventh, emergency funding programs like emergency loans, which are granted to those who hold an entrepreneurship card. Eighth, Postponement of payment of service dues basic (Electricity & Water) in cooperation between SMEs Development Authority, Service Regulation Authority, and General Authority for Water. Thus, entrepreneurs can continue their businesses and cover the costs and losses caused by the pandemic period.

4.3 Finally, Economy and Market Opportunities

The pandemic has created a gap in the market, which entrepreneurs can exploit as a business opportunity. As Sample (C) pointed out, the pandemic has created new markets such as e-marketing, online content creation, transportation, and delivery. Consequently, several companies were established in the field of delivery during the lockdown period. Moreover, the loss of most entrepreneurs in SMEs during the pandemic has negatively affected the economy of Oman, the reason why government seeks to support entrepreneurship sector to promote the economy.

That agreed with Mirzaye, 2021 study which mentioned SMEs make up more than 90% of existing companies worldwide, so they are called the backbone of the global economy. Thus, governments support entrepreneurs through SMEs Development Authority with a range of financial and consultant services which support entrepreneurship.

4.4 *Results Related to the Second Question About What Are the Challenges of COVID-19 for the Entrepreneurs in SMEs?*

The pandemic period was a real dilemma for the economy. As Sample (B) mentioned entrepreneurs have faced many financial and administrative challenges, so the Authority has issued an electronic link to receive complaints and suggestions from their subscribers, in order to reach solutions to the crisis.

There was a lack of demand for services and products due to the lockdown. Therefore, almost all enterprises stopped in that period due to zero revenue. Moreover, the Samples (A) and (C) pointed out, businesses such as beauty centers and private schools stopped. Consequently, several of their workforce were laid off. This is corresponded with Weaver (2022) and Al-Hajj and Othman (2022) study with confirm the lockdown affected workers' payments, wages, which threatened some of them to stop. The closure has caused the suspension of some businesses due to the delay in the arrival of expatriate workers. In addition, the delay of work because of difficulties of delivering goods or resources. In addition, shipment and transportation fees increased the cost and the liabilities of the business. This finding is consistent with the Breish study (2021) which proved the pandemic of Corona increased inventory costs and the costs of storing it, financial flows, supply chains, and the associated difficulty of communicating with suppliers.

4.5 *Results Related to the Third Question About What Is the Statistical Analysis of Entrepreneurship Card Members During the Period (2016–2022)?*

The Entrepreneurship Card issued by the SMEs Development Authority is a document that holders can obtain many facilities in various sectors from the relevant authorities. Its main objectives are to support small and medium enterprises by providing a range of privileges by some government and private entities. The study analyzed the statistics of the entrepreneurship card holders because of their effective role in supporting entrepreneurs in the period of the pandemic. The card containing a package of benefits and facilities was launched for cardholders, to promote recovery from the pandemic. The most prominent of these services is the exemption from the Omanization rate in the first of two years in the workforce authority. Also, it gives them priority in the entitlement of 10% of government tenders and purchases.

The number of SMEs with entrepreneurship card members (27,832) small and medium enterprises divided according to the classification approved by the Authority. It has Increased (10,713) Small Enterprise and medium for the year 2021 by a percentage of (62.6%). Figure 1 shows the growth in the numbers of enterprises members of entrepreneurship cards according to past years.

Muscat was the top Governorate for Entrepreneurship Card member numbers. There were (9126) enterprises with a percentage of (79.32%) of the total enterprises with an Entrepreneurship Card. While Musandam Governorate had the least number. There were about 154 enterprises of the total enterprises with an Entrepreneurship Card due to the population density of the governorate (see Fig. 2).

As can be seen in Fig. 3, the distribution of institutions with an entrepreneurship card came according to the classification of the size of the institution as it is shown in the following. Small enterprises were

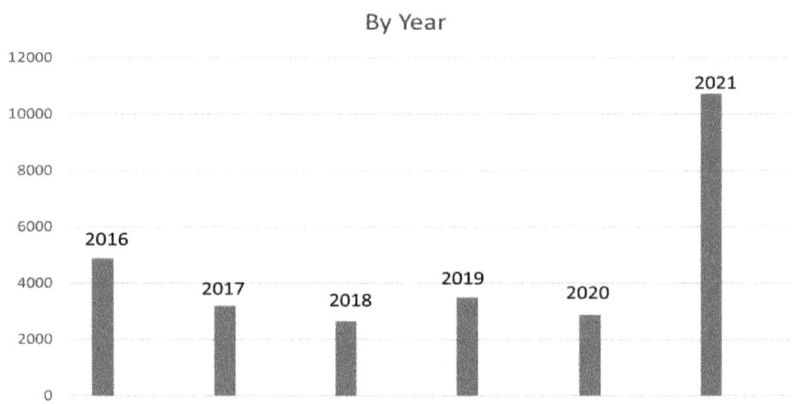

Fig. 1 Distribution of SMEs with entrepreneurship card members per year until the end of 2021

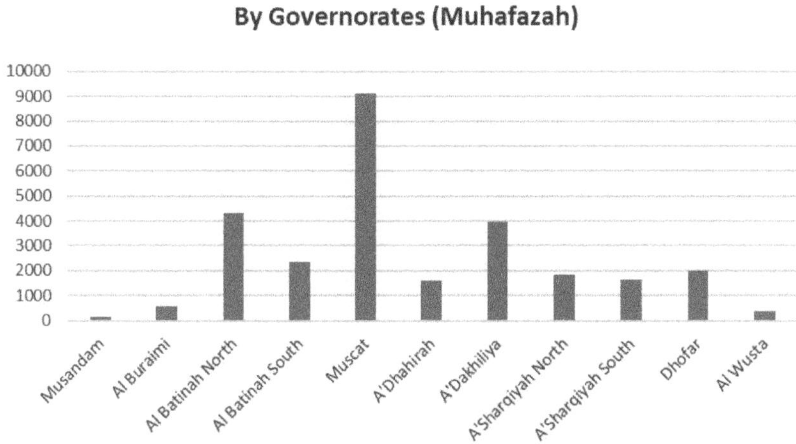

Fig. 2 Distribution of SMEs with entrepreneurship card members by Governorates

the most registered enterprises with a percentage of 27.81%, with a total number of (22,620) small enterprises. While there are only 353 medium enterprises, about 1.27%.

Based on the results in Fig. 4, the wholesale, retail trade, repair of motor vehicles and motorcycles came as the most sectors which obtain an Entrepreneurship Card. There were 8521 enterprises with a percentage of 62.30% of the total registered enterprises. On the other hand, the construction sector came in second with a total of 6519 enterprises.

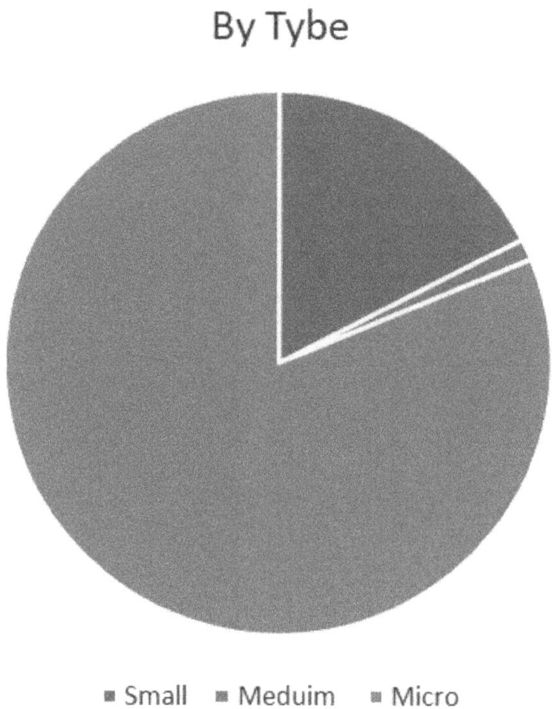

Fig. 3 Distribution of SMEs with an entrepreneurship card depending on the size of the institution

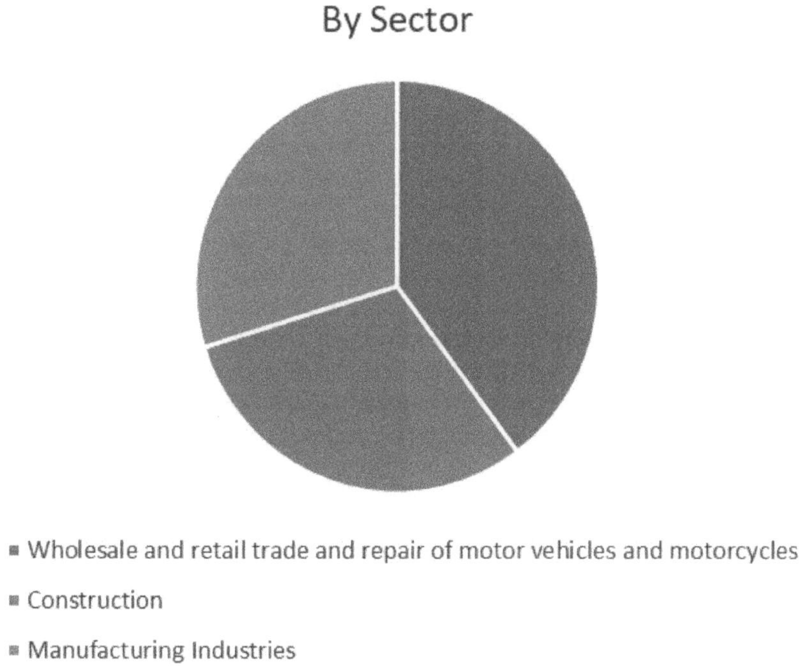

Fig. 4 Distribute SMEs with an entrepreneurship card by the commercial sector

5 Conclusion

There are three main opportunities' sections: Technology support, financial and economy, and market. Technology enhances entrepreneurs to launch online platforms for marketing and providing their services. Banking facilities support, entrepreneurship cards, and emergency loans are the most financial initiatives opportunities for entrepreneurs. There was a gap in the market where entrepreneurs can take the chance to establish their own business such as, e-marketing, content creation, and delivery. Lockdown and quarantine policy stop the operations in some businesses like beauty centers and private schools. Thus, most entrepreneurs go bankrupt. COVID-19 impact in the statistical analysis of entrepreneurship card members, it has increased (10,713) Small Enterprise and medium for the year 2021 by a percentage of (62.6%).

Entrepreneurs' confidence has increased of SMEs Development Authority in COVID-19 period.

The chapter makes some recommendations, including prepare accurate strategy planning in risk management; provide services and facilities to entrepreneurs without lockdown and quarantine policy in another pandemic; and should pay attention to the precautionary process, vaccine, and treatment rather than lockdown.

Finally, this chapter has some theoretical and practical implications. At the theoretical level, it is probably the first initiative to deal with the COVID-19 challenges and opportunities, while providing statistical analysis of entrepreneurship cardholders during the pandemic. As for practical implications, this study helps government officials and company executives in making better risk management decisions through access to information and clear strategy planning and policies.

References

Al-Hajj, A., & Othman A. S. (2022). Challenges and solutions to live with the novel coronavirus (COVID-19) pandemic from the point of view of young entrepreneurs in Oman. *Journal of Social Sciences, 50*(special issue), 113. http://search.mandumah.com/Record/1236453

Askary, M. (2021). *Innovation and entrepreneurship: Alain University: UAE.* https://www.shorturl.at/kprAR

Barashidi, H. (2021). Digital entrepreneurship in Coronavirus (COVID-19): Opportunities and challenges. *Journal of Information and Technology Studies, 2021*(1). https://doi.org/10.5339/jist.2021.5

Gorzelany-Dziadkowiec, M. (2021). COVID-19: Business innovation challenges. *Sustainability, 13*(20), 11439.

Ismael, N. B., Othman, B. J., Gardi, B., Hamza, P. A., Sorguli, S., Aziz, H. M., Ahmed, S. A., … Anwar, G. (2021). The role of training and development on organizational effectiveness. *International Journal of Engineering, Business and Management, 5*(3), 15–24.

Mirzaya, S. (2021). *COVID-19 and crisis management: The necessity of innovation in the business model of SMEs in order to recover and develop fast after the Corona crisis*. Research square. https://doi.org/10.21203/rs.3.rs-1031041/v1

Mustafa, H. (2016). *Business entrepreneurship: Chapter 1: College of business and economy: Salah Al Din University*. https://www.shorturl.at/NVW29

Shaban, G. A. (2021). The impact of digital transformation on achieving sustainable development in Corona pandemic (applied to some Arab countries). *Scientific Journal of Business and Environmental Studies, 12*(v4), 1–30. http://search.mandumah.com/Record/1224193

CHAPTER 3

The Impact of Entrepreneurial Alertness and Innovativeness on SMEs' Crisis Management in Oman: Evidence from A 'Sharqiyah Governorate's Entrepreneurs

Hisham Al Ghunaimi, Ramzi Sallem, Ali Al Hatroshi, and Jawaher Al Balushi

H. Al Ghunaimi · R. Sallem (✉) · A. Al Hatroshi
A'shaqiah University, Ibra, Oman
e-mail: ramzi.sallem@asu.edu.om

H. Al Ghunaimi
e-mail: hisham.alghunaimmi@asu.edu.om

A. Al Hatroshi
e-mail: 2009984@asu.edu.om

J. A. Balushi
University of Technology and Applied Sciences, Muscat, Oman
e-mail: Jawaher.niz@cas.edu.om

A. Mishrif (ed.), *Business Resilience and Market Adaptability*, The Political Economy of the Middle East,
https://doi.org/10.1007/978-981-97-2962-3_3

1 Introduction

Entrepreneurial performance is one of the essential strategies that drive SMEs to achieve the desires and needs of customers and achieve excellence from these institutions (Hassan & Dawood, 2020). However, the performance of entrepreneurship is a practice characterized by planning, decision-making, and actions (Al-Noori & Al-Janabi, 2022). Business performance begins with creating new organizations that may or may not be self-sufficient and never generate significant returns.

The entrepreneur is the fundamental driver of business. There is no such thing as without it, in any case, business. It recognizes holes on the lookout and afterwards changes over them into unique business open doors for entrepreneurs. Once business opportunities are identified, gather, and mobilize the necessary resources to take advantage of the opportunity (Karima & Zohra, 2021).

He oversees the creation, advertising, and faculty, as well as any remaining parts of the association (Hindi & Abdullah, 2020). The entrepreneur additionally carries out the role of supporting the distrust of dangers in the business venture.

There is a duology between entrepreneurs and SMEs. Indeed, entrepreneurs are the main generator of innovation in SMEs, while the latter provide opportunities for entrepreneurs to develop and make a name for themselves in the Business world (Alomani et al., 2021; Basuki et al., 2021; Li et al., 2020). A supportive entrepreneurial ecosystem plays a crucial role in facilitating this relationship and fostering overall financial sustainability of their SMEs (Amoa-Gyarteng & Dhliwayo, 2023).

One of the entrepreneurial features of entrepreneurs is the ability to manage risks and endurance, make quick plans, strive for achievements, innovate, and go about positively performing tasks (Saptono, 2018). Entrepreneurial characteristics are considered an incentive for entrepreneurs to address crisis management, notably during the crisis of the Corona pandemic. In such disasters these traits and skills are for SMEs and entrepreneurs to transform these threats into opportunities (Wolfe, 2016).

The literature in terms of entrepreneurship traits and skills of entrepreneurs is very generous; however, the link between Entrepreneurship and crisis management are under investigation. The current chapter would explore these two research fields to create a logical bridge between the entrepreneurs' main traits and the way they manage their crises. The

COVID-19 pandemic is a real opportunity to investigate empirically such causality link. Drawing the literature, the trait of innovativeness and Alertness was discussed briefly in crisis management. Hence, this chapter may propose a conceptual framework to test empirically, in which a causality link has been created between the innovativeness and the alertness of entrepreneurs' traits and the SMEs crisis management. The Pandemic was a good wind for the investigation, as the interviewees have lived through this disaster, like us, but from an entrepreneurial perspective.

2 Entrepreneurs, SMEs, and Crisis Management

The growing crisis and its constant accumulation of events and things that should not occur at the level of the entire or a part of the system, the effects of which impact the future of the overall system. The managerial crisis is an unsteady peculiarity that addresses an immediate and expressed danger to the endurance and progression of the association. A specific level of hazard describes it and addresses issues faced in the business which are uncertain (Thumiki et al., 2019). A defining moment in unsteady circumstances is because of unwanted outcomes that adversely influence the productivity and viability of the chief and lead to the material, moral and material misfortune that influences the standing of the position and future associations.

It is considered an adverse event which must be addressed, regardless of the preparedness degree of the business, which is indicated by loss of control, acceleration of events, lack of information, and the surprise element. It is an acute and frightening condition of intense pain and bewilderment during a hidden cycle of uncertainty, lack of knowledge, mixed causes and effects, and the resulting repercussions that enhance their acuteness and the level of unknown threat to management reputation and dignity of the CEOs collapse (Al-Manji et al., 2021). It is a situation out of control and a sudden transformation from the usual behaviors that results in an imbalance in society. Addressing this condition needs a specific and quick decision considering restricted information, surprise, and restricted time linked with the identified threat.

Determining a condition as a crisis is a very complex and challenging problem, now that the words disaster, conflict, problem, and shock formally express the concept of crisis and fail to explain the exact and actual meaning of the crisis. It involves the four main elements of threat, uncertainty, surprise, and time pressure that directly impact the business operation and outcomes.

The crisis can reinforce doubts regarding the performance of the organization and result in reduced confidence. Mainly, it negatively impacts businesses; however, sometimes, it has a positive impact, especially if the crisis is an abnormal situation experienced by the organization and threatens its existence due to unexpected internal or external circumstances and the lack of sufficient preparation to avoid damage (Al Kurdi, 2021).

Financial crisis is another concept which is based on the dimensions of cognitive factors depending on the philosophical debate regarding the definition and interpretation of financial crisis content because of various financial market cases which have faced different crises. The risk level causes and repercussions of every financial crisis and the overlap of cognitive concepts associated with interpreting the state of financial markets when the financial activity deteriorates (Al Hijji et al., 2018).

They are political, financial, and social emergencies that possess, as fractional emergencies, a restricted spatial space in structure, content, and results. The crisis was additionally grouped as far as the repeat of the crisis, whether it is occasional or non-recurrent, the profundity of the crisis, whether it is shallow or profound, and terms of the effect of the crisis (Alhazaimeh & Alzoubi, 2020).

The pandemic COVID-19 may be considered the most important crisis in this decade, as it has paralyzed the business activities all over the world, obliging the entrepreneurs, henceforth, to take on various challenges while managing this critical crisis. This pandemic has had a significant impact on the SMEs' financial sustainability (Castro et al., 2020).

Such crisis circumstances can have a significant impact on entrepreneurship, influencing the creation of new ventures as well as those that are already established (Devece et al., 2016). These effects can vary in type and intensity depending on the type of crisis, its duration, and the distinctive characteristics of the entrepreneurial ecosystem (Terstriep et al., 2023). Indeed, recent literature has demonstrated that the crises make it difficult for entrepreneurs to operate, especially when it comes to getting funding and managing economic uncertainty (Davidsson & Gordon, 2016; Kaya, 2019). It has opened doors for exploring creativity, adaptability, and the rise of resilient entrepreneurs who are always pursuing opportunities even in difficult times by prospering in demanding and changing settings. Entrepreneurs may discover new avenues for success if they are able to deftly negotiate the difficulties of the crises.

Transforming the risks of the crisis into opportunities is the mission of any entrepreneur in the era of crisis. Hence, activating their alertness and innovation skills is a must, because they are supposed to be conscious that every problem involves an opportunity that depends on how to look at it. In that sense SMEs take a different approach, based on resilience and coping with emergencies and then recognizing opportunities (Sousa, 2018).

3 Entrepreneurial Innovativeness and Crisis Management

Innovation is characterized as an approach to search for novel answers to the complexities we face, as it is found as any novel insight, thing, or conduct. Because it is subjectively unique to existing structures, it is like the age and perception of groundbreaking thoughts (Tidd & Bessant, 2018). Conflicting points of view and composing activities are essential to epitomize these thoughts and make an interpretation of them into innovations. SMEs through their entrepreneurs are setting up coordinated courses of getting and assessing ideas to decide on the one that empowers the making of added value for their entities (Leonidou et al., 2020). This proactive attitude in the period of crisis may aid in tracking down different ways of actuating and incrementing the deal volume (Johnsson, 2018). Therefore, innovation helps develop a perception of the product and helps the SMEs to be continually listening to their customers even in these critical periods.

There are many types of innovation that may support the SMEs crisis management. Technical innovations remain the most important ones in the period of crises. Entrepreneurs are invited to use their innovativeness to foster the technical execution of their SMEs by adding new products or services and by integrating novel administrative processes (Toms et al., 2020). Indeed, there are many different facets and a complex relationship between crisis management and entrepreneurial innovativeness. Indeed, during the crisis period, identifying innovative opportunities is capital for the entrepreneurs and SMEs. Crisis management is not only an effort for the entrepreneurs to be content to manage the risks, but it is one in which they are in continual pursuit of opportunities while adopting a positive perspective (Ali, 2022; Hong & Shin, 2021; Zaidan et al., 2022). For the

SMEs to struggle and ensure sustainability is very challenging, especially in hard times (Abdelfattah et al., 2023). The COVID-19 pandemic had been a real source of inspiration to these entrepreneurs, while managing their SMEs, have learned a lot about the way to manage any crisis innovatively, this period was tough but very instructive (Durugbo et al., 2022; Krishnan et al., 2022).

H1: The more the Omani entrepreneurs are innovative, the more they have succeeded in managing the COVID-19 crisis.

4 Entrepreneurial Alertness and Crisis Management

Entrepreneurial alertness is a strategic cycle that furnishes the association with data that qualifies it to confront contests considering logical establishments and guidelines more readily (Yeşilkaya & Yıldız, 2022). Hence, the association's examination of its inner and outer climate through strategic alertness is considered essential. Strategic alertness works as a system which involves sub-systems that are impacted by the flow of information received from the entire environment and with the same trade through which the organization listens and anticipates weak signals. In the environment, to find coverage of business opportunities and reduce uncertainty, this process is open to what is going on outside the organization. It revolves around the exploitation of a particular type of information called weak signals. It is information that allows anticipating an event before it is finally achieved. As Njoroge et al. (2020) opined, entrepreneurial alertness is the query on the behavior of competitors and technological innovations, monitoring these strategies, especially marketing strategies, knowing the new desires of customers, and in general, monitoring the environment. He has also opined that entrepreneurial alertness acts as a tool that helps organizations overcome challenges between other institutions by improving the organization's competitiveness. The competitiveness of the organization also affects the strategic thought through the information provided by strategic alertness, as it is a process of permanent monitoring of the environment, which inevitably leads to occupying a high place in its field of activity, as it is represented in an informational path within a prior and anticipatory work of events as well as the changes that can occur in the future. It has a continuous approach of collecting information, starting with targeting strategic alertness, then analyzing, processing, and publishing it at the appropriate time for the person to make the appropriate decisions, the competitiveness of the organization, as it also affects the strategic thought through the information provided by strategic alertness (Jalod et al., 2021).

In the future, it will have a continuous and integrated approach to collecting information, starting with identifying the topics and dealers that matter to it, or what is called targeting strategic alertness, then analyzing, processing, and publishing it at the appropriate time for the person to make the appropriate decisions (Alshaer, 2020). Strategic alertness is an informational process open to the organization's surroundings, as it begins in the stage of searching for information to understand and interpret the targeting stage, which is to identify the surrounding part that the organization wants to follow up on and determine the required information. Later, the monitoring stage includes the appointment of the entrepreneurs involved in pioneering alertness and mission identification. The information is collected and transmitted to the store's in-charge and is published later.

H2: The more the Omani entrepreneurs are innovative the more they have succeeded in managing the COVID-19 crisis.

5 Methodology and Findings

5.1 *Sample*

The study used the quantitative methodology by administrating a survey to 166 respondents through a random sampling technique. The interviewees are entrepreneurs owning small and medium-scale organizations and who are settled at A 'Sharqiyah Governorate in Oman (Table 1).

Table 1 Demographics

Entrepreneurial experience		**Gender**	
More than 15 years	49.4%	Male	84.3%
From 10 to 15 years	15.7%	Female	15.7%
5 to 10 years	24.7%	**Nationality**	
less than 5 years	7.2%	Omani/Non Omani	95.8% vs 4.2%

Most of the interviewees are Omani males who are owning their SME for more than 5 years, which is reflecting that they have a big entrepreneurial experience, allowing them to be more ready to absorb any accidental circumstances or crisis.

5.2 *Measures*

The survey instrument was composed of 40 items. The interviewees were asked to indicate to what extent they agreed or disagreed with each of the items using a 5-likert scale: (1) strongly agree, (2) agree, (3) neither agree or disagree, (4) disagree, and (5) strongly disagree. Of the 40 items, 28 were used to construct scales for innovativeness (8 items), alertness trait (10 items), and crisis Management (10 items). Items for the innovativeness scale were adapted from the Jackson Personality Inventory (Jackson 1994) like (Gürol & Atsan, 2006; Mueller & Thomas, 2001), while items used for the alertness scale were taken from (Kaish & Gilad, 1991) like (Tang et al., 2012) and finally crisis management capability was adopted from the crisis management index created by (Kim et al., 2008). Reliability test results indicate that Cronbach's alpha scores were significative for all the three scales. Alpha scores for the innovativeness scale 076, for alertness scale 0.82, and for crisis management scale 0.88. All scales were also determined to be unidimensional based on results obtained from principal component analysis.

5.3 *Data*

The Kolmogorov–Smirnov test was used to test whether the data follow a normal distribution or not, and the results are as shown in Table 2.

It is clear from the results shown in the normality test table that the probabilistic value of all fields of study was more significant than the significance level (= 0.05). α) so the data for these domains follows a normal distribution.

5.4 *Hypothesis Analysis*

Simple regression analysis is a statistical procedure that is utilized to analyze the effectiveness of an independent variable (influencing) on a dependent variable (affected), and it mainly emphasizes building a model

Table 2 Normality Test

Tests of Normality

	Kolmogorov-Smirnova			*Shapiro–Wilk*		
	Statistic	*Df*	*Sig*	*Statistic*	*df*	*Sig*
Pioneering Awakening	0.077	151	0.027	0.980	151	0.030
Innovation	0.060	151	0.200*	0.990	151	0.355
Crisis Management	0.043	151	0.200*	0.990	151	0.397

Source Author's work

which indicates the association between the dependent and the independent variable. This model assumes linearity in the parameters (and) the shape of this model $\beta_0 \beta_1$

$$y = \beta_0 + \beta_1 x + e$$

y : Dependent variable

x: the independent variable

β_0: It is the value of the dependent variable if the independent variable is zero.

β_1 : It is the value by which the dependent variable changes if the independent variable increases by one unit.

e: Random error

There is a statistically significant impact of the independent variables (innovativeness and alertness On crisis management, where the value of the morale level was 0.00 less than $0.05 = \alpha$; therefore the causality link is significant (Table 3).

6 Discussion and Future Research Implications

The study has been restricted to Oman and has collected data from the small and micro business entrepreneurs of Oman. It has incorporated information from only micro and SMEs of experienced entrepreneurs established at A 'Sharqiyah governorate which may not reflect all the Omani context. The sample should be extended to the other regions in Oman, which may contribute better to understand this pandemic impact on the Omani entrepreneurs. Furthermore, if the study had collected

Table 3 Simple Linear Regression Analysis

	Unstandardized Coefficients		*Standardized Coefficients*	*t*	*Sig*
	B	*std. Error*	*Beta*		
(Constant)	8.276	3.353		2.468	0.015
Alertness	0.334	0.087	0.299	3.843	0
Innovativeness	0.612	0.112	0.423	5.438	0

information before COVID-19, it would have given better visibility about the crisis management capability of these entrepreneurs.

The alertness and innovativeness traits among entrepreneurs are essential in achieving the SMEs strategic vigilance system to manage the crisis well. The study has several implications which can be helpful for both entrepreneurs and policymakers. The results of the research can be helpful for policymakers to develop a conducive environment which promotes these skills among entrepreneurs. Moreover, this aids in creating programs and events for entrepreneurial activities like mentorship opportunities and training. The study also focuses on discussing alertness and innovativeness not only in entrepreneurship but also in crisis management research. Indeed, it is a question of how to improve these two important traits among entrepreneurs. The entrepreneurial ecosystem may awaken those who aspire to become entrepreneurs to the importance of managing situations of crisis which may arise during their entrepreneurial trip. When facing a crisis, they must be capable of getting alert to the situation and innovative to create opportunities to ensure the sustainability of their SMEs.

7 Conclusion

Entrepreneurial traits among the entrepreneurs support the SME planning process, whether in the short, medium, or long term and contribute to the formation and crystallization of strategies and the evaluation of the resulting objectives. There was a genuinely massive impact on certain qualities of a forerunner in crisis management, and the alertness and innovativeness were of the main qualities of the entrepreneur in SMEs crisis management in Oman. Supporting the component of positive reaction to the occasion. Supporting creativity and innovation methodologies a strategic vigilance is essential for these small companies to compare their crisis management aptitude with other organization. This comparison stimulates the elements of innovation and adaptation, provides services and products with added value, and then supports its competitive position and acquires multiple competitive advantages. Problem-Solving and Decision Support: Strategic vigilance gives decision producers exact and informed gauges about contender patterns, regulations and innovation, security, political and ecological dangers, and so forth, and accordingly decreases the strength of vulnerabilities related to significant, little routine decisions and even assists with understanding Those problems and their answers.

References

Abdelfattah, F., Malik, M., Al Alawi, A. M., Sallem, R., & Ganguly, A. (2023). Towards measuring SMEs performance amid the COVID-19 outbreak: Exploring the impact of integrated supply chain drivers. *Journal of Global Operations and Strategic Sourcing, 16*(2), 520–540. https://doi.org/10.1108/JGOSS-11-2021-0094

Al Hijji, K. Z., AlHarrasi, N. H., & Alissaee, H. S. (2018). The role of information in strategic planning & decision-making: Overview on economic organizations in Oman. *Journal of Economics, Business, & Accountancy Ventura, 21*(1), 143–150.

Al Kurdi, O. F. (2021). A critical comparative review of emergency & disaster management in the Arab world. *Journal of Business & Socio-Economic Development, 1*(1), 24–46.

Alhazaimeh, A. S., & Alzoubi, M. O. (2020). The impact of human resources management practices as an entry point in crisis XE "Crisis" management. *Journal of Asian Scientific Research, 10*(4), 238–254.

Ali, H. S. (2022). The role of firm XE "Firms" innovativeness in the time of Covid-19 crisis XE "Crisis" : Evidence from Chinese manufacturing firms XE "Firms." *Asian Journal of Technology Innovation, 30*(3), 689–714. https://doi.org/10.1080/19761597.2021.1976063

Al-Manji, S., Lovett, J., & Mitchell, G. (2021). Factors affecting disaster resilience in Oman: Integrating stakeholder analysis & fuzzy cognitive mapping. *Risk, Hazards & Crisis in Public Policy, 12*(1), 29–50.

Al-Noori, A. A., & Al-Janabi, A. A. (2022). The role of marketing alertness in crisis management. *Journal of Positive School Psychology,* 7725–7732.

Alomani, A., Baptista, R., & Athreye, S. S. (2021). SBE paper AA_RB_SA. *Small Business Economics,* 1–25.

Alshaer, S. A. (2020). The effect of strategic alertness on organizational ambidexterity in Jordanian Commercial Banks. *Modern Applied Science, 14*(6), 82–89.

Amoa-Gyarteng, K., & Dhliwayo, S. (2023). Capital structure, profitability, and short-term solvency of nascent SMEs in Ghana: An empirical study. *Journal of Entrepreneurship, Management and Innovation, 19*(4), 83–110. https://doi.org/10.7341/20231943

Basuki, Widyanti R., & Rajiani, I. (2021). Entrepreneurs of millennial generations in the emerging market of Indonesia. *Entrepreneurial Business and Economics Review, 9*(2), 151–165. https://doi.org/10.15678/EBER.2021.090210

Castro, M. P., Scheede, C. R., & Zermeño, M. G. (2020, April). Entrepreneur profile & entrepreneurship skills: Expert's analysis in the Mexican entrepreneurial ecosystem. In *2020 International Conference on Technology & Entrepreneurship-Virtual (ICTE-V)* (pp. 1–6). IEEE.

Davidsson, P., & Gordon, S. R. (2016). Much Ado about nothing? The surprising persistence of nascent entrepreneurs through macroeconomic crisis. *Entrepreneurship: Theory and Practice, 40*(4), 915–941. https://doi.org/10.1111/etap.12152

Devece, C., Peris-Ortiz, M., & Rueda-Armengot, C. (2016). Entrepreneurship during economic crisis XE "Crisis": Success factors and paths to failure. *Journal of Business Research, 69*(11), 5366–5370. https://doi.org/10.1016/j.jbusres.2016.04.139

Durugbo, C. M., Almahamid, S. M., Budalamah, L. H., Al-Jayyousi, O. R., & Bendimerad, B. (2022). Preparedness for Innovation in Times of Crisis: Lessons From the Initial COVID-19 Pandemic Response. *International Journal of Innovation and Technology Management, 19*(6). https://doi.org/10.1142/S0219877021400125

Gürol, Y., & Atsan, N. (2006). Entrepreneurial characteristics amongst university students Some insights for entrepreneurship XE "Entrepreneurship" education and training in Turkey. *Education þ Training, 48*(1), 25–38.

Hassan, S. M., & Dawood, F. S. (2020). Marketing alertness & its role in ambidexterity performance applied research in Baghdad Company for soft drinks. *International Journal of Management (IJM), 11*(12).

Hindi, D., & Abdullah, H. (2020). Strategic alertness towards anticipating the future of library & information institutions: A prospective study. *International Journal of Library & Information Sciences, 7*(2), 112–138.

Hong, S., & Shin, H. D. (2021). Organizational slack and innovativeness: The moderating role of institutional transition in the Asian financial crisis XE "Crisis." *Asian Business and Management, 20*(3), 370–389. https://doi.org/10.1057/s41291-019-00094-y

Jalod, K. M., Hasan, A. J., & Hussain, A. N. (2021). Strategic alertness & its role in entrepreneurial performance: An analytical study of the views of a sample of managers in the Ur Company in Nasiriyah, Iraq. *Multicultural Education, 7*(1), 92–103.

Johnsson, M. (2018). The innovation XE "Innovation" facilitator: Characteristics & importance for innovation XE "Innovation" teams. *Journal of Innovation Management, 6*(2), 12–44.

Kaish, S., & Gilad, B. (1991). Characteristics of opportunwies search of entrepreneurs versus executives: Sources, interests, general alertness. *Journal of Business Venturing, 6*, 45–61.

Karima, K., & Zohra, D. (2021). The impact of strategic alertness on e-management in the National Railway Transport Company (SNTF). *Journal of Information Technology Management, 13*(2), 202–230.

Kaya, H. D. (2019). The impact of the 2008–2009 global crisis on entrepreneurial aspirations and attitudes. *Studies in Business and Economics, 14*(1), 111–126. https://doi.org/10.2478/sbe-2019-0009

Kim, Y., Cha, H., & Kim, J. R. (2008). Developing a crisis XE "Crisis" management index: Applications in South Korea. *Journal of Public Relations Research, 20*(3), 328–355. https://doi.org/10.1080/10627260801962962

Krishnan, C. S. N., Ganesh, L. S., & Rajendran, C. (2022). Entrepreneurial Interventions for crisis XE "Crisis" management: Lessons from the Covid-19 Pandemic's impact on entrepreneurial ventures. *International Journal of Disaster Risk Reduction, 72*. https://doi.org/10.1016/j.ijdrr.2022.102830

Leonidou, E., Christofi, M., Vrontis, D., & Thrassou, A. (2020). An integrative framework of stakeholder engagement for innovation XE "Innovation" management & entrepreneurship XE "Entrepreneurship" development. *Journal of Business Research, 119*, 245–258.

Li, C., Murad, M., Ashraf, S. F., Syed, N., & Riaz, M. (2020). Entrepreneurial nascent behaviour: The role of causation process in opportunity discovery and creation. *Entrepreneurial Business and Economics Review, 8*(4), 183–200. https://doi.org/10.15678/EBER.2020.080410

Mueller, S. L., & Thomas, A. S. (2001). Culture and entrepreneurial potential. *Journal of Business Venturing, 16*(1), 51–75. https://doi.org/10.1016/s0883-9026(99)00039-7

Njoroge, M., Anderson, W., Mossberg, L. & Mbura, O. (2020). Entrepreneurial orientation in the hospitality industry: Evidence from Tanzania. *Journal of Entrepreneurship in Emerging Economies, 12*(4), 523–543.

Saptono, A. (2018). Entrepreneurship education & its influence on financial literacy & entrepreneurship XE "Entrepreneurship" skills in college. *Journal of Entrepreneurship Education, 21*(4), 1–11.

Sousa, M. J. (2018). Entrepreneurship skills development in higher education courses for teams leaders. *Administrative Sciences, 8*(2), 18.

Tang, J., Kacmar, K. M., & Busenitz, L. (2012). Entrepreneurial alertness in the pursuit of new opportunities XE "Opportunities." *Journal of Business Venturing, 27*(1), 77–94. https://doi.org/10.1016/j.jbusvent.2010.07.001

Terstriep, J., David, A., Ruthemeier, A., & Elo, M. (2023). The role of embeddedness of migrant start-ups in local entrepreneurial ecosystems during the COVID-19 crisis. In *Journal of Comparative International Management,* 26(1).

Thumiki, V. R. R., Jovancai-Stakić, A., & Al, B. R. S. S. (2019). The resultant effect of crisis XE "Crisis" -driven HR strategies applied during the current economic crisis XE "Crisis" in Oman: An HR manager XE "Managers" 's perspective. *The European Journal of Applied Economics, 16*(1), 77–98.

Tidd, J., & Bessant, J. (2018). Innovation management challenges: From fads to fundamentals. *International Journal of Innovation Management, 22*(05), 1840007.

Toms, S., Wilson, N., & Wright, M. (2020). Innovation, intermediation, & the nature of entrepreneurship XE "Entrepreneurship" : A historical perspective. *Strategic Entrepreneurship Journal, 14*(1), 105–121.

Wolfe, A. W. (2016). Organizing collective action amid the ripple effects of change: Narratives of crisis XE "Crisis", disaster, and opportunity. *Journal of Applied Communication Research, 44*(1), 1–21. https://doi.org/10.1080/00909882.2015.1116704

Yeşilkaya, M., & Yıldız, T. (2022). Optimistic expectations & proactivity: Can they be the key to successful strategies in entrepreneurship? *Journal of Industrial Integration & Management, 7*(1), 113–132.

Zaidan, A. S., Khaw, K. W., & Alnoor, A. (2022). The influence of crisis management, risk-taking, and innovation in sustainability practices: Empirical evidence From Iraq. *Interdisciplinary Journal of Information, Knowledge, and Management, 17*, 413–442. https://doi.org/10.28945/5019

CHAPTER 4

Evaluating Opportunities in E-Entrepreneurship: The Role of Self-Perceived Creativity

Fadi Abdelfattah, Hussam Al Halbusi, Raya Al-Brwani, and Khalid Abed Dahleez

1 Introduction

The significance of the entrepreneurial phenomenon in regional economic and social growth is increasingly evident due to its role in reducing unemployment and enhancing completeness (Weiss et al., 2019). With technological advancements, e-business, particularly e-entrepreneurship,

F. Abdelfattah (✉)
Department of Business and Economics,
Modern College of Business and Science, Muscat, Oman
e-mail: fadi.abdelfattah@mcbs.edu.om

H. Al Halbusi
Department of Management, Ahmed Bin Mohammed Military College (ABMMC), Doha, Qatar

A. Mishrif (ed.), *Business Resilience and Market Adaptability*, The Political Economy of the Middle East,
https://doi.org/10.1007/978-981-97-2962-3_4

has garnered heightened attention from both researchers and practitioners (Lai & To, 2020; Fattah et al., 2022). E-entrepreneurship involves establishing a new enterprise with an original business proposal in Net Economics and delivering products and/or services electronically within network systems (Uzir et al., 2021a, 2021b).

As entrepreneurship practices and accelerators gain momentum, a growing number of individuals express interest in entrepreneurship research (Abdelfattah & Al Halbusi, 2022). Simultaneously, global interest in e-entrepreneurship is on the ascent, playing a critical role in employment creation, innovation, and overall economic growth (Hoong et al., 2019; Weiss et al., 2019). E-entrepreneurs embark on ventures with an eye on minimizing expenses and risks while seeking revenue and growth opportunities (Klofsten et al., 2019; Lai & To, 2020). Entrepreneurial characteristics, such as a desire for responsibility, self-reliance, perseverance, a need for immediate feedback, high energy levels, thinking expansively, and motivation for achievement, distinguish them (Uzir et al., 2021a, 2021b; Wartiovaara et al., 2019).

A successful entrepreneurial venture necessitates innovation and persistence (Jung et al., 2020; Naveed et al., 2022). While previous studies primarily focused on the intention to engage in entrepreneurship, a fundamental belief in one's ability to persevere and achieve is crucial, considering the labor and risks involved (Alnoor et al., 2022; Schmutzler et al., 2019). The effectiveness of entrepreneurship education programs in fostering the desire to start businesses remains uncertain, with some studies suggesting limited impact (Anjum et al., 2021).

In the evolving paradigm, e-entrepreneurship represents a departure from traditional approaches, emphasizing value addition through societal, environmental, and technological outcomes (Cruz-Cárdenas et al., 2021). Being an e-entrepreneur involves quickly identifying connections, and business opportunities, and allocating resources for value creation and sustainable innovations (Commission et al., 2012; Krishnan et al., 2022). Entrepreneurs, frequently perceived as creative, are proposed to possess

---

R. Al-Brwani · K. A. Dahleez
College of Business Administration (COBA), A'Sharqiyah University, Ibra, Oman

necessary but insufficient conditions for entrepreneurship (Anjum et al., 2021). This chapter aims to enhance understanding of the relationship between opportunity evaluation decisions and e-entrepreneurial intentions through self-perceived creativity, serving as a critical mechanism for assessing the attractiveness of future resources.

2 Literature Review

2.1 Opportunity Evaluation Process

The initiative is an essential component of entrepreneurship, where personal drive often has a cascading impact on broader actions and results within the entrepreneurial ecosystem (Chandra, 2017; Lumpkin & Dess, 1996). Entrepreneurship is strongly associated with innovation, whether it involves the development of novel technologies or processes (Schumpeter & Nichol, 1934) or the progression of existing innovative enterprises (Gartner, 1985). Consequently, entrepreneurship requires proactive engagement to identify and seize valuable opportunities (Guth & Ginsberg, 1990).

McMullen and Shepherd (2006) proposed a model consisting of two distinct stages in the entrepreneurial process: "opportunity concentration" and "opportunity appraisal." This framework established a foundation for understanding entrepreneurial action and the inherent ambiguity that accompanies it. The concept of opportunity recognition, specifically why and how opportunities are perceived and pursued, has been the focus of research into "opportunities focus" or third-person opportunities (McCann & Vroom, 2015; Tehseen et al., 2021). However, the study of "opportunity assessment" goes a step further by examining why certain individuals identify and act on opportunities personally, known as first-person opportunities (Marks & Batev, 2021). Despite these distinctions, the existing portrayal of the attention and assessment phases lacks details on the cognitive processes involved and the motivating factors behind entrepreneurial behavior. In a subsequent investigation, McMullen and Shepherd (2006) delved into these aspects, culminating in a model explaining how individuals form their beliefs about opportunities. This highlights that the development of first-person opportunity perspectives is a complex cognitive process influenced by an individual's knowledge, motivation, and available resources (Autio et al., 2013).

While recognizing and assessing opportunities are fundamental prerequisites for entrepreneurial action, there is a notable scarcity of empirical research on how individuals identify and evaluate third-party opportunities and the circumstances under which opportunity assessment leads to entrepreneurial action (Haynie et al., 2009). Most current studies on opportunity evaluation have concentrated on the construction and indication perspectives, with limited exploration into how entrepreneurs perceive and manage risk (Welter & Scrimpshire, 2021).

In both contexts, the entrepreneurial process encompasses the various roles, processes, and behaviors involved in recognizing innovations and establishing enterprises to exploit them (Asante & Affum-Osei, 2019; Packard & Burnham, 2021). Consequently, this framework aims to be more operational, enhancing our comprehension of the transition from entrepreneurial intent to opportunity assessment. Thus, in line with this objective, the following hypothesis is formulated.

2.2 *Self-Perceived Creativity*

Individual creativity holds significant importance in personal cognitive processing as it enables the generation of novel and valuable ideas through the recombination and synthesis of previously acquired information and skills (Kreitler & Casakin, 2009; Laguia et al., 2019). The foundational components of creativity, encompassing the process, product, person, and environment, exert a profound influence on the creative endeavor (Harris et al., 2014). The cognitive approach endeavors to elucidate the mechanisms and technologies underlying creative thinking, highlighting that creativity entails more than mere traits like openness, hierarchy, autonomy, and exploratory behavior (Nguyen et al., 2021).

In the present context, self-perceived creativity assumes a critical mediating role in the nexus between the opportunity evaluation process and e-entrepreneurial intention. Self-perceived creativity is defined as the "creative capacity, skills, and abilities that the individual possesses" (Hinton, 1970, p. 211). Particularly noteworthy is individuals' confidence in their capacity to generate innovative ideas as their skills progress (Laguia et al., 2019; Luo et al., 2021). Entrepreneurs are often associated with creativity, and entrepreneurship is acknowledged to demand a notable level of creative prowess (Akbari et al., 2021; Frese & Gielnik, 2014). Innovation, integral to the entrepreneurial stereotype (Lampel & Germain, 2016), intertwines closely with entrepreneurship, especially concerning creativity and motivation for self-employment, where those with heightened perceived creativity are inclined toward entrepreneurial pursuits (Ip et al., 2018; Leal-Rodriguez & Albort-Morant, 2019). Therefore, self-perceived creativity plays a pivotal role in the decision-making process of choosing entrepreneurship as a career path, with individuals harboring high self-perceptions aligning with the attributes of successful entrepreneurs, rendering entrepreneurship an appealing choice. Conversely, those with lower self-perceived creativity may dismiss entrepreneurship as a viable career option, perceiving a misalignment between their characteristics and the entrepreneurial profile (Duckworth et al., 2016; Leal-Rodriguez & Albort-Morant, 2019).

Furthermore, empirical evidence suggests that individuals who perceive themselves as more creative exhibit a greater inclination to initiate their entrepreneurial ventures. Multiple studies affirm the substantial impact of creativity on an individual's interest and motivation to commence a business. The present chapter posits the following hypotheses based on the aforementioned rationale (Fig. 1).

- **Hypothesis on: Opportunity evaluation decisions positively impact self-perceived creativity.e (H1)**: Opportunity evaluation decisions positively influence e-entrepreneurial intention.
- **Hypothesis two (H2)**: Opportunity evaluation decisions positively impact self-perceived creativity.
- **Hypothesis three (H3)**: Self-perceived creativity positively influences e-entrepreneurial intention.

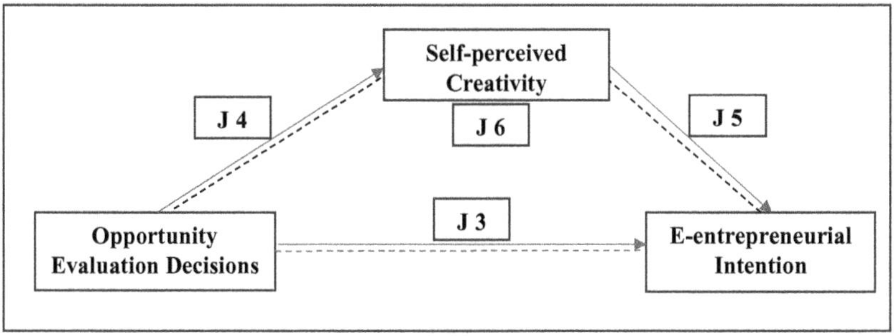

Fig. 1 Research framework (Self developed)

- **Hypothesis four (H4)**: Self-perceived creativity mediates the relationship between opportunity evaluation decisions and e-entrepreneurial intention.

3 Methodology

3.1 *Material and Procedure*

This cross-sectional study adhered to a positivist and quantitative research approach aligned with its objectives. The research framework incorporated both primary and secondary data sources. Primary data, pivotal for achieving the study goals, were gathered from entrepreneurs across diverse regions in Oman. Given the varied backgrounds and experiences of these entrepreneurs in the realm of entrepreneurial endeavors, the survey encompassed inquiries concerning self-perceived creativity boundary conditions (entrepreneurial role model, opportunity evaluation decision, and entrepreneurship education) and e-entrepreneurship intention.

Considering the absence of a comprehensive list of entrepreneurs with associated addresses, a non-probabilistic, purposive sampling strategy was employed to distribute a structured closed-ended questionnaire. Non-probability purposive sampling was chosen due to its applicability to various non-probability sample schemes, especially when a complete sampling frame for theory generalization is unavailable. While the findings from purposive sampling may limit generalizability, empirical evidence supports the reliability of data collected through such methods. In this context, Omani business owners were selected as study participants to assess the hypotheses derived from the literature.

Data collection employed a Google form survey distributed via social media platforms (e.g., Facebook and WhatsApp) and emails. The questionnaire, divided into three sections, sought respondents' permission, addressed respondent profiles, and delved into study variables (entrepreneurship role model, opportunity evaluation decision, and entrepreneurship education) and e-entrepreneurship intention. Considering language diversity among Omani respondents, questionnaires were developed in both English and Arabic, adhering to recommended translation protocols (Brislin, 1986). The questionnaire underwent pilot testing with ten professors, resulting in minor adjustments to enhance clarity, validity, and reliability.

A total of 305 voluntary responses were collected, ensuring confidentiality and exclusive use for research purposes. The received data underwent initial processing to eliminate bias or outliers, followed by descriptive analysis in SPSS to present participant profiles in frequency and percentage.

Upon data cleaning, Structural Equation Modeling by Partial Least Squares (SEM-PLS) was employed to scrutinize the proposed hypotheses. Data computation utilized SPSS and SmartPLS3.2.8 software (Hernández-Perlines, 2016), with techniques such as the PLS Algorithm and Bootstrapping applied for analysis.

3.2 Variables Measurement

All variables in our study—opportunity evaluation decisions, self-perceived creativity, and e-entrepreneurial intention—were sourced from established and reliable studies. Given the Arabic-speaking nature of our participants, the items underwent translation from English to Arabic. This translation was executed by two bilingual experts using Brislin's translation–back-translation technique, ensuring semantic equivalence with the original English versions (Brislin, 1986).

Opportunity evaluation decisions were assessed using a 5-item scale adapted from Welter and Scrimpshire (2021). Self-perceived creativity was measured with a 6-item scale sourced from DiLiello and Houghton (2008) and Fattah et al. (2022). E-entrepreneurial intention, denoting a person's inclination to establish an e-business, was gauged with a 5-item scale adapted from Lai and To (2020) and Abdelfattah et al. (2022). All measures employed a five-point Likert response format (1 = strongly disagree; 5 = strongly agree).

4 Data Analysis and Results

Structural Equation Modeling (SEM) analysis was chosen for its efficiency and reliability. The study utilized SEM by Partial Least Squares (PLS) through Smart PLS 3.2.8 software. This method, recognized for its practicality and robustness, is suitable for complex causal analyses involving both first- and second-order constructs, as it doesn't necessitate strict assumptions about variable distribution. Bootstrap t-statistics were generated with 5,000 subsamples to evaluate the statistical significance of path coefficients, with n – 1 degrees of freedom.

4.1 *Confirmatory Factor Analysis*

To validate the measurement model, criteria for construct level reliability, reliability and validity, convergent validity, and discriminant validity were assessed. Table 1 presents the results of item consistency, indicating no significant issues, with most items surpassing the suggested 0.5 threshold. Internal consistency, assessed through Cronbach's alpha and composite reliability (CR), exceeded the 0.70 cut-offs, as shown in Table 1. Convergent validity, measured by the average variance extracted (AVE), met the criteria, with all values surpassing the 0.5 threshold. Regarding discriminant validity, AVE values for each variable significantly exceeded the common variance with other latent variables. Additionally, HTMT standards below 0.90 confirmed the discriminant validity for each pair of variables (see Tables 2 and 3).

Table 1 Measurement Model

Constructs	*Items*	*Loading (> 0.5)*	*CA (> 0.7)*	*CR (> 0.7)*	*AVE (> 0.5)*
Opportunity Evaluation Decisions	OPED1	0.815	0.775	0.878	0.672
	OPED2	0.861			
	OPED3	0.751			
	OPED4	0.891			
	OPED5	0.855			
Self-Perceived Creativity	SPC1	0.752	0.818	0.948	0.741
	SPC2	0.745			
	SPC3	0.814			
	SPC4	0.855			
	SPC5	0.856			
	SPC6	0.856			
E-Entrepreneurial Intention	E-EI1	0.898	0.811	0.898	0.688
	E-EI2	0.805			
	E-EI3	0.834			
	E-EI4	0.865			
	E-EI5	0.875			

Notes CA = Cronbach's Alpha, CR = Composite Reliability, AVE = Average Variance Extracted
Source Author's own work and Author's calculations

Table 2 Discriminant validity (Fornell-Larcker)

Variables	*1*	*2*	*3*
1. Opportunity Evaluation Decisions	**0.842**		
2. Self-Perceived Creativity	0.478	**0.746**	
3. E-Entrepreneurial Intention	0.363	0.499	**0.745**

Source Author's own work and Author's calculations

Table 3 Discriminant validity (HTMT)

Variables	1	2	3
1. Opportunity Evaluation Decisions			
2. Self-Perceived Creativity	0.547		
3. E-Entrepreneurial Intention	0.389	0.612	

Source Author's own work and Author's calculations

4.2 *Hypothesis Testing*

The findings related to H1–H3 are presented in Table 4. In support of H1, opportunity evaluation decisions were found to be significantly and positively related to e-entrepreneurial intention ($\beta = 0.386$, $t = 6.467$, $p < 0.000$), confirming the acceptance of H1. The second direct effect (H2) revealed a positively significant relationship between opportunity evaluation decisions and self-perceived creativity ($\beta = 0.198$, $t = 3.119$, $p < 0.001$), supporting H2. Similarly, for H3, self-perceived creativity was significantly related to e-entrepreneurial intention ($\beta = 0.280$, $t = 3.990$, $p < 0.000$), leading to the acceptance of H3. These results are summarized in Table 4.

As predicted in H4, the positive influence of opportunity evaluation decisions on e-entrepreneurial intention was examined for mediation by self-perceived creativity. The bootstrapping method, employing 5,000 subsamples, revealed a significant indirect effect (indirect effect = 0.255, $t = 3.571$, $p < 0.000$, Table 18). The 95% confidence interval (CI), not containing 0 (lower limit = 0.088, upper limit = 0.278), substantiates the existence of mediation (Preacher & Hayes, 2008). The mediating effect

Table 4 Structural path analysis: Direct and indirect effects

#H	*Relationship*	*SB*	*SD*	*t-value*	*p-values*	*[Lower; Upper Level]*	*Decision*
H1	Opportunity Evaluation Decisions → E-Entrepreneurial Intention	0.386	0.060	6.467	0.000	[0.275; 0.475]	Supported
H2	Opportunity Evaluation Decisions → Self-Perceived Creativity	0.198	0.066	3.019	0.001	[0.075; 0.293]	Supported
H3	Self-perceived creativity → E-Entrepreneurial Intention	0.280	0.070	3.990	0.000	[0.166; 0.404]	Supported
Mediating Test (Indirect Effect)							
H4	Opportunity Evaluation Decisions → Self-Perceived Creativity → E-Entrepreneurial Intention	0.255	0.031	3.571	0.000	[0.088; 0.278]	Supported

Source Author's own work and Author's calculations

of self-perceived creativity in the relationship between opportunity evaluation decisions and e-entrepreneurial intention is substantial, providing robust support for H4.

5 Discussion and Conclusions

The findings of this study underscore a noteworthy correlation between opportunity evaluation decisions and e-entrepreneurial intentions, revealing a significant mediating role played by self-perceived creativity. This revelation accentuates the pivotal role of creativity in shaping entrepreneurial objectives, positioning the decision-making process in opportunity appraisal as a catalyst for enhancing e-entrepreneurial intentions.

This chapter contributes substantially to the existing literature by advancing research that delves into the intricate interplay between opportunity evaluation decisions and e-entrepreneurial intentions, elucidating the mediating influence of self-perceived creativity. Notably, the scarcity of studies exploring and substantiating this particular relationship is acknowledged, with only a handful of published articles addressing this nexus (e.g., Abdelfattah et al., 2022; Lai & To, 2020). Consequently, our study contributes robust evidence supporting the generalizability of these relationships, thereby piquing significant interest among researchers, educators, and entrepreneurship advocates. The study sheds light on how entrepreneurs navigate risk, generate innovative ideas, and translate them into actionable initiatives, particularly in the context of their e-entrepreneurial goals.

The practical implications of this chapter extend to policymakers, offering insights that can inform strategic initiatives to cultivate entrepreneurship. Notably, the findings emphasize the importance of self-confidence and the potential for entrepreneurial engagement among Omani entrepreneurs. Policymakers can leverage this understanding to make informed decisions regarding the allocation of resources and the implementation of supportive measures to foster entrepreneurship. Furthermore, the study recommends a nuanced approach to managing e-business variables, urging policymakers to adopt effective strategies for e-business marketing. It highlights the need for a robust IT governance framework to ensure channel control, compliance to mitigate individual idiosyncrasies, and a governance structure that incentivizes high levels of individual commitment. The analysis also underscores the importance of individuals recognizing the distinct effects of structural dimensions in e-business aspects on the adoption of various marketing techniques, advocating for tailored approaches that consider beneficial combinations and potential conflicts between different marketing plans.

5.1 *Practical Implications*

The research on evaluating opportunities in E-entrepreneurship, particularly with a focus on the role of self-perceived creativity, carries significant practical implications for aspiring entrepreneurs, educators, policymakers, and business leaders alike. Firstly, for individuals contemplating or embarking on an entrepreneurial journey, understanding the pivotal role of self-perceived creativity can serve as a source of motivation and self-assurance. This knowledge can inspire prospective entrepreneurs to recognize their creative potential and bolster their confidence in pursuing innovative business ideas. Moreover, it underscores the importance of nurturing and developing creative skills, offering practical pathways for self-improvement in creativity to enhance opportunity evaluation and entrepreneurial success. Educational institutions and training programs can benefit from these findings by incorporating creativity development into their entrepreneurial curricula. Encouraging students to hone their creative thinking abilities, problem-solving skills, and lateral thought processes can better prepare them for the challenges and opportunities of E-entrepreneurship. It underscores the need for educational initiatives that go beyond traditional business instruction to foster a holistic entrepreneurial mindset.

For policymakers, this research underscores the value of supporting initiatives that promote creativity and innovation, providing incentives for research and development, and facilitating access to resources for innovative startups. Creating an environment that fosters creative thinking and risk-taking is essential for nurturing a robust ecosystem of E-entrepreneurship, which can, in turn, drive economic growth, create jobs, and foster technological advancement. Business leaders and established companies can take away insights about harnessing the creative potential of their workforce. Encouraging intrapreneurship, where employees are given the freedom to explore innovative ideas and innovative solutions, can lead to novel opportunities and improved competitiveness within the rapidly evolving digital landscape. The practical implication is that fostering a culture of creativity and offering resources for idea exploration can be an asset for any organization. Thus, the practical implications of this research underscore the need to acknowledge and cultivate self-perceived creativity in aspiring and established entrepreneurs, educational institutions, policymakers, and organizations. Recognizing the role of creativity in opportunity evaluation and entrepreneurial success can guide practical actions to enhance E-entrepreneurship, innovation, and economic growth in an increasingly digital world.

5.2 *Limitations and Future Research*

While this chapter sheds light on the crucial role of self-perceived creativity in opportunity evaluation within the realm of E-entrepreneurship, it is essential to acknowledge certain limitations that pave the way for future research. Firstly, this research primarily focuses on the individual's self-perceived creativity as a key determinant in the opportunity evaluation process. However, entrepreneurial ecosystems are complex, dynamic, and influenced by a multitude of internal and external factors. Future research can delve deeper into the relationship between self-perceived creativity and other variables such as risk perception, information processing, and environmental context, offering a more comprehensive understanding of the opportunity evaluation process in E-entrepreneurship. Moreover, this chapter adopts a cross-sectional research design, capturing a specific moment in time. To capture the dynamic nature of entrepreneurial activities and opportunities, longitudinal research can be employed to explore how self-perceived creativity evolves and how it influences opportunity evaluation at various stages of an entrepreneurial venture. This would provide a more nuanced understanding of the temporal aspects of creativity and opportunity assessment. Furthermore, the research primarily focuses on the individual entrepreneur. Future investigations can broaden the scope to explore the role of self-perceived creativity within entrepreneurial teams and collaborations. Understanding how creativity is collectively nurtured and harnessed in group dynamics can be instrumental, especially in the context of digital entrepreneurship, where innovation often involves collaborative efforts. Finally, while this research highlights the role of creativity in recognizing and seizing opportunities, it does not explore the potential challenges or downsides of high self-perceived creativity, such as over-optimism or potential biases. Future studies could investigate the potential pitfalls associated with excessive self-perceived creativity and how entrepreneurs can effectively manage these challenges.

Acknowledgements The research leading to these results has received funding from the Ministry of Higher Education, Research, and Innovation (MoHERI) of the Sultanate of Oman under the Block Funding Program with agreement no. MoHERI/BFP/ASU/01/2021.

References

Akbari, M., Bagheri, A., Imani, S., & Asadnezhad, M. (2021). Does entrepreneurial leadership encourage innovation work behavior? The mediating role of creative self-efficacy and support for innovation. *European Journal of Innovation Management, 24*(1), 1–22. https://doi.org/10.1108/EJIM-10-2019-0283

Alnoor, A., Al-Abrrow, H., Al Halbusi, H., Khaw, K. W., Chew, X., Al-Maatoq, M., & Alharbi, R. K. (2022). Uncovering the antecedents of trust in social commerce: An application of the non-linear artificial neural network approach. *Competitiveness Review, 32*(3), 492–523.

Anjum, T., Farrukh, M., Heidler, P., & Tautiva, J. A. D. (2021). Entrepreneurial intention: Creativity, entrepreneurship, and university support. *Journal of Open Innovation: Technology, Market, and Complexity, 7*(1), 1–13. https://doi.org/10.3390/joitmc7010011

Asante, E. A., & Affum-Osei, E. (2019). Entrepreneurship as a career choice: The impact of locus of control on aspiring entrepreneurs' opportunity recognition. *Journal of Business Research, 98*, 227–235.

Autio, E., Dahlander, L., & Frederiksen, L. (2013). Information exposure, opportunity evaluation, and entrepreneurial action: An investigation of an online user community. *Academy of Management Journal, 56*(5), 1348–1371.

Brislin, R. W. (1986). The wording and translation of research instruments. In W. J. Lonner & J. W. Berry (Eds.), Field methods in cross-cultural research. (pp. 137–164). Sage Publications, Inc. DiLiello, T. C., & Houghton, J. D. (2008). Creative potential and practiced creativity: Identifying untapped creativity in organizations. *Creativity and Innovation Management, 17*(1), 37–46.

Chandra, Y. (2017). A time-based process model of international entrepreneurial opportunity evaluation. *Journal of International Business Studies, 48*(4), 423–451.

Commission, E., From, C., Commission, THE., The, T. O., Council, THE., Economic, THE E., Committee, T. H. E., & The, O. F. (2012). Committee and the Committee of The Regions Social Protection in European Union Development Cooperation.

Cruz-Cárdenas, J., Zabelina, E., Guadalupe-Lanas, J., Palacio-Fierro, A., & Ramos-Galarza, C. (2021). COVID-19, consumer behavior, technology, and society: A literature review and bibliometric analysis. *Technological Forecasting and Social Change, 173.* https://doi.org/10.1016/j.techfore.2021.121179

Duckworth, A. L., Gendler, T. S., & Gross, J. J. (2016). Situational strategies for self-control. *Perspectives on Psychological Science, 11*(1), 35–55.

Abdelfattah, F., Al Halbusi, H., Dahleez, K. A., Al Sinawi, S., & Al Wahibi, G. (2021). An Investigation of Components Deriving Entrepreneurial Activities in Duqm City: A Special Economic Zone in Oman. *International Journal of Entrepreneurship, 25*, 1–14.

Abdelfattah, F., & Al Halbusi, H. (2022). Understanding How Entrepreneurship Innovation Solves Women's Challenges in the Arab Region: Omani Women Entrepreneurs Model. In *Innovative Economic, Social, and Environmental Practices for Progressing Future Sustainability* (pp. 269–283). IGI Global.

Abdelfattah, F., Al Halbusi, H., & Al-Brwani, R. M. (2022). Influence of self-perceived creativity and social media use in predicting e-entrepreneurial intention. *International Journal of Innovation Studies*. https://doi.org/10.1016/j.ijis.2022.04.003

Frese, M., & Gielnik, M. M. (2014). The psychology of entrepreneurship. *Annual Review of Organizational Psychology and Organizational Behavior, 1*(1), 413–438.

Gartner, W. B. (1985). A conceptual framework for describing the phenomenon of new venture creation. *Academy of Management Review, 10*(4), 696–706.

Guth, W. D., & Ginsberg, A. (1990). Guest editors' introduction: Corporate entrepreneurship. *Strategic Management Journal,* 5–15.

Harris, T. B., Li, N., Boswell, W. R., Zhang, X. A., & Xie, Z. (2014). Getting what is new from newcomers: Empowering leadership, creativity, and adjustment in the socialization context. *Personnel Psychology, 67*(3), 567–604. https://doi.org/10.1111/peps.12053

Haynie, J. M., Shepherd, D. A., & McMullen, J. S. (2009). An opportunity for me? The role of resources in opportunity evaluation decisions. *Journal of Management Studies, 46*(3), 337–361. https://doi.org/10.1111/j.1467-6486.2009.00824.x

Hinton, H. E. (1970). Insect eggshells. *Scientific American, 223*(2), 84–91.

Hoong, C. W., Qureshi, Z. H., Sajilan, S., & Halbusi, H. Al. (2019). A study on the factors influencing social entrepreneurial intention among undergraduates. MACS 2019 - 13th International Conference on Mathematics, Actuarial Science, Computer Science and Statistics, Proceedings, 1–7. https://doi.org/10.1109/MACS48846.2019.9024818

Ip, C. Y., Liang, C., Wu, S.-C., Law, K. M. Y., & Liu, H.-C. (2018). Enhancing social entrepreneurial intentions through entrepreneurial creativity: A comparative study between Taiwan and Hong Kong. *Creativity Research Journal, 30*(2), 132–142.

Jung, K. B., Kang, S. W., & Choi, S. B. (2020). Empowering leadership, risk-taking behavior, and employees' commitment to organizational change: The mediated moderating role of task complexity. *Sustainability (Switzerland), 12*(6). https://doi.org/10.3390/su12062340

Klofsten, M., Fayolle, A., Guerrero, M., Mian, S., Urbano, D., & Wright, M. (2019). The entrepreneurial university as driver for economic growth and social change-Key strategic challenges. *Technological Forecasting and Social Change, 141*, 149–158.

Kreitler, S., & Casakin, H. (2009). Self-perceived creativity: The perspective of design. *European Journal of Psychological Assessment, 25*(3), 194–203. https://doi.org/10.1027/1015-5759.25.3.194

Krishnan, S. N., Ganesh, L. S., & Rajendran, C. (2022). Entrepreneurial Interventions for crisis management: Lessons from the Covid-19 Pandemic's impact on entrepreneurial ventures. *International Journal of Disaster Risk Reduction, 102830*. https://doi.org/10.1016/J.IJDRR.2022.102830

Laguía, A., Moriano, J. A., & Gorgievski, M. J. (2019). A psychosocial study of self-perceived creativity and entrepreneurial intentions in a sample of university students. *Thinking Skills and Creativity, 31*, 44–57. https://doi.org/10.1016/j.tsc.2018.11.004

Lai, L. S., & To, W. M. (2020). E-Entrepreneurial intention among young Chinese adults. *Asian Journal of Technology Innovation, 28*(1), 119–137.

Lampel, J., & Germain, O. (2016). Creative industries as hubs of new organizational and business practices. *Journal of Business Research, 69*(7), 2327–2333.

Leal-Rodriguez, A. L., & Albort-Morant, G. (2019). Promoting innovative experiential learning practices to improve academic performance: Empirical evidence from a Spanish Business School. *Journal of Innovation & Knowledge, 4*(2), 97–103.

Lumpkin, G. T., & Dess, G. G. (1996). Clarifying the entrepreneurial orientation construct and linking it to performance. *Academy of Management Review, 21*(1), 135–172.

Luo, H., Cheng, S., Zhou, W., Song, W., Yu, S., & Lin, X. (2021). Research on the impact of online promotions on consumers' impulsive online shopping intentions. *Journal of Theoretical and Applied Electronic Commerce Research, 16*(6), 2386–2404. https://doi.org/10.3390/jtaer16060131

Marks, J., & Batev, T. (2021). Temporal mediation of uncertainty within entrepreneurial opportunity evaluation. *Journal of Developmental Entrepreneurship, 26*(01), 2150007.

McCann, B. T., & Vroom, G. (2015). Opportunity evaluation and changing beliefs during the nascent entrepreneurial process. *International Small Business Journal, 33*(6), 612–637.

McMullen, J. S., & Shepherd, D. A. (2006). Entrepreneurial action and the role of uncertainty in the theory of the entrepreneur. *Academy of Management Review, 31*(1), 132–152.

Naveed, R. T., Alhaidan, H., Al Halbusi, H., & Al-Swidi, A. K. (2022). Do organizations really evolve? The critical link between organizational culture and organizational innovation toward organizational effectiveness: Pivotal role of organizational resistance. *Journal of Innovation & Knowledge, 7*(2), 100178.

Nguyen, T. T., Phan, H. T. T., & Pham, V. T. (2021). Impact of creativity on student entrepreneurial intention. *International Journal of Innovation, 9*(3), 646–663. https://doi.org/10.5585/iji.v9i3.19659

Packard, M. D., & Burnham, T. A. (2021). Do we understand each other? Toward a simulated empathy theory for entrepreneurship. *Journal of Business Venturing, 36*(1), 106076.

Preacher, K., & Hayes, A. (2008). Asymptotic and resampling strategies for assessing and comparing indirect effects in multiple mediator models. *Behavior Research Methods, 40*, 879–891. The sage handbook of advanced data analysis methods for communication research, 1354. https://doi.org/10.3758/brm.40.3.879

Schmutzler, J., Andonova, V., & Diaz-Serrano, L. (2019). How context shapes entrepreneurial self-efficacy as a driver of entrepreneurial intentions: A multilevel approach. *Entrepreneurship Theory and Practice, 43*(5), 880–920.

Schumpeter, J. A., & Nichol, A. J. (1934). Robinson's economics of imperfect competition. *Journal of Political Economy, 42*(2), 249–259.

Tehseen, S., Johara, F., Halbusi, H. A., Islam, M. A., & Fattah, F. A. M. A. (2021). Measuring dimensions of perceived business success among Malaysian and Bangladeshi SME owners. *Rajagiri Management Journal*. https://doi.org/10.1108/RAMJ-05-2021-0045

Uzir, M. U. H., Al Halbusi, H., Lim, R., Jerin, I., Hamid, A. B. A., Ramayah, T., & Haque, A. (2021a). Applied Artificial Intelligence and user satisfaction: Smartwatch usage for healthcare in Bangladesh during COVID-19. *Technology in Society, 67*, 101780.

Uzir, M. U. H., Al Halbusi, H., Thurasamy, R., Hock, R. L. T., Aljaberi, M. A., Hasan, N., & Hamid, M. (2021b). The effects of service quality, perceived value and trust in-home delivery service personnel on customer satisfaction: Evidence from a developing country. *Journal of Retailing and Consumer Services, 63*, 102721.

Wartiovaara, M., Lahti, T., & Wincent, J. (2019). The role of inspiration in entrepreneurship: Theory and the future research agenda. *Journal of Business Research, 101*, 548–554.

Weiss, J., Anisimova, T., & Shirokova, G. (2019). The translation of entrepreneurial intention into start-up behavior: The moderating role of regional social capital. *International Small Business Journal, 37*(5), 473–501.
Welter, C., & Scrimpshire, A. (2021). The missing capital: The case for psychological capital in entrepreneurship research. *Journal of Business Venturing Insights, 16*, e00267.

PART II

The Impact of COVID-19 on the Business Sector

CHAPTER 5

The Impact of COVID-19 on E-Commerce According to the Results and Recommendations of Previous Studies

Khaled Medekhel

1 Introduction

The Covid-19 pandemic has had a great impact on all societies in the world, without making a difference between a developed country and a developing country, and on all sectors, especially the economic business sector, under the conditions of social confinement imposed by various governments in the world, and this measure was accompanied by the cessation of various economic and social activities, countries separated from each other and companies stopped all forms of direct transactions as they faced a difficult situation due to people staying in their homes, and transactions between individuals and groups of one country also stopped, as places of worship, schools, and universities were closed, as well as shops

K. Medekhel (✉)
Echahid Hamma Lakhdar University, El Oued, Algeria
e-mail: medekhel-khaled@univ-eloued.dz

A. Mishrif (ed.), *Business Resilience and Market Adaptability*, The Political Economy of the Middle East,
https://doi.org/10.1007/978-981-97-2962-3_5

and public transport, and electronic dealing became the urgent alternative for individuals. The whole world led him towards the use of Internet technology and various means of communication to continue their lives from a distance. Shopping has become practiced remotely for fear of people contacting each other, and the global economy has plunged into an unprecedented and unexpected crisis.

Hence, the shift towards electronic commerce has become the most effective solution to continue daily life, and on this basis, the biggest beneficiary of this situation is the technology and Internet sector companies, especially with the need for more than one billion people to their homes and everyone resorting to electronic services and various new applications that allow them to adapt to the circumstances. Currently prevailing.

In this emergency situation on the world, scientists and researchers in various disciplines have taken to studying the impact of Covid-19 on humanity and what is related to their lives and work and how they can overcome the current crisis, and among the most important results of those studies we find this pandemic and contributed to raising the pace of dealing with electronic commerce in various countries of the world, online shopping has become one of the most important means that consumers use to meet their consumer needs and purchase their basic needs.

In our current chapter, we are trying to discuss the results and recommendations of a significant group of research concerned with the impact of Covid-19 on electronic commerce and published on the "Algerian Portal of Scientific Journals" platform known as "ASJP" (www.asjp.cerist.dz), and their number reached 30 studies to date 15/12/2022.

We can ask the following questions:

What are the results of studies that dealt with the impact of Covid-19 on e-commerce published on the Algerian "ASJP" platform, and how can we benefit from its recommendations?

2 The Importance of Chapter

The importance of this chapter in Koha focuses on analyzing the results of studies that dealt with the impact of Covid-19 on electronic commerce through the "Algerian Portal of Scientific Journals ASJP" platform, and how the rules of commerce have changed in light of this crisis and how governments and companies have tried to take advantage of it and turn it into an opportunity to highlight the importance of technology in everyday life.

The importance of our chapter also lies in clarifying the future of e-commerce through the recommendations that came from studies in the Algerian "ASJP" platform, and that the spread of the Covid-19 virus hastened this future, as researchers agreed on an increase in the use of e-commerce patterns, and despite the presence of many risks and many obstacles that stand in the way of the prosperity and growth of e-commerce, but the rapid global growth in the application and use of e-commerce will be a catalyst for fortifying the infrastructure of this commercial style, in addition to strengthening legal protection for it, and this will motivate investors, creators, and innovators to develop its procedures and raise the level of confidence among consumers to deal with it.

3 Aim of the Chapter

The chapter seeks to shed light on the reality of electronic commerce in light of the Covid-19 pandemic through 30 studies that focused on the impact of Covid-19 on electronic commerce and published on the "Algerian Portal of Scientific Journals" platform, from on January 18, 2020, and the last study published was on December 15, 2022. There is no after it, and we will try to clarify the gains. We also summarize the challenges, risks, and obstacles of electronic commerce through studies published on the mentioned platform.

On the other hand, our current chapter aims at summarizing and organizing a set of recommendations on the development of electronic commerce considering Covid-19 and beyond.

next:

- Recommendations for governments
- Recommendations for international bodies
- Recommendations for companies
- Recommendations for banks
- Recommendations for institutional supporters
- Recommendations for civil associations

4 Search Tools

To reach good results in our current chapter, the researcher used a number of important and irreplaceable approaches to discuss the results and recommendations of 30 studies (in the Table 1 given) that were previously published on the "Algerian Portal of Scientific Journals" platform known as "ASJP", among those curricula are the following:

The historical method: It is concerned with collecting past data and information, then classifying, arranging, and criticizing them, to help the scientific researcher understand a social problem or scientific topic. By looking at past events, a person can identify past mistakes and try to avoid them and discover different ways to improve the reality that he can live in now or in the future (www.bts-academy.com).

Analytical descriptive approach: This type of method is specifically used to know all information about phenomena that are related to scientific research, and this type of method works on analyzing them as well as knowing an explanation of them. The researcher also used survey studies, which are considered one of the types of descriptive approach, and careful observation of the members of the chapter community is used. The focus through survey studies is on one of the aspects of the research problem, and this problem is analyzed and working to show many results. Moreover, through studies the survey introduces a set of reforms on the surface of scientific research (www.maktabtk.com).

Research that focused on the impact of Covid-19 on e-commerce published on the platform.

"Algerian Portal of Scientific Journals" "ASJP", until 15/12/2022 (Sorted by date of publication).

5 Results of Research on Electronic Commerce Considering the Covid-19 Pandemic

5.1 *Results about the Reality of Electronic Commerce Considering the Covid-19 Pandemic*

The study (Seham, 2021) confirmed that it was Chinese and American companies that captured the largest market shares in electronic commerce by sweeping the markets in light of the increasing consumer access to websites, and at the forefront of these companies, the jd site, Alibaba site, Amazon site, and other sites whose activity flourished in this crisis.

Table 1 Research that focused on the impact of COVID-19 on e-commerce published on the platform. "Algerian Portal of Scientific Journals" "ASJP", until 15/12/2022 (Sorted by date of publication)

No.	*Article title and author name*	*Journal*	*Date of publication*
1	The reality of the performance of e-commerce companies considering the spread of the Corona virus—A case study of the Amazon company as a model Milud ben Khayra, Fawaz Hudhli, Dinawi 'Anfal Eayisha	Journal of Value-Added Business Economics, Volume 02 / Issue: 01 (2020), pp. 9–23	12/03/2020
2	The repercussions of the emerging corona virus on the labor market, "E-commerce as a model" Samiat Aleayib	Journal of Labor and Employment Law, Volume 05 / Issue 04 (November 2020), pp. 01–20	15/11/2020
3	The performance of e-commerce companies considering the spread of the Corona virus between reality and challenges—Amazon as a model Milud bin Khayra, Masnueat Asma	Afaq Journal for Research and Studies, Volume 04 / Issue: 01 (2021), pp. 151–165	18/01/2020
4	The impact of the Corona pandemic on the growth of electronic commerce in the world, an analytical study Seham Moussa	Organization and Labor Journal, Volume 9 / Issue 4 (2021)	10/03/2021
5	The E-commerce business in time of Covid-19: Positive impact Afifa Arrouf	Revue des sciences humaines de l'université Oum El Bouaghi, Number 02 (June 2021)	16/04/2021
6	The containment effect caused by the COVID-19 pandemic on the e-commerce sector in Algeria Chanoune Nadjet. Boukrif Moussa	Algerian Review of Economy and Management, Volume 15, No. 02 (2021)	18/06/2021
7	E-commerce in Algeria between reality and challenges in light of the repercussions of the Corona pandemic (Covid 19) Salman Husayn	Locality of Economic Studies, Volume: 21 / Issue: 01 (2021), pp. 339–356	30/06/2021
8	E-commerce in Algeria: Obstacles and development requirements with reference to the COVID-19 pandemic Abd Alkamil Bialhabib, Yusif Miduiki, Adil Zaqrir	Journal of Administrative and Financial Sciences, Volume: 05 / Issue: 01 (2021), pp. 11–30	30/06/2021

(continued)

Table 1 (continued)

No.	*Article title and author name*	*Journal*	*Date of publication*
9	E-commerce and its impact on the corona pandemic, a field study at the level of Jijel Suarayat Buridih	Al-Manhal Al-Iqtisadi Magazine, Volume 04 / Issue 01 (June 2021), pp. 359–374	30/06/ 2021
10	The impact of the Corona pandemic on the implementation of contractual obligations and on e-commerce Raha Bariq, Muhamad Alkhadaedlaj	Journal of Rights and Humanities, Volume 13 / Issue 3 (October 2022), pp. 68–77	30/10/ 2020
11	The reality of e-commerce in the Corona pandemic Dali Bashir, Bwkhari Asma	Journal of Legal Studies, Volume 8 / Issue 02 (2021), pp. 491/470	08/11/ 2021
12	The reality of e-commerce in Algeria before and after the Corona pandemic, a statistical analytical study for the period 2016–2021 Ben Nama Fatim Alzuhrati, Eida Muhamad, Ben Nama Nuria	Journal of Economics and Environment, Volume 04 / Issue: 03 Special (2021), pp. 76–89	10/11/ 2021
13	Global e-commerce transactions in light of the repercussions of the Corona pandemic "Covid 19" Sadiqi Ahmad, Alttybi Abd Allah	Irtiqaa Journal for Research and Economic Studies, Volume 02 / Issue: 02, 2021, pp. 1–17	25/11/ 2021
14	The repercussions of the Corona pandemic on electronic commerce—with reference to the case of Algeria– Yaequbin Saliha	Economic Dimensions Journal, Volume (11) / Issue 02 (2021), pp. 851–875	30/12/ 2021
15	E-commerce gains in light of the Corona pandemic—A glimpse of e-commerce in Saudi Arabia during the pandemic Yasaminat Tawil	The Economic Researcher Journal, Volume 09 / Issue 02 (2021), pp. 435–451	30/12/ 2021
16	The effects of the Corona pandemic (Covid-19) on small and medium enterprises and the inevitability of their integration into e-commerce in Algeria Khaled Barish	Economics of Money Business Journal, Volume 6 / Issue 02 (December 2021), pp. 187–196	31/12/ 2021
17	COVID-19: The explosion of E-commerce TABET DERRAZ Bessouh Nadiral	The MECAS Notebooks, Volume: 17 / No. 4 (December 2021)	31/12/ 2021

(continued)

Table 1 (continued)

No.	*Article title and author name*	*Journal*	*Date of publication*
18	The impact of the Covid-19 pandemic on e-commercein Algeria Benai Mustapha. Guettafi Said. Larab Sarah	Journal of administrative and financial sciences, Volume: 05 / No. 02 (2021), pp. 560–573	31/12/2021
19	E-commerce in light of the COVID-19 pandemic: opportunities and challenges Shadli Shawqi. Amal Mahawa	Journal of Economic Growth and Entrepreneurship JEGE Spatial and entrepreneurial development studies laboratory. \ 2022, Volume 05, No. 1, pp. 167–176	28/02/2022
20	Predicting the Direction of E-Commerce Stock Prices during COVID 19 Using Machine Learning Bouriche Nouria. Benbouziane Mohamed	Journal of Economic Integration. Vol. 10, No. 01 / (March 2022), pp: 462–473	31/03/2022
21	The impact of the Corona pandemic on e-commerce in the clothing sector in Hebron Governorate Abd Alqadir Darawish, Fadl Eida, Majid Milh	Journal of Banking Financial Economics and Business Administration, Volume: 11 / Issue: 01 (2022), pp. 156–184	12/04/2022
22	Global E-Commerce in the Light of COVID-19—A Case Study of Algeria Fadilat Faniya	Journal of Banking Financial Economics and Business Administration, Volume: 11 / Issue: 01 (2022), pp. 185–201	12/04/2022
23	The repercussions of the Covid-19 pandemic on e-commerce in the Kingdom of Saudi Arabia Asma Ben Tarad	Journal of the Research Unit in Human Resources Development Volume 17 / Issue 1 (Special) May 2022	–/05/2022
24	The impact of COVID-19 pandemic on the development of e-commerce in World Allali Fatiha. Allali Zahra	Journal of Economic Growth and Entrepreneurship, Volume: 05 / No. 2 (2022), pp. 1–11	31/05/2022

(continued)

Table 1 (continued)

No.	*Article title and author name*	*Journal*	*Date of publication*
25	Algerian public banks and the challenges of e-commerce under the Corona pandemic Ben Khaledi Nawal	Journal of Economic and Administrative Research, Volume 16 / Issue: 01 (2022), pp. 351–366	03/06/2022
26	Duality between online and offline shopping in the age of Covid-19. What future for e-commerce in Algeria? Tebache Djamal. Chetbani Saida	International journal of economic performance, Volume: 05 / Issue: 01 (2022), p. 399	04/06/2022
27	The recovery of electronic commerce in Algeria in light of the Corona pandemic (Covid 19) Eamir Buekaaz, Wadie Qasim	Horizons of Management Sciences and Economics, Volume 06 / Issue: 01 (2022), pp. 432–451	16/06/2022
28	The reality and contributions of E-Commerce in light of the Corona pandemic—International experiences madani hassiba, Seddaoui noura	Journal of Contemporary Economic Research, Volume 5 / Issue 2, pp. 1–18	30/10/2022
29	E-commerce challenges and their impact on marketing activity during the Corona Virus pandemic Qatar's e-commerce portal as a model for success and challenge during the Corona Virus Pandemic (2019–2021) lihawl fatum, nahar khaled bin alwalid	Forum Journal for Economic Studies and Research, Volume 06 / Issue: 02 (2022), pp. 591–608	04/11/2022
30	The contribution of coexistence with the Corona pandemic in activating e-commerce inAlgeria Kermia toufik, sebti hamza	Scientific Journal of Economic Dialogue, Volume 01 / Issue: 02 (2022), pp. 55–57	15/12/2022

Source Author's calculations

At the level of continents and countries (Seham, 2021) concluded that electronic commerce witnessed unprecedented growth, and Asia topped the first rank in terms of the volume of income generated from electronic commerce, amounting to 2.448.3 billion dollars, followed by the Americas with 832.63 million dollars, then Europe with 591.230 billion dollars.

The study (Seham, 2021) says that the Covid-19 pandemic revealed the fragility of the e-commerce infrastructure in many countries, especially African countries.

The study (Arroof, 2021) says that Covid-19 has changed the attitudes of consumers who have increased their consumption of necessities, such as food, and reduced the consumption of other goods such as clothing.

In the study (Arroof, 2021), the largest increase in online sales was recorded in the food sector (+20%) in Italy (+32.7%) in China (28%) in the USA (17.9%) in Italy during March 2020.

The most important and largest e-commerce markets in the world are, in order, according to a study (Ben Khaira et al., 2020, January 18), the Chinese market topped the e-commerce market in 2019 with an estimated amount of 867.9 billion US dollars, while the American market was estimated at 365.2 billion dollars in revenues US$1 billion in 2019. As for the Global Online Markets Online Market Ranking by Gross Goods Value (GMV) for 2019, the top five global online markets are Annazou, Tiall, Taobao, JD.coin, and eBay.

The study of (Faniya, 2022) and (Seham, 2021) confirmed that most of the global economic sectors (oil, tourism, transport, ...) were affected in light of the health crisis that cast a shadow at all levels, and recovery from it is not in the short term, especially after emergence of new strains of the virus.

The study (Ben Tarad, 2022) says that Covid-19 contributed to the growth of e-commerce by accelerating the digital transformation of various industries and companies and changing the behavior of individuals by moving towards platforms that were available for communication but were previously underused.

According to (Buridih, 2021), electronic commerce is linked to a certain level of sophistication, learning, and individual income, while most of the Algerian society is from fragile groups, low-income groups, workers and heads of families from various middle and poor social strata. These groups are not expected to deal in this way of trade, as they resort to most of them buy with a loan or pay the term, and therefore they are not interested in electronic payment or electronic commerce, especially with the terrible decline of commercial activity and the low public spending and the suspension of most public projects.

The situation of e-commerce in Algeria, according to the study (Salman, 2021) is still far from the aspirations and the actual capabilities that it has, especially in the period preceding the Covid-19 pandemic.

Amazon is the largest online market in the US according to (Ben Khaira et al., 2020, January 18) with $275 billion in US GMV, followed by eBay at $96 billions. The world's best online market sold $2.03 trillion.

5.2 *Results about the Gains and Opportunities of Electronic Commerce Considering the Covid-19 Pandemic*

A study (Brish, 2021) recorded that the fear of transmission through contact made many individuals move towards the option of paying through credit cards, prepaid cards, or online payment. Many countries have encouraged individuals to use digital money instead of chapter money, which has restored a kind of confidence to such financial transactions.

The shift to online purchases in most countries, according to a study (Bin Khaira et al., 2020, January 18) due to the Covid-19 epidemic, which increased e-commerce activity by providing the most demanded products such as alcohol and hand soap.

E-commerce in many countries of the world was in a state of growth before the emergence of the Covid-19 pandemic, but the pandemic, according to (Salman, 2021) gave it a strong impetus and acceleration, so retail sales increased at a steady pace and acquired a broader market share than traditional sales channels.

Under these exceptional circumstances, the world witnessed a significant growth in the volume of e-commerce after the rapid and sudden shift in the consumer trend from the traditional purchase model to the e-shopping model, thus, according to (Sadiqi et al., 2021), remote shopping sites and e-commerce platforms became the only outlet to revitalize the economy. Global economic growth stimulus, an effective solution to mitigate HIV infection.

E-commerce, according to a study (Seham, 2021), contributed to providing employment opportunities for individuals whose activities were suspended due to the pandemic, and from here it is expected that new jobs will appear in the future.

The pandemic has created a consumer e-commerce habit that is expected to be difficult to abandon in the future (Yaequbin, 2021).

Many traders and companies in the world have been affected by the quarantine procedures, and the biggest beneficiary under the current circumstances has become the companies most dependent on electronic commerce, according to a study (Buekaz et al., 2022).

A study (Darawish, et al., 2022) stated that there is a smart system employed by the Garment Trade Department in the Palestinian Hebron to motivate consumers to buy through social networking sites, during various promotional campaigns, which led to an increase in the demand for electronic commerce.

According to (Tawili, 2021), Saudi Arabia has replaced many efforts and initiatives aimed at developing and strengthening the e-commerce business system and overcoming its difficulties. e-commerce to protect consumers from fraud, deception, or misrepresentation.

The pandemic enabled the Saudi market to raise challenges, which helped it move towards the use of e-commerce by opening electronic applications for traditional stores to provide needs commensurate with these conditions to maintain customers (Ben Tarad, 2022).

A study (Bin Khaira et al., 2020, January 18) recorded an increase in electronic product demand on Amazon, and ordering products ordered online has become a common habit in light of this pandemic, in line with the imposed quarantine to reduce the risk of infection.

The consumer was dependent on e-commerce sites because of the great discounts and offers that they offer on some goods and products, but with the spread of Covid-19, a study (Ben Nama et al., 2021) says that purchase invoices often include more than one commodity, regardless of discounts and offers.

According to a study (Benai et al., 2021) that in Algeria expands the scope of online commerce to new categories of companies and consumers (for the elderly and food products for example).

E-commerce can help preserve jobs during a crisis. And creating new jobs (such as Amazon), which is what was stated in the study (Arroof, 2021).

According to Arroof, the e-commerce sector benefited from the boom in the pharmaceutical and food sector, which flourished during the crisis.

The study (Allali & Allali, 2022) found that e-commerce has witnessed an amazing leap in the advancement of technological innovations for brands, creating new ways to respond to a faster pace of digitization of e-commerce procedures.

5.3 *Results on the Performance of Electronic Commerce in Light of the Covid-19 Pandemic*

A study (Tawili, 2021) recorded that in June 2020, due to the Covid-19 virus, the global e-retail business recorded a record number of 22 billion monthly visits.

According to a study (Tawili, 2021): Health and Medicine achieved 581.37 million visits in May 2020, while e-commerce websites for books achieved 1.51 billion visits in March 2020, also websites that sell home decor and furniture products online in turn achieved 1.7 1 billion visits in March 2020.

In the opinion of (Dali et al., 2021), merchants resorted to the websites of companies to conclude deals and commercial contracts in an electronic way, provided that there is satisfaction between the contracting parties, because they are in the case of necessity.

E-commerce benefited from this pandemic to witness a 57% increase in global electronic transactions during the first quarter of 2020 only (Tabet & Bessouh, 2021).

According to the study (Benai et al., 2021), online sales transactions have partially shifted from luxury products and services to everyday consumer products that many people use.

According to a study (Seham, 2021), developed countries, especially China and the United States of America, Britain, Germany, and France, witnessed a significant increase in online retail revenues during the second semester of the year 2020 compared to previous years.

It was stated in the study (Salman, 2021) that Algeria has taken a number of measures that have been taken in order to improve the situation of e-commerce and address the effects of the Covid-19 pandemic, which contributed to improving its global ranking within the e-commerce index, but despite that it has not yet reached the level of aspirations that correspond to the capabilities available in comparison with other countries.

The study (Buridih, 2021) concluded that establishing facts about electronic commerce in Algeria in general was possible to benefit from electronic commerce as a measure to avoid the spread of the Covid-19 pandemic, and to confront the lack of cash-flow, but this did not happen despite the positive effects that would have been achieved if it had been seized this opportunity on the financial and health fronts;

It was stated in a study (Boukrif et al., 2022) that Algeria recorded in the years 2020 and 2021 an increase in the volume of electronic payment transactions and an increase in online purchases as a result of the spacing imposed by the pandemic.

The study (Darawish et al., 2022) indicated that the credibility and reliability of electronic commerce in light of a pandemic was moderate in the clothing sector in the Hebron Governorate in Palestine.

Since the outbreak of the Covid-19 virus, according to (Tawili, 2021) 48% of respondents from Saudi Arabia have used online shopping to purchase products frequently, which is a high percentage compared to the rest of the countries in the Middle East and North Africa region.

A study (Tawili, 2021) stated that the market value of the e-commerce industry in the Kingdom of Saudi Arabia amounted to about 4.9 billion US dollars in 2019, rising to 6.07 billion dollars in 2020 due to the spread of the Covid-19 virus.

E-commerce reflected a new historical stage in the march of the Saudi economy, where, according to (Tawili, 2021) it achieved great success locally and internationally, and this is reflected in the positive numbers that made it rank ninth in the field of improving e-commerce growth among Asian countries.

Despite the decline in Amazon's revenues in the first quarter of 2020, it achieved, according to (Ben Khaira et al., 2020, December 3), the weakness in the second quarter, due to the outbreak of the epidemic and the inevitable resort of dealers to electronic commerce.

As stated in the study (Ben Khaira et al., 2020, December 3) that the profits of Amazon shares increased to the limits of double in the second quarter of 2020 due to the recovery of electronic commerce, which may be among the reasons for the decline in revenues despite the profits achieved in the quarter The first of 2020 witnessed an increase in investment and spending on workers to protect their health and an increase in the number of workers to meet the demand.

According to (Bin Khaira et al., 2020, January 18), Amazon achieved an increasing net income in light of the spread of the Covid-19 pandemic and was not affected by it despite all the difficulties, despite the decrease in net income for the first quarter of 2020 compared to the year 2019, but the net profit in the quarter The second and third far outnumber her;

The largest e-commerce companies have achieved strong growth in sales according to a study (Arroof, 2021) which is respectively + 15.88%, +26%, −1.25% for Alibaba, Amazon and ebay, but the revenue is declining due to the cost of delivering more goods and protecting laborers.

It was found through a study (Darawish et al., 2022) that most of the dimensions of electronic commerce in light of the Covid-19 pandemic led to a noticeable increase in sales for many companies working in the field of electronic commerce during the pandemic.

5.4 *Findings on the Challenges and Risks of Electronic Commerce in Light of the Covid-19 Pandemic*

Despite the efforts made by some governments to encourage e-commerce during the pandemic, according to (Benai et al., 2021) it remains out of reach for some groups due to entrenched digital divides.

The study (Arroof, 2021) recorded that disrupted delivery (due to containment and prevention measures) and supply difficulties are the main negative impact of Covid on e-commerce.

Despite the prevalence of online commerce, it has not replaced traditional commerce (Allali & Allali, 2022) in many LDCs, the advantages of e-commerce are well known for its presentation, home delivery, and attractive prices. However, the majority of consumers and businesses have not taken advantage of the opportunities available, due to many persistent obstacles.

The study (Brish, 2021) warned of the development of economic and financial risks facing the countries of the world to include risks of liquidity, financing, and bankruptcy for some sectors, including small and medium industries, as a result of the repercussions of the Covid-19 pandemic.

The behavior of most citizens in Arab countries, according to a study (Ben Tarad, 2022) still faces fear of using the Internet, which constitutes an obstacle to the success of Arab e-commerce. The lack of awareness of the means of electronic marketing, especially the means of electronic payment, as a result of the lack of confidence in the security aspects of protecting their information through e-shopping and the lack of credibility of the published data, which leads them to become victims of fraud and fraud.

Seham (2021) confirmed that electronic commerce in the countries of the Arab Mashreq and Africa is still lagging the economic progression, and the gap between the economies of the countries in this pandemic has become clearer, as electronic commerce revenues amounted to 41.56

billion dollars, which represents 1.06 percent of the incomes achieved globally.

Despite the efforts made by Algeria to promote e-commerce and give a strong impetus to its advancement, in the opinion of (Yacoubin, 2021) it is declining compared to the rest of the countries, due to the lack of confidence in the e-commerce in the products offered to it remotely.

It was found through a study (Shadli et al., 2022) that not all sectors of activity benefited from trade.

It (Darawish et al., 2022) was found that the obstacles to electronic commerce were high in light of the Covid-19 pandemic in general, especially with regard to payment methods through electronic credit cards, and their rise indicates the presence of challenges facing clothing merchants in the Hebron Governorate in Palestine.

The conclusions of the study (Darawish et al., 2022) that clothing merchants in the Hebron Governorate in Palestine regarding the website indicate that it is possible that there may be a decline in consumer behavior and a limitation of purchase through websites with the end of the Covid-19 pandemic.

According to what was stated in a study (Bin Khaira et al., 2020, January 18), Amazon believes that in the current circumstances there are a number of potential challenges such as exchange rate fluctuations, changes in global economic conditions, customer spending volume, global events, growth rate Internet, online commerce and cloud services, depending on the duration and scope of the pandemic.

He warned (Buraidah, 2021) that the spread of many sellers who are not necessarily commerce on the level of social networking sites, and their illegal trading operations, in addition to the cases of fraud that consumers are exposed to, contributed to the decline in consumer confidence in general in this type of business. Trading.

The study (Buraidah, 2021) also showed that banks and postal agencies do not have a protective and secure policy for the electronic accounts of their customers, which contributed to the reluctance of large groups of account holders from using their card for electronic payments.

The pandemic has changed the principles of the online game according to (Seham, 2021). The ability to meet the growing needs of the consumer, provide services of quality and reliability, and reach the consumer wherever he is found is the main factor in maintaining market shares.

5.5 *Findings about the Obstacles of Electronic Commerce in Light of the Covid-19 Pandemic*

What the current situation required of precautionary measures and decisions taken by most countries to avoid the spread of the Covid-19 virus, this was reflected, according to the study (Glamor et al., 2022), negatively and directly on the implementation of contractual obligations, some of which were impossible to implement completely under these exceptional circumstances, including its implementation has become burdensome for the debtor, and this will undoubtedly raise a large number of cases of exemption from liability on the basis of force majeure before the courts.

It was stated in the study (Allali & Allali, 2022) that e-commerce is still far from reach for some because of the inappropriate regulations for it in some countries. However, networks, software, and human components are the basis of this complexity in e-commerce. In addition, issues of online payment security and data privacy, including an overreliance on cash and a shared mistrust.

The image of e-commerce for some Arab countries, according to (Ben Trad, 2022) differs from the rest of the world, as many Arab companies are far from the process of online commerce, and the reason is that they are left behind in electronic transactions.

The Covid-19 epidemic did not contribute to the adoption of electronic payment in the Algerian state of Jijel, according to a study (Buridih, 2021), as the lack of infrastructure made the completion of electronic commerce operations through postal and bank cards unsecured and its results unsafe, and it was only available to interbank card holders. CIB" as the majority of employees and wage earners do not have such cards.

The results reveal a study (Chanoune & Boukrif, 2021) on the state of the e-commerce market in Algeria. This sector still suffers from obstacles such as the distrust of the Algerian consumer and the lack of habit of buying online although the latter can be an alternative or complement to traditional buying, especially in this global health crisis.

He warned (Benai et al., 2021) that inappropriate regulations for e-commerce in Algeria could create obstacles for companies.

6 Research Recommendations on the Development of Electronic Commerce in Light of the Covid-19 Pandemic

6.1 *Recommendations Addressed to Governments on the Development of Electronic Commerce in Light of the Covid-19 Pandemic*

In the opinion of the study (Brish, 2021) the need for state intervention by urging banks to facilitate the granting of new loans to support working capital in small and medium enterprises, and to encourage loan renewal processes through regulatory leniency and guarantees.

According to the study (Ben khalidi, 2022), it is necessary to work on building a strong infrastructure for electronic commerce and to pay attention to the quality of the Internet flow to facilitate the process of communication, whether between banks or customers.

According to (Ben Khalidi, 2022) it is necessary to work on developing the banking environment in line with electronic transactions.

Work to activate the practice of e-commerce and add an element of security according to (Faniya, 2022) by enacting laws that protect the consumer from being subjected to fraud;

In order to benefit from the benefits of e-commerce, it is recommended (Salman, 2021) that decision makers at all levels should think about providing the necessary mechanisms to adopt dealing with it and provide the necessary environment for its development.

It is also recommended (Salman, 2021) that Algeria should make more efforts and work to update the legal texts related to commerce in general and e-commerce in particular, and to punish violators of dealing in the latter.

A study on governments (Shadli et al., 2022) indicated the establishment of facilities by reducing taxes and fees on electronic business transactions.

Expanding the scope of legal texts to include, according to (Buraidah, 2021) the relationships between the economic operators themselves.

In the opinion of (Seham, 2021), work to introduce the remote work system in anticipation of future crises similar to the current one.

The study (Yaequbin, 2021) encouraged more investment in information and communication technology to keep pace with the development taking place in the economies of developed countries.

It recommended (Ben Trad, 2022) to stimulate the private sector to e-commerce, reduce cultural and legal obstacles, introduce facilities, and prepare the legal environment to be clear of use and keep pace with technology and laws governing trade.

It also recommended (Aleayiba, 2020) that judges should be flexible when adjudicating labor disputes related to the termination of the work relationship due to the Covid-19 virus, until the legislative texts are amended in line with environmental changes and natural developments that go beyond the natural estimate.

According to (Aleayiba, 2020), it is important to establish special committees or exceptional funds at the level of social security funds, to take charge of workers' wages in crises that are imposed due to the health emergency and emerging viruses.

According to (Tabet & Bessouh, 2021) it is necessary to know that this type of trade as a real engine of economic recovery can have a promising future provided that an efficient and modern payment system is established;

According to the study (Chanoune & Boukrif, 2021), a clear policy and a coherent strategy must be developed by the state, companies, banks, and specialized associations in order to launch e-commerce in this way and follow successful experiences.

According to (Allali & Allali, 2022) it is necessary to accelerate the digitization of small companies and pay more attention to digital entrepreneurship and encourage the creation of start-ups in this field.

6.2 *Recommendations Addressed to International Bodies on the Development of Electronic Commerce Considering the Covid-19 Pandemic*

It is very necessary, according to the study (Aleayiba, 2020) to reconsider the environmental dimension in all areas of communication, communications, transactions, and individual and collective human behaviors, because all human relations in direct contact with the environment are affected and affected by it.

It is recommended according to (Buraidah, 2021) to establish partnerships with international bodies and organizations, as is the case with the United Nations Conference on Trade and Development "unctad" to benefit from its plans to develop a strategic partnership to develop the e-commerce sector;

The need to reconsider, according to (Seham, 2021) information technology projects and the infrastructure of electronic commerce in the third world countries and work to reduce the technological gap between countries so that there are no obstacles during the practice of electronic commerce.

Work must be done to activate the practice of electronic commerce according to (Seham, 2021) and to enact international laws governing foreign electronic commerce.

Giving the Arab countries that know a delay in the field of e-commerce, and in particular Algeria, according to (Tawili, 2021) the greatest attention to this concept because of its importance, by providing infrastructures of digitization and technology, in addition to taking from Saudi Arabia's success in the field of e-commerce and what it has reached impressive results and figures, an example and a model for it.

A study (Faniya, 2022) recommended reducing the technological gap between countries, especially African countries, by reconsidering their infrastructure and proposing projects that would support e-commerce.

After the Covid-19 virus revealed the weakness of electronic trading in some Arab countries, it is necessary, according to (Ben Tarad, 2022) to expedite the study of the reasons for the delay in electronic commerce in these countries, and to develop effective, rapid and tested solutions to activate this trade in their countries.

6.3 Recommendations to Companies Regarding the Development of Electronic Commerce Considering the Covid-19 Pandemic

In light of the development in the field of informatics, a study (Ben Khaira et al., 2020, December 3) recommended dropping what successful companies in the field of e-commerce, such as Amazon, do on Algerian companies to ensure their sustainability in light of the Covid-19 crisis and not to fall into bankruptcy.

According to the opinion of (Ben Khaira et al., 2020, December 3), electronic commerce should be taken care of as an alternative to real commerce, as it generates important returns for companies.

Opinion (Bresh, 2021) on the need for an early response to the integration in electronic commerce after the pandemic, which requires continuous reformulation of models and action plans.

Adapting according to (Brish, 2021) to current needs, making quick decisions, abandoning traditional work plans, and trying new ways of doing business according to electronic platforms are among the main factors for the success of companies after the pandemic.

It is important, according to (Bialhabib et al., 2021) the availability of a strategic management vision for the company that is active in the field of e-commerce transactions, which ensures the continuity of activity accompanied by strengthening customer confidence in e-shopping.

The necessity of creating powerful digital platforms for each company, according to the opinion of (Tabet & Bessouh, 2021).

In the opinion of (Allali & Allali, 2022), companies need bold and smart regulatory frameworks to work with governments and the private sector to take advantage of e-commerce opportunities.

The need to focus on developing companies' websites to face, according to the recommendation of (Darawish et al., 2022) the challenges imposed by internal and external competition.

It is necessary in the recommendations of (Darawish et al., 2022) to promote the allocation of budgets to enhance promotional campaigns to increase methods of consumer communication and to overcome obstacles related to contacting consumers through companies, access to marketing sectors, bypassing closures, and increasing its market share in those sectors.

According to the opinion of (Darawish et al., 2022) it is better to preserve the advantages of exploiting disasters and turn them into strengths, as happened in the Covid-19 pandemic, where many companies emerged with high profits as a result of their exploitation of the current circumstances.

6.4 *Recommendations Addressed to Banks Regarding the Development of Electronic Commerce in Light of the Covid-19 Pandemic*

I recommend (Yacoubin, 2021) in his study that electronic payment methods must be developed and their use in shops generalized so that citizens can complete the stages of electronic purchase.

It is necessary to link the merchant's account, according to the recommendation of (Darawish et al., 2022) with local banks, which will facilitate payment through websites.

It is necessary to provide protection and security devices according to (Ben Khalidi, 2022) to gain the confidence of customers in bank cards.

According to the study (Boukas et al., 2022), banks should be encouraged to establish an advanced banking system that accepts electronic commercial transactions, adopt electronic payment systems, and use the various available modern payment methods.

6.5 Recommendations Addressed to the Organizations Supporting Institutions Regarding the Development of Electronic Commerce in Light of the Covid-19 Pandemic.

Among the recommendations of the study (Darawish et al., 2022) is the need to qualify commerce and customers to deal with electronic payment cards through workshops organized by the required authorities such as local banks and chambers of commerce.

He also recommended (Darawish et al., 2022) the necessity of coordinating with the various authorities to make the e-commerce system a success, to obtain legal permissions, and to give the legal character to e-commerce.

According to (Darawish et al., 2022) the consumer must be made aware of the importance of electronic shopping and facilitate the task of obtaining electronic payment cards.

6.6 Recommendations Addressed to Civil Associations on the Development of Electronic Commerce in Light of the Covid-19 Pandemic

It is necessary to cultivate a culture of e-marketing among the segments of society, according to (Buraidah, 2021) through conducting awareness-raising campaigns to inform the media about the importance of this type of marketing.

Strengthening the electronic commerce system and showing the advantages it obtains in the opinion of (Darawish et al., 2022) through commercial transactions through the electronic system.

In my opinion (Faniya, 2022), it is necessary to spread the culture of remote dealing among merchants and consumers and work to raise awareness through training programs in the field of digitization and electronic commerce.

Also recommended (Shadli et al., 2022) to develop awareness programs on the importance of electronic commerce.

7 Conclusion

Finally, through this chapter, the results and recommendations of 30 studies concerned with the impact of Covid-19 on electronic commerce published on the "Algerian Portal of Scientific Journals" platform, from the year 2020 to 15 October 2023, have been shed light on the reality of electronic commerce. In light of the Covid-19 pandemic, our chapter clarified the gains and opportunities of electronic commerce and its performance in light of the Covid-19 pandemic, through the reference studies, and we also summarized the challenges, risks, and obstacles of electronic commerce through the studies published on the mentioned platform.

As for the recommendations, our current chapter was keen to summarize and organize a set of recommendations on the development of electronic commerce in light of the Covid-19 pandemic and beyond, which were brought by the research published on the "Algerian Portal of Scientific Journals" platform, which focused on the impact of Covid-19 on electronic commerce, as those recommendations were directed to a number of different parties, including: governments and international bodies, as it was directed to companies and their supporters, banks and even civil associations.

References

Aleayiba samia. (2020, November). The repercussions of the emerging corona virus on the labor market, "E-commerce as a model". *Journal of Labor and Employment Law, 5*(4).

Allali, F., & Allali, Z. (2022). The impact of COVID-19 pandemic on the development of e-commerce in world. *Journal of Economic Growth and Entrepreneurship, 5*(2).

Arroof, A. (2021, June). The E-commerce business in time of Covid-19: Positive impact. *Revue des sciences humaines de l'université Oum El Bouaghi, 2.*

Ben khalidi nawal. (2022). Algerian public banks and the challenges of e-commerce under the Corona pandemic. *Journal of Economic and Management Research, 16*(1).

Ben khaira milud et masnueatun asma. (2020, January 18). The performance of e-commerce companies in light of the spread of the Corona virus between reality and challenges—Amazon as a model. *Afaq Journal for Research and Studies, 4*(1).

Ben khaira Miloud, Hathli Fawaz et Dinawi Anfal Aisha. (2020, December 3). The reality of the performance of e-commerce companies in light of the spread of the Corona virus—Amazon case study as a model. *Value Added Journal of Business Economics, 2*(1).

Ben nama fatimat alzuhrati, eidat muhamadu et ben nama nuria. (2021). The reality of e-commerce in Algeria before and after the Corona pandemic, a statistical analytical study for the period 2016–2021. *Journal of Economics and Environment, 4*(3).

Ben tarad asma. (2022, May). The repercussions of the Covid-19 pandemic on e-commerce in the Kingdom of Saudi Arabia. *Journal of Research Unit in Human Resource Development, 17*(1).

Benai, M., Guettafi, S., & Larab, S. (2021). The impact of the Covid-19 pandemic on e-commerce in Algeria. *Journal of Administrative and Financial Sciences, 5*(2).

Bialhabib Eabd Alkamli, Miduki Yusif et Zaqrir Eadil. (2021). E-commerce in Algeria: Obstacles and development requirements referring to the covid-19 pandemic. *Journal of Administrative Sciences, 5*(1).

Bouriche Nouria et Benbouziane Mohamed. (2022, March). Predicting the direction of e-commerce stock prices during COVID 19 using machine learning. *Journal of Economic Integration, 10*(1).

Brish Khaled. (2021, December). The effects of the Corona pandemic (Covid-19) on small and medium enterprises and the inevitability of their integration into e-commerce in Algeria. *Business Finance Magazine, 6*(2).

Buekaz Eamir et Qasima Wadie. (2022). The recovery of electronic commerce in Algeria in light of the Corona pandemic (Covid 19). *Horizons Journal of Management Sciences and Economics, 6*(1).

Buridih Suraya. (2021, June). E-commerce and its impact on the corona pandemic, a field study at the level of Jijel state. *Al Manhal Economic Magazine, 4*(1).

Chanoune, N., & Boukrif, M. (2021). The containment effect caused by the COVID-19 pandemic on the e-commerce sector in Algeria. *Algerian Journal of Economics and Management, 15*(2).

Dali Bashir et Bukhari Asma. (2021). The reality of e-commerce in the Corona pandemic. *Journal of Legal Studies, 8*(2).

Darawish Eabd Alqadir, Fadl Eidatun et Mulaha Majid. (2022). The impact of the Corona pandemic on e-commerce in the clothing sector in Hebron Governorate. *Journal of Banking Financial Economics and Business Administration, 11*(1).

Faniya Fadila. (2022). Global e-commerce in the light of COVID-19—A case study of Algeria. *Journal of Banking Financial Economics and Business Administration, 11*(1).

Glamor Mercy et Dalaj Muhammad Al-Khidr. (2022, October). The impact of the Corona pandemic on the implementation of contractual obligations and on e-commerce. *Journal of Law and Human Sciences, 13*(3).

Sadiqi Ahmadu et Altiybi Abd Allah. (2021). Global e-commerce transactions in light of the repercussions of the Corona pandemic "Covid 19". *Irtiqa Journal for Research and Economic Studies, 2*(2).

Salman Husayn. (2021). E-commerce in Algeria between reality and challenges in light of the repercussions of the Corona pandemic (Covid 19). *Journal of Economic Studies, 21*(1).

Seham Musiun. (2021). The impact of the Corona pandemic on the growth of electronic commerce in the world, an analytical study. *Organization and Work Magazine, 9*(41).

Shadli Shawqi et Mahawatu Amal. (2022). E-commerce in light of the COVID-19 pandemic: Opportunities and challenges. *Journal of Economic Growth and Entrepreneurship, 5*(1).

Tabet, D., & Bessouh, N. (2021, December). COVID-19: The explosion of e-commerce. *The MECAS Notebooks, 17*(4).

Tawili Yasmina. (2021). E-commerce gains in light of the Corona pandemic—A glimpse of e-commerce in Saudi Arabia during the pandemic. *Journal of the Economic Researcher, 9*(2).

Tebache, D., & Chetbani, S. (20222). Duality between online and offline shopping in the age of Covid-19: What future for e-commerce in Algeria? *International Journal of Economic Performance, 5*(1).

www.asjp.cerist.dz [En ligne].

www.bts-academy.com [En ligne].

www.maktabtk.com [En ligne].

Yaequbin Saliha. (2021). The repercussions of the Corona pandemic on electronic commerce—With reference to the case of Algeria. *Economic Dimensions Magazine, 11*(2).

CHAPTER 6

The Role of Tarassud Plus Application in Serving the Government and Society During COVID-19 Pandemic

Kawther Al Abri, Laila Al Sibani, Abdullah Al Yarubi, and Faten Hamad

1 Introduction

Coronavirus disease 2019 (Covid-19) is highly contagious, with a rapid high death rate, originating in Wuhan. It was confirmed by the World Health Organization (WHO) in January 2020 and became an outbreak all over the world. Globally, there have been 559,469,605 confirmed cases of Covid-19, including 6,361,157 deaths, reported to World Health Organization as of 11 July 2022, a total of 12,130,881,147 vaccine doses have been administered (WHO Coronavirus [COVID-19] Dashboard, 2022). Governments took different measures to prevent and control the spread of Covid-19 starting from closing schools to a complete closure of some businesses and total lockdown. However, technology played a vital role in supporting the government during the pandemic. Currently,

K. Al Abri (✉)
Business Administration, Sultan Qaboos University, Al-Khoud, Oman
e-mail: kawtheralabri@squ.edu.om

A. Mishrif (ed.), *Business Resilience and Market Adaptability*, The Political Economy of the Middle East,
https://doi.org/10.1007/978-981-97-2962-3_6

governments tend to digitize their transactions and services. Digitalization has the potential to significantly improve the delivery of health care to individuals and communities. Hospitals have been digitizing their services and remodeling the entire health-care system. Digitalization not only improves patient safety and satisfaction, but it also keeps population health statistics current. Because approximately 6 billion people (roughly 75% of the world's population) have access to mobile phones, mobile health applications have become an important channel for healthcare service providers to provide healthcare services (Islam et al., 2020).

2 Problem Statement

The term health technologies appeared as one of the new era terms. It is defined by the World Health Organization as "the application of organized knowledge and skills in the form of devices, medicines, vaccines, procedures, and systems developed to solve a health problem and improve quality of life" (Kushendriawan et al., 2021). In addition, Digital Contact Tracing (DCT) developed and promoted in many countries in the context of the Covid-19 pandemic. It was considered as a valuable tool to help the fight against the virus. It allows health authorities to react quickly and limit contagion (Lavorgna et al., 2021). This study chose to shed light on Tarassud plus application to be evaluated due to its significant role as an essential platform for contacts and case listing to ensure proper follow-up and documentation by public health authorities.

This chapter explores how the technology represented by Tarassud Plus Application supported the government in Oman and served the society during the Covid-19 pandemic. It assessed the user experience of the health technology services in Tarassud Plus App which is provided by the

L. Al Sibani
Omani Studies Centre, Sultan Qaboos University, Al-Khoud, Oman
e-mail: laila.zahran@squ.edu.om

A. Al Yarubi
Information System Administration, Caledonian College, Seeb, Oman

F. Hamad
Information Studies, Sultan Qaboos University, Al-Khoud, Oman
e-mail: f.hamad@squ.edu.om

government. In addition, the research assessed Omani society's readiness to embrace technology. The research ended up with recommendations related to the effective employment of technology to manage similar crises in the future.

3 Research Objectives

The main aim of this research was to investigate the role of technology provided by Emushrif in supporting the government and society in Oman during the Covid-19 pandemic, to assess the UX (User Experience) of Tarassud Plus App, to assess the Omani society's readiness to embrace technology and to come up with recommendations related to the effective employment of technology crisis management in the future. The research questions are (1) How Technology based services represented by Tarassud Plus Application supported the government to manage the crisis in Oman? and (2) What is the user experience with health technology-based services (Tarassud Plus App) provided during Covid-19 pandemic?

4 Literature Review

4.1 The Use of Technology to Manage Covid-19 Pandemic.

Timely monitoring, screening, investigations, and stringent isolation appear to be common tactics used by nations with low Covid-19 per-capita survival rates. The most prosperous countries have depended on incorporating technological innovation and incorporating it into healthcare policies and care to the extent of collaboration and information systems needed for the efficient adoption of these policies. With the use of cloud computing and business communication tools like Zoom and Skype, it is possible for an individual to pose confronted by a simulated environment while still being at their own home. Less migration and societal dissemination will arise as a result (Ruktanonchai et al., 2020). Working remotely not only reduces Covid-19 virus spread but also saves time and offers more versatility. If telecommuting becomes more widespread after the Covid-19 pandemic, businesses may decide to reduce lease costs and recruit workers from regions with cheap labor costs (Zhao et al., 2021). Moreover, the Covid-19 had significantly changed the world's distribution network. Several companies were forced to close due to biosecurity and distance rules. Despite rising consumer desire for food, medical supplies, and personal protection equipment, some nations imposed varied degrees of trade restrictions on these items (Jiang, 2021). Taiwan was especially susceptible to Covid-19 because of its closeness to Wuhan, China, but its effective use of big data is attributed with the region's low incidence of illnesses and fatalities (Wang et al., 2020).

A network created by Swedish Health Services, a US-based medical company allowing healthcare professionals to provide real-time information regarding patient numbers with Covid-19, individual protective equipment, personnel, respiratory utilization, and other supplies and equipment (Drees, 2021). To monitor the condition of buildings, distribute medical resources, and boost inpatient bed occupancy, this knowledge disseminated throughout its facilities (Drees, 2021). China employed inexpensive web- and cloud-based solutions to vet people and point them in the direction of the proper help (Hu et al., 2020a, 2020b).

A commercial entity in the USA utilized electronic thermostats to gather actual information on rheumatic fever clusters, and nationwide research is using wearable software to record heart rates at rest in an effort to detect Covid-19 developing pandemics (Whitelaw et al., 2020). These projects lack integration into practices and policies since they are primarily corporate or investigative. In order to provide immediate information and better timeframes of people's transportation, South Korea has incorporated tools for forceful contact marking that use global positioning system (GPS) data from automobiles and cellular phones, surveillance camera footage, facial recognition technology debit card documents, and other data sources (Fisher & Sang-Hun, 2020). Urgent SMS notifications sent to South Koreans especially with new Covid-19 instances in their area, and those who may have come into touch with the sick are told to go to testing facilities and quarantine themselves. South Korea managed to keep its per-capita fatality rates among the smallest in the world by recognizing and treating illnesses promptly (Fisher & Sang-Hun, 2020).

A wristwatch app has been introduced in Germany that monitors sleeping patterns, heat, and heartbeat to check for viral sickness symptoms (Busvine, 2020). Regulators can estimate the possibility of Covid-19 occurrence nationwide using statistics from the software shown on an electronic, online version (Busvine, 2020). Germany kept its per-capita fatality rate modest in comparison to other economies while having a high frequency of diseases thanks to ubiquitous screening and electronic health initiatives (Busvine, 2020).

Government-issued cell devices with GPS tracking are used in Taiwan to spy on people under residential isolation electronically (Wang et al., 2020). If someone violates the isolation, this "digital fence" sends them notifications and imposes a penalty (Wang et al., 2020). People under self-isolation in Hong Kong are compelled to wear wristbands connected via cloud infrastructure to a computer that notifies officials if containment is violated.

Machines were also employed to cleanse objects and regions where the disease is thought to have been considerably damaged, as well as in public spaces where many people utilize or congregate. In some nations, they employed to transport food to homes when they were under confinement. Drones used to keep an eye on individuals and carry supplies to hospitals so that patients can receive care. Many believe that considering these developments, social communication will become more limited and industrial occupations will be replaced by robots. Additionally, it will lead to the development of new jobs in the ICT sector (Renu, 2021).

4.2 Covid-19 in Oman

As of the given time frame from January 3, 2020, to November 22, 2023, Oman reported a total of 399,449 confirmed cases of Covid-19 with 4628 deaths to the World Health Organization. Additionally, by October 24, 2022, a total of 7,086,050 vaccine doses had been administered in Oman as part of efforts to vaccinate the population against Covid-19. This data reflects the country's vaccination campaign progress in immunizing individuals against the virus up to that specific date (*Oman: Who coronavirus disease (covid-19) dashboard with vaccination data, 2023*).

The government of Oman, based on supreme directives, formed a supreme committee to examine the mechanism of dealing with developments resulting from the spread of Covid-19 in light of the emerging health indicators. In addition to the World Health Organization information and instruction, the supreme committee ensured the provision of care and protection to members of the Omani society and foreigners residing in the country, several directives, and administrative decisions by the Supreme Committee. A significant role was played by Oman Technology Fund in partnership with UNICEF office encouraging initiatives of young people to confront Covid-19.

The Ministry of Health in Oman introduced a contact tracing (CT) system based on three complementary digital tools as part of its digital transformation from traditional paper-based methods: Tarassud plus, Medical Scout and HMushrif applications. All contacts in the laboratory confirmed or possible Covid-19 cases were advised to install all three applications that synergistically manage the various steps of CT on their smartphones. However, Tarassud plus application was developed by MoH, While Medical Scout application developed by a global company (Al Burkan Company), and HMushrif application was developed by E Mushrif Company which is a local company (Al Manji et al., 2022).

4.3 *Tarassud Plus Application*

Tarassud Plus is Oman's official Covid-19 application for citizens, residents, and visitors. The application's authority is restricted to the country until the pandemic is declared over. This application provides data on infectious diseases to citizens and residents. The Ministry of Health developed and ran the application. It includes features such as quarantine tracking, digital vaccination certificates, RT PCR results, and Covid-19-related statistics (Fig. 1).

The Ministry of Health has used artificial intelligence technology by launching the Tarassud Plus system of epidemiological investigation based on artificial intelligence technology, which is supported by the medical

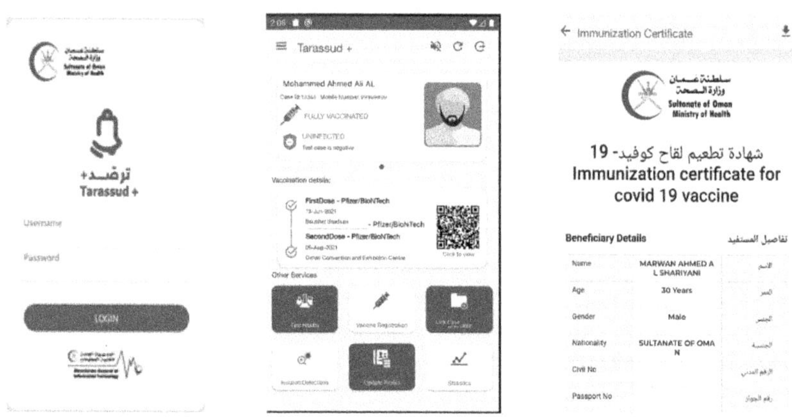

Fig. 1 Tarassud Plus application

detector and medical supervisor programs. Individuals use this application because the system is distinguished by the ability to communicate with the virtual support team via the medical detector icon. It has a role in the evaluation of an individual's health status through symptom analysis, allowing for continuous follow-up. It is useful in tracking infected and isolated people or contacts and directing them to health institutions. The medical detector app is also available in five languages: Arabic, English, Hindi, Bengali, and Urdu, allowing it to be used by people of all nationalities who live in the Sultanate of Oman. The system aims to limit disease spread by increasing the efficiency of geographical tracking of cases where isolation has been applied and assessing the extent of their commitment and adherence to the isolation instructions, as well as tracking contacts, especially given the growing number of cases and geographical expansion. It also enables automatic identification of the isolated identity using face recognition technology. If a smart bracelet is detected nearby, the system notifies the user, and the GPS and Bluetooth services are activated (Al Balushi, 2022). According to Wahaj Alkhaleej electronic newspaper (June 28, 2022), The Sultanate of Oman, represented by the Ministry of Health won the His Highness Sheikh Salem Al-Ali Al-Sabah Informatics Award in Kuwait for (Trassed Plus), in its 20th session this year 2022 as the best projects concerned with developing human capabilities in the field of information development, Under the patronage of His Highness Sheikh Nawaf Al-Ahmad Al-Jaber Al-Sabah, Emir of the State of Kuwait (Al-Jaradi, 2022) (Fig. 2).

4.4 *Tarassud Plus Application Advantages*

Mobile Health technology allows the use of real-time data to prevent and control pandemic and diseases that are constantly changing (Salehinejad et al., 2020). Dr. Sulien al Khalili from the Ministry of Health (2020) indicated that the system has been useful in communicating with and guiding people. People who have used the app have given it a positive response. She explained: "I think the main reason is that the individuals have the support when they really need it, and for us it has made our lives easy because nowadays the geographical data such as where they are located and how many are infected as well as how many have been in contact area now easier to comprehend. It is also convenient to communicate with the people" (Kothaneth, 2020). The main strength of this data management platform is its accessibility to users. Community members

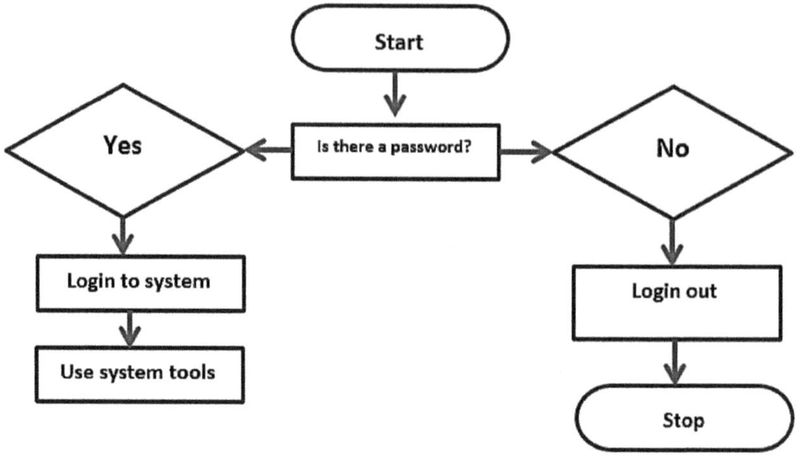

Fig. 2 Tarassud Plus mechanism

have free access to the platform to update information and see Covid-19 test results and vaccination status. Another advantage is easy access to key stakeholders such as private hospitals and laboratories. This allows for collaboration between departments and reduces the burden on health ministry staff. Prior to its implementation in Oman, this approach was not widely used in Electronic Medical Records (EMR). However, similar approaches to CT are used around the world, each using its own tools to ensure the highest possible level of data protection. Although the implementation of CT remains a challenging process, Oman's experience was remarkable as an evidence-based model adapted to the dynamic nature of the pandemic and could be replicated in other countries (Al Manji et al., 2022).

4.5 *Tarassud Plus Application Challenges*

Given the limited offline operability of the applications, managing contacts data was one of the key issues that arose. Operators used a two-step process in places with poor internet connectivity, first gathering data on paper before entering it into the system. Furthermore, the Oman Ministry of Health lacked national risk communication guidelines to address community concerns and widespread rumors. Fatigue associated with the implementation of Covid-19 PHSMs tended to increase a sense of distrust, which manifested itself with a higher proportion of respondents expressing fear, anxiety, and distrust, and who can be aggressive or reluctant to cooperate at times. Community leaders, on the other hand, played a significant role in calming such situations and facilitating tracers' access to cases and contacts within their communities. Another problem is that the system is extremely centralized, with all data stored on a single server. This exposes the system to privacy violations (piracy) and raises ethical concerns. However, measures have been put in place to limit operator and supervisor access. At the moment, access restrictions have been implemented based on geographical location, which means that district level operators can only see data from cases within their district, governorate level supervisors can only manage data from their governorate, and national level operators serve as system administrators (Al Manji et al., 2022).

4.6 User Experience Evaluation

Usability, also known as user testing, refers to how well an app works and whether or not it fulfills its intended purpose. User ratings of app flexibility, operability, understandability, learnability, efficiency, satisfaction, attractiveness, consistency, and error rates are commonly used to assess usability (Jake-Schoffman et al., 2017). Evaluating app usability can assist developers in meeting the needs of users by designing simple and useful apps. Previous research has looked at apps that can help patients with chronic diseases. A reliable and objective tool for app evaluation is required to rate the degree to which mHealth apps satisfy quality criteria. One of the tools is The Mobile Application Rating Scale (MARS), it is simple to use and provides a multidimensional measure of app quality indicators such as engagement, functionality, aesthetics, and information quality, as well as app subjective quality (Salehinejad et al., 2020). This research evaluates the user experience in Tarassud Plus App in order to reach the extent of user satisfaction with this service provided by the government during the pandemic.

5 Methodology

The Quantitative approach based on the survey method was adopted. It is an approach that helps researchers to collect, analyze, compare, and conclude findings. "The selection of a research approach is also based on the nature of the research problem or issue being addressed, the researchers' personal experiences, and the audiences for the study" (Creswell, 2014). By selecting a quantitative approach for this survey-based research, the researchers aimed to gather numerical data to analyze and draw conclusions about the society's response to technological services and user experiences during Covid-19 Pandemic as this method is suitable for evaluating trends, patterns, and correlations within the collected data.

5.1 Data Collection Tool

For this purpose, a questionnaire was prepared and disseminated using Google forms. The questionnaire was prepared based on reviewing the literature and based on some features and characteristics of Tarassud applications. The types of questions were multiple choice, checkboxes, and likert scale. This diversity in question types allows for collecting both categorical and ordinal data. The survey was designed using Google Forms and included various types of questions such as multiple choice, checkboxes, and Likert scale items. The questionnaire was organized over three sections, which are: The first section aimed to gather demographic information about the respondents, which is crucial for understanding the sample characteristics. The second section targeted opinions and perceptions of the society toward technological services managed by the government. While the third and last section focused on evaluating the user experience of the Tarassud application. The survey was distributed in both Arabic and English languages to maximize the response rate and cater to a wider audience.

5.2 Population and Sample

The research adopted convenient sampling technique to target 1000 respondents from Oman, encompassing citizens and expatriates of both

Table 1 Age, area of residence, and the qualifications of the respondents

		Frequency	*Percent*
Age	18–24	39	12.3
	25–34	120	37.9
	35–44	114	36.0
	45–54	36	11.4
	55–64	6	1.9
	65+	2	0.6
	Total	317	100.0
Area of Residence	Al Batinah North	33	10.4
	Al Batinah South	34	10.7
	Al Buraimi	7	2.2
	Al Dakhiliya	61	19.2
	Al Dhahira	16	5.0
	Al Sharqiya North	8	2.5
	Al Sharqiya South	5	1.6
	Dhofar	18	5.7
	Musandam	1	0.3
	Muscat	134	42.3
	Total	317	100.0
Qualification	Less than High School	7	2.2
	High school	49	15.5
	Diploma	50	15.8
	Bachelor	140	44.2
	Master	55	17.4
	PhD	16	5.0
	Total	317	100.0

Source Authors calculations

genders aged between 18 and 65. However, the actual number of respondents was 317, representing a variety of individuals from different regions of the country, making the response rate 31.7% as indicated in Table 1.

5.3 *Data Analysis*

The collected data was analyzed using Statistical Package for the Social Sciences (SPSS), a statistical software commonly used for quantitative analysis. This software assists in interpreting and drawing conclusions from the gathered data.

6 Findings and Discussion

Table 1 represents the distribution of respondents across different age brackets. Understanding the demographics of the respondents provides insights into how different age groups vary in experiences and preferences concerning the technological services being studied. The majority of respondents lie in the 25–34 age bracket (around 38%). 36% of respondents are between 35 and 44 years old. Participants with ages between 55 and 64 represent about 2%, while only 0.6% of them are older than 65 years old. Different age groups perceive and interact with technological services or applications differently.

The respondents living in Muscat represent 42.3% which is the highest. The number of respondents living in Al Batinah North and Al Batinah South are nearly the same, accounting for 10.4% and 10.7% respectively. Respondents living in Dhofar, Al Dhahira, Al Sharqiya North, Al Buraimi, and Al Sharqiya South represent 5.7%, 5%, 2.5%, 2.2%, and 1.6% respectively.

Most of the respondents have a bachelor's degree, representing 44.2%. Respondents with diploma or high school are approximately the same, with 15.8% and 15.5% respectively. Respondents holding postgraduate degrees (i.e., master and Ph.D.) are 22.4%. Very few respondents are less than high school qualified, representing only 2.2%.

Table 2 shows that most participants have used Tarrasud App during Covid-19, representing 92.1%. Other services, such as Rased, Sahala Platform, and Tracking bracelet, have been used by about 8% of participants.

Table 2 Types of E-Systems used during Covid-19 pandemic

System		*Frequency*	*Percent*
Valid	Rased	3	0.9
	Sahala Platform	1	0.3
	Tarrasud App	292	92.1
	Tarrasud App, Rased	3	0.9
	Tarrasud App, Sahala Platform	4	1.3
	Tarrasud App, Tracking bracelet	12	3.8
	Tracking bracelet	2	0.6
	Total	317	100.0

Source Authors calculations

This data offers insights into the demographics of the respondents based on their geographic locations, educational qualifications, and their utilization of specific services during the pandemic. The results clearly show that the highest percentage of respondents were located in Muscat, with a bachelor degree and used Tarrasud App as the most used technological service during the pandemic by 92.1%.

The high percentage of users who used the Tarassud Plus Application indicated the importance of the application as a source of information to society individuals and families during Covid-19 pandemic taking into consideration that it is the official government system and the mode of communication between the society and the government.

Table 3 shows that 83.6% of the users are satisfied with the services provided by the government during Covid-19. About 69% of participants think that the technology was implemented appropriately to control the spread of Covid-19 compared to approximately 32% of respondents with opposite opinions. Around 88% of participants think that Omani society is ready and capable to utilize advanced technologies. This high percentage might be in relation with the respondent's level of education as 66.6% of respondents were bachelor, Master, and Ph.D. degree holders. 77.6% of respondents believed that E-health services decreased the rumors and misinformation during Covid-19 pandemic as all announcements and clauses from the governmental supreme committee are accessible in application.

Around 82% of participants think that the use of technology was effective to control the pandemic. Around 74% of participants believe that Oman performance is better than other countries regarding pandemic management. This percentage is supported by (Al Raqadi, 2020) as some countries around the world were approaching the government representatives to know and learn about the system used in the Sultanate of Oman to manage the crisis in the health sector. Moreover (Al Manji et al., 2022) confirmed that Oman's experience was remarkable and could be replicated in other countries.

6.1 User Experience with Health Technology Services (Tarassud App) Provided by the Government to Manage Covid-19 Pandemic

For assessing the user experience, the mean and standard deviations of the opinions of the surveyed individuals were extracted, as shown in Table 4. The table indicates the mean and standard deviation of 18 questions

Table 3 The response of the society

Survey Question	*Yes*		*No*	
	Frequency	*Percentage*	*Frequency*	*Percentage*
Are you satisfied about the services provided by the government during Covid-19 pandemic?	265	83.5	52	16.4
Do you think the technology was employed properly in Oman to control the spread of Covid-19?	217	68.5	100	31.5
Do you think the Omani society is ready and able to use advanced technologies?	278	87.7	39	12.3
Do you think the e-health services provided by the government reduced the rumors and misinformation?	246	77.6	71	22.4
The effect of using technology to control the pandemic was good	259	81.7	58	18.3
Oman's performance is better than other countries to manage the pandemic?	235	74.1	82	25.9

Source Authors calculations

answered by the respondents. The responses were measured on Likert scale, ranging from 1 = strongly disagree to 5 = strongly agree. Generally, the mean of the responses is above the average except for questions 8 and 14, where the mean was 2.68 and 2.63 respectively. Regarding the standard deviation, it was within the moderate range, ranging between 0.97 and 1.25.

The statement "It is easy to learn how to use the app" came in the first place and with the highest mean which is (4.12), and a standard deviation (0.97) with a high degree of appreciation. This indicates that the app is interested in providing usability and simplicity features, which makes the user stay longer using it without deciding to exit. As for the second highest arithmetic average, the paragraph stating "This application is highly reliable" with the mean (3.864), and a standard deviation (1.08) with a high degree of appreciation. An app's reliability is defined by its ability to be available when needed. By the way, about the following statement "One of the most important features of the application is that my profile is constantly updated", with the mean (3.858), and a standard deviation (1.08) with a high degree of appreciation. This feature confirms

Table 4 Respondents experience in Tarassud Plus App

Question	*Mean*	*Std. Deviation*
I think Tarassud Plus application is efficient	3.719	1.02
I think Tarassud Plus is practical	3.716	1.05
I think the quality of the content is high	3.625	1.06
I think the instructions and the information in the app is valuable	3.839	1.06
Navigating between pages is fast	3.637	1.14
It is easy to learn how to use the app	4.123	0.97
It is easy to find what I'm looking for in the main navigation menu	3.808	1.05
I experienced some confusion in using the app	2.675	1.22
This application is highly reliable	3.864	1.08
This app is useful, and it meets my expectations	3.707	1.03
I think that the application is accessible to all segments of society (people with special needs, the elderly)	3.262	1.23
I'm satisfied with the features of the App	3.707	1.02
One of the most important features of the application is that my profile is constantly updated	3.858	1.08
I think "statistics" feature in the App is not that important	2.631	1.25
The application provides a map of the nearest medical center	3.388	1.08
The application provides public safety information and means of prevention in a clear and easily accessible place	3.546	1.08
Sufficient health assistance data is available in the app	3.274	1.07
In case that I need technical assistance for the application, sufficient contact information is available	3.341	1.10

Source Authors calculations

what was mentioned by one of the literatures (Alqahtani & Orji, 2020) which indicates that the users liked to see new activities, backgrounds, pictures, quotes, and dashboard features added frequently.

while the paragraph that states "I think statistics feature in the App is not that important" ranked the eighteenth and last, with an arithmetic mean (2.63) and a standard deviation (1.25) with a medium degree of appreciation. However, these results in general agree with what the literature has indicated "users liked apps that are usable, offer a variety of features and options, are personalized, affordable, informative, credible, and secure. They also like apps that offer some form of social support, customer service, and emergency support. Users also preferred apps that allow them to have some control over the app features and functionalities" (Alqahtani & Orji, 2020). The limitations of the application are the unavailability of the offline mode that allows users to use the Tarassud Plus app in emergency or panic situations. Moreover, it will be in the patient's interest if the application provides a map of the nearest health institution that can provide the required service to the patient.

7 Conclusion

The pandemic has provided an opportunity for countries to develop technology-based solutions, including and use technologies and information management. The provision of online telehealth is a response to the threat of Covid-19 and has been a reminder that technology plays an essential role in minimizing the spread of the pandemic and managing the risks arising from lockdowns during the pandemic and even after the pandemic (Richter, 2020). This research investigated the role of Tarassud application in supporting the government and society in Oman during the Covid-19 pandemic and assessed the user experience of Tarassud Plus App. The results revealed the remarkable efforts and initiatives made by the government to employ the technology in controlling the spread of Covid-19. Society satisfaction was high as the platform was developed to meet individual's expectations. Moreover, the results indicated the Omani society's readiness to embrace advanced technology.

7.1 Limitations

Limitations of this research might be related to the methodology followed, as mixed method data will be more accurate to gain more comprehensive understanding of behavior and attitude. Potential extended research should consider quantitative and qualitative approaches. Qualitative in a form of interviews with Ministry of Health senior officials could add a better understanding of what was expected from the technological services and whether the service provided satisfied the government officials and provided the required assistance during the pandemic. Moreover, extended research should target a larger sample size a as it is always desirable to increase the results validity and increases the likelihood of representing diverse characteristics within the population, leading to more generalizable results.

8 Recommendations

Research implications for government officials can vary widely based on required services. The chapter highlights the following to be considered by government in Oman:

- To have a contingency plan to reduce the efforts during similar pandemics.
- To consider the end user expectation and requirements before and during the service to increase the level of the satisfaction.
- To develop user-friendly technology tools with an active customer support team to ensure that individuals can access and use new technology.
- To make use of IoT technologies in the healthcare sector as the technology is core of any business currently.
- To continue encouraging the youth to come up with new solutions, systems, and platforms to ease the process of providing services to the community.
- Providing the employees with training and resources so that they can fully utilize new technology.

References

Al Balushi, A. (2022, April 10). Tarassud plus helped the fight against Covid-19. *Oman Observer*. Retrieved July 21, 2022, from https://www.omanobserver.om/article/1117556/oman/health/tarassud-plus-helped-the-fight-against-Covid-19

Al-Jaradi, U. (2022, June 28). يفوز بجائزة الشيخ سالم العلي الصباح للمعلوماتية.
تطبيق "ترصد بلس". صحيفة وهج الخليج الإلكترونية. Retrieved July 20, 2022, from https://www.wa-gulf.com/988121

Al Manji, A., Tahoun, M., Chi Amabo, F., Alabri, M., Mahmoud, L., Al Abri, B., Aboushady, A. T., Jabbour, J., Nabeth, P., & Sadek, M. (2022). Contact tracing in the context of Covid-19: A case study from Oman. *BMJ Global Health, 7*(Suppl. 3), 1–6. Retrieved July 7, 2022, from https://doi.org/10.1136/bmjgh-2022-008724

Al Raqadi, A. (2020). *Tarassud, Ministry of Health*. Al Wisal. https://www.youtube.com/watch?v=ztWpK6QJ92s

Alqahtani, F., & Orji, R. (2020). Insights from user reviews to improve mental health apps. *Health Informatics Journal, 26*(3), 2042–2066. https://doi.org/10.1177/1460458219896492

Busvine, D. (2020, April 7). Germany launches smartwatch app to monitor coronavirus spread. *Reuters*. https://www.reuters.com/article/us-health-coronavirus-germany-tech-idUSKBN21P1SS

Creswell, J. W. (2014). *Research design: Qualitative, quantitative and mixed methods.*

Drees, J. (2021, July 12). *Telehealth use stabilizing at levels 38 times higher than before pandemic*. https://www.beckershospitalreview.com/telehealth/telehealth-use-stabilizing-at-levels-38-times-higher-than-before-pandemic.html

EMushrif About Us. (2022). Retrieved August 4, 2022, from https://www.emushrif.com/en/about-us

Fisher, M., & Sang-Hun, C. (2020, March 23). How South Korea flattened the curve. *The New York Times*.

Hu, Z., Ge, Q., Li, S., Jin, L., & Xiong, M. (2020a). *Artificial Intelligence forecasting of Covid-19 in China*. ArXiv:2002.07112 [Q-Bio]. https://arxiv.org/abs/2002.07112

Hu, Y., Liang, W., Liu, L., & Li, L. (2020b). Clinical characteristics of coronavirus disease 2019 in China. *New England Journal of Medicine, 18*, 1708–1728. https://doi.org/10.1056/NEJMoa2002032

Islam, M. N., Karim, M. M., Inan, T. T., & Islam, A. K. (2020). Investigating usability of mobile health applications in Bangladesh. *BMC Medical Informatics and Decision Making, 20*(1). https://doi.org/10.1186/s12911-020-1033-3

Jake-Schoffman, D. E., Silfee, V. J., Waring, M. E., Boudreaux, E. D., Sadasivam, R. S., Mullen, S. P., Carey, J. L., Hayes, R. B., Ding, E. Y., Bennett, G. G., & Pagoto, S. L. (2017). Methods for evaluating the content, usability, and efficacy of commercial mobile health apps. *JMIR MHealth and UHealth, 5*(12), 1–12. https://doi.org/10.2196/mhealth.8758

Jiang, P. (2021). Spatial-temporal potential exposure risk analytics and urban sustainability impacts related to COVID-19 mitigation: A perspective from car mobility behaviour. *Journal of Cleaner Production, 279*, 123673. https://doi.org/10.1016/j.jclepro.2020.123673

Kothaneth, L. (2020, June 16). Moh develops app that alerts about Covid positive people around you. *Oman Observer*. Retrieved July 21, 2022, from https://www.omanobserver.om/article/12581/CORONAVIRUS/moh-develops-app-that-alerts-about-Covid-positive-people-around-you

Kushendriawan, M. A., Santoso, H. B., Putra, P. O. H., & Schrepp, M. (2021). Evaluating user experience of a mobile health application 'halodoc' using user experience questionnaire and usability testing. *Jurnal Sistem Informasi, 17*(1),

58–71. Retrieved July 7, 2022, from https://doi.org/10.21609/jsi.v17i1.1063

Lavorgna, A., Ugwudike, P., Carr, L., Benitez, Y. S., & Rekha, G. S. (2021). To app or not to app? Understanding public resistance to COVID-19 digital contact tracing and its criminological relevance. *Law, Technology and Humans, 3*(2), 28–45. Retrieved July 6, 2022, from https://search.informit.org/doi/10.3316/informit.20220201061375

Oman: Who coronavirus disease (covid-19) dashboard with vaccination data. (no date). *World Health Organization*. https://covid19.who.int/region/emro/country/om. Accessed 27 November 2023.

Renu, N. (2021). Technological advancement in the era of COVID-19. *SAGE Open Medicine, 9*(1), 205031212110009. https://doi.org/10.1177/20503121211000912

Richter, A. (2020). Locked-down digital work. *International Journal of Information Management, 55*, 102157. https://doi.org/10.1016/j.ijinfomgt.2020.102157

Ruktanonchai, N. W., Floyd, J. R., Lai, S., Ruktanonchai, C. W., Sadilek, A., Rente-Lourenco, P., Ben, X., Carioli, A., Gwinn, J., Steele, J. E., Prosper, O., Schneider, A., Oplinger, A., Eastham, P., & Tatem, A. J. (2020). Assessing the impact of coordinated COVID-19 exit strategies across Europe. *Science*, eabc5096. https://doi.org/10.1126/science.abc5096

Salehinejad, S., Niakan Kalhori, S. R., Hajesmaeel Gohari, S., Bahaadinbeigy, K., & Fatehi, F. (2020). A review and content analysis of national apps for COVID-19 Management Using Mobile Application Rating Scale (MARS). *Informatics for Health and Social Care, 46*(1), 42–55. Retrieved July 22, 2022 from https://doi.org/10.1080/17538157.2020.1837838

Wang, C. J., Ng, C. Y., & Brook, R. H. (2020). Response to COVID-19 in Taiwan. *JAMA, 323*(14). https://doi.org/10.1001/jama.2020.3151

Whitelaw, S., Mamas, M. A., Topol, E., & Spall, H. G. C. V. (2020). Applications of digital technology in COVID-19 pandemic planning and response. *The Lancet Digital Health, 2*(8). https://doi.org/10.1016/S2589-7500(20)30142-4

WHO Coronavirus (COVID-19) Dashboard. (2022). Retrieved July 19, 2022, from https://Covid19.who.int/

Zhao, J., Ahmad, Z., Khosa, S. K., Yusuf, M., Alamri, O. A., & Mohamed, M. S. (2021). The role of technology in COVID-19 pandemic management and its financial impact. *Complexity, 2021*, 1–12. https://doi.org/10.1155/2021/4860704

PART III

The Impact of COVID-19 on Logistics, Supply Chain, and Food Security

CHAPTER 7

Global Supply Chain Disruptions: Lessons From the COVID-19 Pandemic Crisis

Othmane Touat

1 Introduction

In a period already marked by trade and unilateral tensions and institutional decline, the global supply chain system and the trade transport and logistics sector have faced severe difficulties as a result of the Coronavirus (COVID-19) pandemic. Sudden pauses in economic activity and unprecedented declines in world trade have caused global recessions in most countries. The economic disruptions resulting from the COVID-19 pandemic have also affected some sectors much more than others, reflecting sectoral differences related to demand, labor intensity, and global value chain operations.

Global supply chains are becoming highly sophisticated and interconnected. It is also more exposed to widespread risks, with greater potential failures. The disruption caused by the COVID-19 pandemic has

O. Touat (✉)
Faculty of Economics, Commercial Sciences and Management, University of Algiers 3, Algiers, Algeria
e-mail: touatabdou@yahoo.fr

A. Mishrif (ed.), *Business Resilience and Market Adaptability*, The Political Economy of the Middle East,
https://doi.org/10.1007/978-981-97-2962-3_7

tested existing supply chains and basic business models, which include considerations of transportation, logistics networks, and trade facilitation capabilities.

Following the initial shock, signs of recovery appeared at multiple rates in late 2020 and continued until 2022, with some setbacks during 2021, and with the recovery of commodity trade, especially the trade of containerized consumer goods, at a faster pace than expected while maintaining the strength of the momentum. However, intersecting trends in supply chains, workforce availability, equipment and transport capabilities, seafarers' crisis, as well as freight costs, continue to affect the prospects for transport and logistics chains and the sector's long-term sustainability and resilience. These trends are occurring against the backdrop of increasing requirements for climate change mitigation and adaptation, as well as pressures related to the energy transition, natural disasters and devastating weather patterns, uncertain pandemic and vaccination paths, uneven economic recovery, and growing geopolitical risks, such as the war in Ukraine that affect the Black Sea region.

Hence the Problem that This Chapter Attempts to Answer, as Follows:

- How has the COVID-19 pandemic affected global supply chain systems in light of the measures taken by various countries of the world to respond and mitigate the effects of the pandemic? What is the future of this system in the post-pandemic stage?

2 Literature Review

The COVID-19 pandemic has triggered unprecedented disruptions in global supply chains, affecting various industries and raising critical challenges for the transport and trade logistics sector. Scholars have extensively explored the multifaceted impact of the pandemic on supply chain dynamics, emphasizing the need for a comprehensive understanding of these challenges.

Research by Ivanov and Das (2020) emphasizes the profound impact of COVID-19 on global supply chains, with disruptions ranging from manufacturing delays to distribution challenges. The study underscores the vulnerabilities exposed within supply chains and the imperative for adaptive strategies.

Kumar et al. (2020) delve into the logistical bottlenecks and port congestion resulting from the pandemic. The research highlights how these disruptions have led to increased delays and costs, affecting the efficiency of transportation networks and logistical operations.

Exploring the broader implications, Sharma et al. (2020) discuss the economic consequences and geopolitical risks associated with the disruptions. The study illuminates the interconnectedness of global economies and the need for strategic measures to mitigate risks arising from geopolitical uncertainties.

On a more optimistic note, Van Hoek (2020) investigates the opportunities that arise amid challenges. The research focuses on the potential for digital transformation, climate change mitigation, and sustainability initiatives within the transport and logistics sectors.

McKinsey & Company (2022) contributes insights into policy responses, advocating for proactive measures to enhance the resilience of global supply chains. The study discusses the role of governments and international organizations in formulating strategies to address future uncertainties.

In conclusion, the literature reflects a rich tapestry of research on the disruptions caused by COVID-19 in global supply chains and the associated challenges faced by the transport and trade logistics sector. These studies collectively emphasize the need for adaptive strategies, policy interventions, and innovation to navigate the complexities of the post-pandemic landscape.

3 Methodology

To comprehensively investigate the impact of the COVID-19 pandemic on global supply chains, a mixed-methods approach was employed to triangulate insights from various sources. Firstly, quantitative data was collected through a systematic review of industry reports, trade publications, and governmental databases, were gathered from reputable databases such as the World Bank, International Monetary Fund (IMF), UNCTAD, and WTO. This allowed for the aggregation of statistical information related to disruptions, such as changes in production outputs, trade volumes, and logistics performance indicators. Concurrently, qualitative data was gathered through in-depth data of key industry agents, supply chain actors, and policymakers to provide a nuanced understanding of the challenges and adaptations within the sector.

Data analysis involved a combination of statistical techniques for quantitative data, such as trend analysis and comparative assessments, while qualitative data underwent thematic analysis to identify recurring patterns and emergent themes. The use of both data types and complementary analytical tools facilitated a comprehensive exploration of the multifaceted aspects of global supply chain disruptions during the COVID-19 crisis.

4 Evolution of the Global Supply Chain Pattern

In its simplest sense, supply chains are a connected network of people, companies, resources, and technologies involved in the manufacture and sale of a product or service. It is in the form of activities distributed internationally, and the supply chain begins with the delivery of raw materials from the supplier to the manufacturer and ends with the delivery of the service or the final product to the final consumer. With regard to operational aspects, trade across global supply chains is defined as including trade in goods that cross at least two international borders (IMF, 2022).

From a historical perspective, supply chains were simple and operated within limited geographic ranges. It was often easy to obtain all the ingredients used to make a product from a location close to where the final product was consumed. However, today's supply chains are extremely complex and involve many producers from all over the world. As companies get their inputs from all over the world to be able to take advantage of the most appropriate ingredients needed to assemble their products. Several factors have also contributed to this development. Technological breakthroughs have allowed companies to communicate seamlessly with other companies on the other side of the world, thus reducing transportation costs. International agreements have also made international business easier, by facilitating contract enforcement, and lowered their cost by reducing tariff and non-tariff barriers. In addition, the structural reforms of commercial enterprises in various countries of the world allowed investment in foreign factories. This advancement in technology, institutions, and policies has allowed commercial enterprises to fragment their production processes, which has led to the flourishing of international trade in production inputs (or so-called intermediate goods) (Dollar, 2019).

These profound changes have affected almost every country, with both advanced and emerging market economies becoming more integrated into global supply chains. The change was radical in the nineties of the last century and the first decade of the new millennium, until this merger stabilized to some extent in the second decade of the current millennium.

However, over the past years, global supply chains have faced the increasing impact of unilateral policies. The trade tensions that began in 2017 between major trading powers have been a powerful test of the solidity of the pattern of trade supply chains. The most important thing to note is that the United States and China clashed in the midst of these escalating tensions, which led to a decline in the value of trade between the United States and China by more than 15% in 2019 compared to the previous year. As of June 2019, about $400 billion in bilateral trade between the United States and China was subject to additional tariffs. The direct result of the tariffs between the two countries is the diversion of some bilateral trade to other countries with firms that are fiercely competitive with firms in China or the United States (BBC News, 2019).

Beyond the countries directly involved, trade tensions have implications for global and regional supply chains. The tariffs penalize not only the company that assembles the product, but also suppliers along the value chain, wherever they are, and ultimately will provide strong incentives for companies to restructure their supply chains. Some estimates suggest that US tariffs on China have significantly affected upstream suppliers to China in other East Asian countries. Similarly, China's tariffs on imports from the United States have had negative effects on North American suppliers (Fig. 1). Once again, other regions of the world will benefit from this restructuring, especially Europe. The data indicates that the European Union benefited most from this situation, taking in about $70 billion in bilateral trade ceded by the United States and China, with other major beneficiaries from Japan, Mexico, and Canada, each taking in more than $20 billion (China Briefing, 2019).

5 The COVID-19 Pandemic and Its Repercussions on Global Supply Chains

More than two years after the onset of the COVID-19 pandemic, the coronavirus crisis has triggered the biggest economic recession in 90 years and rolled back hard-earned development progress, threatening the achievement of the Sustainable Development Goals by 2030, exposing deep fissures in the global economic system.

High levels of uncertainty continue to surround the global economic outlook, with global gross domestic product declining by an estimated

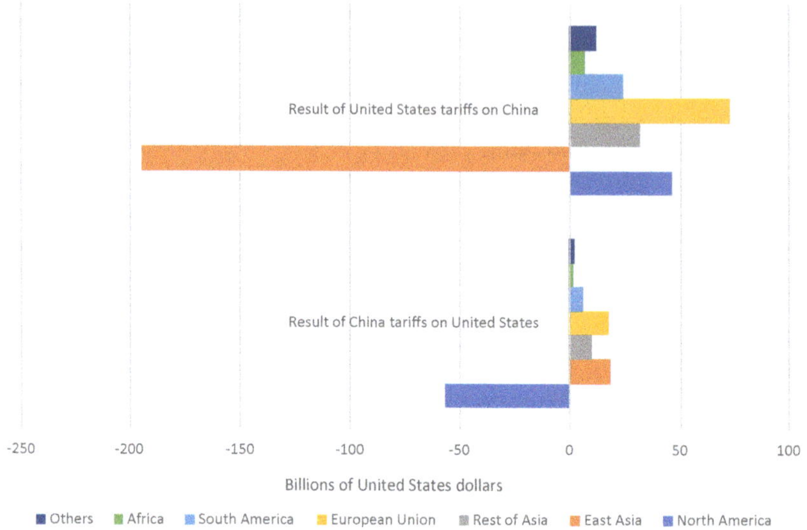

Fig. 1 Impact of trade tensions on supply chains 2017–2019 (*Source* United Nations, 2019)

4.3% in 2020, the largest contraction in global output since the Great Depression. According to the "World Economic Outlook 2022" report, data indicates that the output of developed economies shrank by 5.6% in 2020, with a recovery of 4.0% in 2021. However, the renewed outbreak of the pandemic and the emergence of new mutations led to take new measures of comprehensive lockdown during successive periods of 2021 and the beginning of 2022 in many countries, which makes a quick recovery less likely (IMF, 2022).

Future developments will depend on the course of the health crisis and the potential repercussions of the Russian-Ukrainian war, including whether it is possible to control the new strains of the COVID-19 virus with currently available vaccines, or whether these strains will cause a prolongation of the pandemic.

The economic and social turmoil caused by the COVID-19 pandemic also led to an unprecedented collapse of international trade in the first half of 2020. With the values of international trade declined by about 9% (with a decline in trade in goods by about 6% and services by about 16%), the economic disruptions resulting from the COVID-19 pandemic have affected some sectors much more than others, reflecting sectoral differences related to demand and intensity in terms of labor and global supply chain operations (WTO, 2020a, 2020b).

Trade in goods that are highly dependent on global supply chains (GVC-intensive goods) was more volatile than trade in other goods (Fig. 2), in January–April 2020—exports of GVC-intensive goods fell by % 30, while exports of other goods fell by about 18%. Global value chain-intensive goods also saw a faster recovery. However, some sectors, such as the automotive sector, experienced a relatively sharper decline initially with major inputs such as semiconductors being cut off. It was also greater in sectors implementing complementary processes (close to the end user) than in sectors implementing core processes (input). However, the ability to work from home (the ability to Tele-work) in partner countries mitigated the effects of the general shutdown. The effects of these repercussions have also diminished over time, and in light of the fluctuations in commodity trade that is heavily dependent on global value chains, calls have emerged to explore policy options available to increase the resilience of global supply chains in the face of shocks (IMF, 2022).

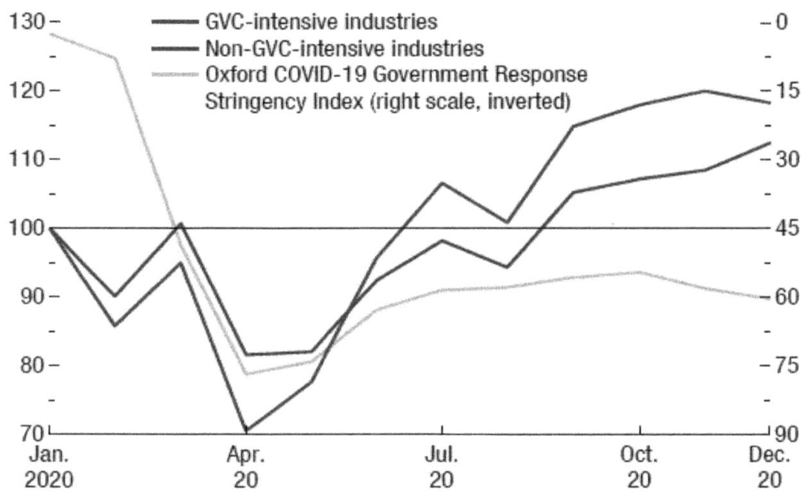

Fig. 2 Volatility of trade in sectors that are highly dependent on GVCs versus sectors that are not dependent on GVCs January–December 2020 (*Source* IMF, 2022, p. 88)

6 Effects of the Pandemic on the International Transport and Trade Logistics Sector

The COVID-19 pandemic has underscored the importance of transportation and logistics for global supply chains, trade, and interconnected economies. This health crisis has shown how vulnerable the sector is to shocks and imbalances.

International transport and logistics have been severely affected by the pandemic. Shipping companies, airlines, road transport companies, and railways have seen a sharp drop in demand for their services, especially for passenger transport. Meanwhile, transport workers must cross borders that may be closed as part of the national health response measures. Aircrews are forced not to move, and truck drivers are stuck at the border, where it is estimated that up to 300,000 seafarers a month need international flights to enable a change of crews (UNCTAD, Maritime Transport Review, 2021b).

Considering that most of the international trade is carried out by sea, the total volume of world trade transported by sea is 80%. With more than half shipped in sea containers, the COVID-19 pandemic has affected international maritime trade as it disrupted operations and put pressure on the supply chain. Despite the sector's performance was better than initially expected, the volumes of sea trade and container port traffic in 2020 decreased by 3.8% (Fig. 3).

Many ports have suffered from reduced ship arrivals due to the modification or cancelation of cruise routes. The improved connectivity of some ports reflects a change in container shipping patterns and an increase in vessel sizes. This has offset the negative effects of "changing or canceling the sailing route," that is, the shipping companies' decision to cancel scheduled services due to the pandemic. Figure 4 shows a decrease in the number of ships that arrived at ports per week during the first five months of 2020, compared to the average for the same period in the previous year. All major ship types recorded fewer port stops. Oil tankers saw the largest drop among cargo vessel types, while passenger ships reduced port stops by nearly 30%. The restrictions and controls caused by the pandemic, along with labor shortages caused by illness or imposed quarantines, have also undermined customs services. In addition, delays, including in the assignment of bills of lading, affected the performance of commercial contracts.

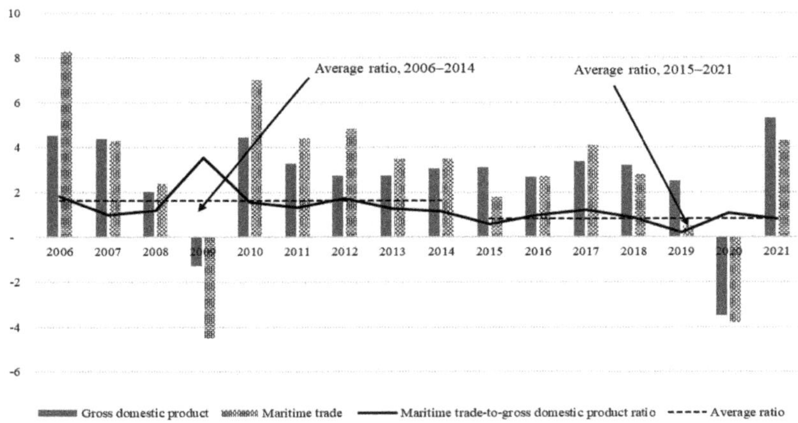

Fig. 3 International Maritime Trade, World GDP, and maritime trade to GDP ratio (Annual and average percentage change) (*Source* UNCTAD, 2022).

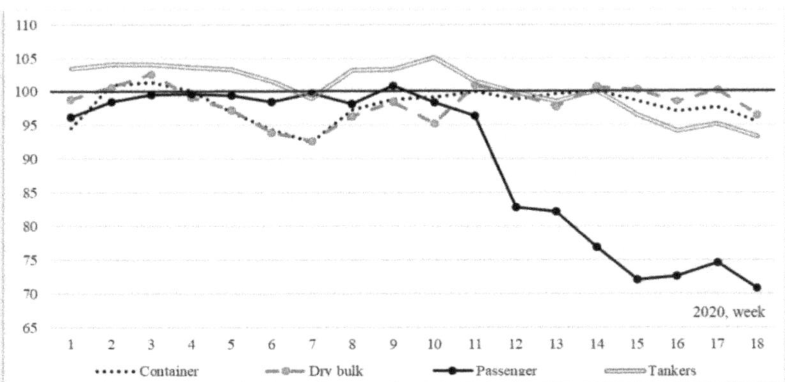

Fig. 4 Weekly port stops for selected types of ships in 2020, compared to the first 18 weeks of 2019 (*Source* MarineTraffic, 2021)

The concerned authorities across the maritime supply chain took immediate measures to ensure the continuity of port operations and shipping services. General rules and protocols were also imposed on all economic activities in the field of maritime transport and ports. Pre-existing plans and guidelines on how to respond to crises have proven useful. It was essential to ensure effective communication between all relevant actors, and access to transparent, accurate, and correct information. In addition to the role played by worker and employee support initiatives, the adoption of "supply chain" approaches that assist all stakeholders across the entire chain (UNCTAD, 2022).

7 Supply Chain Crisis Caused by rising Freight Costs

With trade flows recovering faster than expected in the third quarter of 2020, rising demand combined with slower growth in cargo capacity supplies, including in sea and air transportation, has led to frictions across the supply chain coupled with a decrease in service reliability and an increase in freight costs. At the same time, ocean container carriers have benefited from difficult market conditions, and the profitability of container carriers is expected to reach $35 billion in 2021. Increased demand in the second half of 2020 and the first half of 2021 was accompanied by disruptions in the supply chain, including a shortage of capacity Tonnage of ships and equipment, port congestion, long waiting times and delays. A week-long wait for container ships in choked ports and a blocked Suez Canal exacerbated logistical challenges. Together, these factors led to increases in container freight rates of 23% in 2021 (UNCTAD, Maritime Transport Review, 2021b).

The asymmetric recovery in maritime trade at the end of 2020 was reversed by disrupted supply chain bottlenecks that would have boosted the profitability of shipping and increased pressure on supply chains, ports, shipping, and trade. Supply chains have come under severe strain in 2021 due to the increase in e-commerce, along with capacity constraints, equipment shortages, and renewed virus infections in some parts of the world, including at a critical international container terminal in China (Yantian Port) and the lockdown Suez Canal for a week. Extreme congestion means that an estimated 15% of ships' carrying capacity is affected by delays in harbor or slow sailing (Fig. 5).

These pressures continued, as the first quarter of 2022 witnessed severe congestion in ports and disruption of logistics and transportation networks. Although the significant increase in e-commerce may have kept commerce going, it also required distribution centers and transportation capacity. Cautious estimates suggest that cross-border e-commerce will expand to nearly $1 trillion in value by 2030, compared to its current

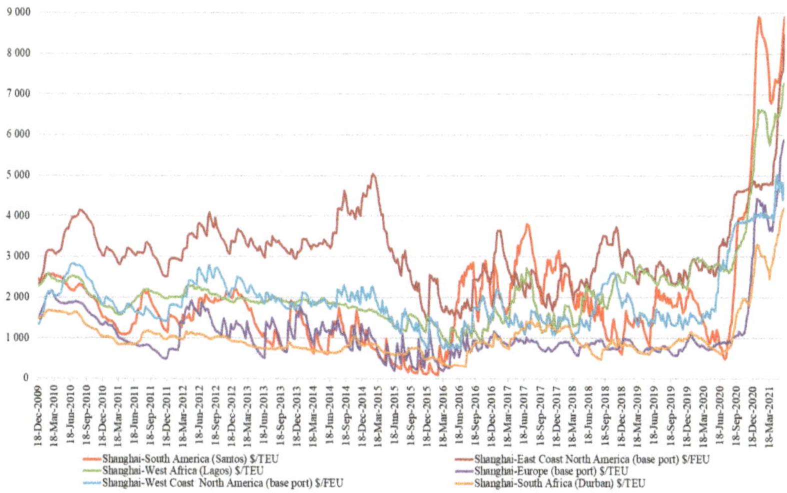

Fig. 5 Shanghai containerized freight (Index, weekly spot rates, 18 December 2009 to 21 May 2021, selected routes) (*Source* MarineTraffic, 2021)

value of about $300 billions. It is estimated that five to seven years of growth in e-commerce to have compressed into one year (McKinsey & Company, 2022).

Freight rates increased significantly, surcharges were imposed, and the reliability of transport services declined, while delays and port stay times increased (Fig. 6). New disruptions, such as the halting of manufacturing and port activities in China in March 2022 due to new COVID-19 infections, as well as the war affecting the Black Sea region, may further disrupt transportation (CRSL, 2022).

Increasing costs pose a challenge to trade patterns and supply chains, particularly for smaller shippers who are less able to bear the extra costs and are the weakest link when negotiating prices and booking space on ships. A simulation model prepared by UNCTAD indicates that world import price levels will increase on average by 11.9% as a result of continued increases in freight rates. Small island developing States will be the hardest hit, given their dependence on shipping (Fig. 7). Import prices to SIDS will face a cumulative increase of 26.7%, with a time lag of about a year.

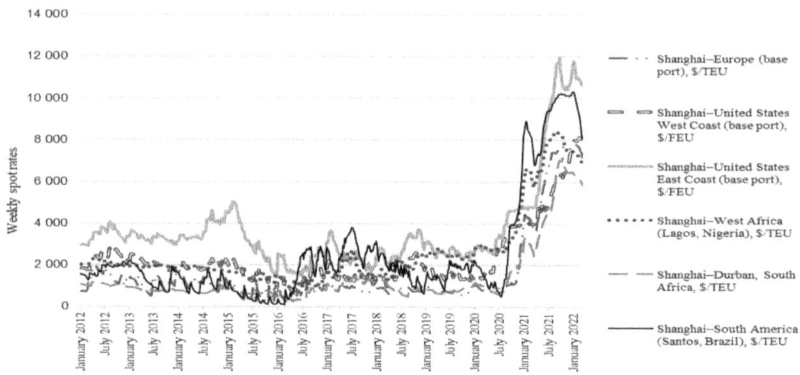

Fig. 6 Shanghai Container Shipping Index, selected routes, January 2012–January 2022 (*Source* CRSL, 2022)

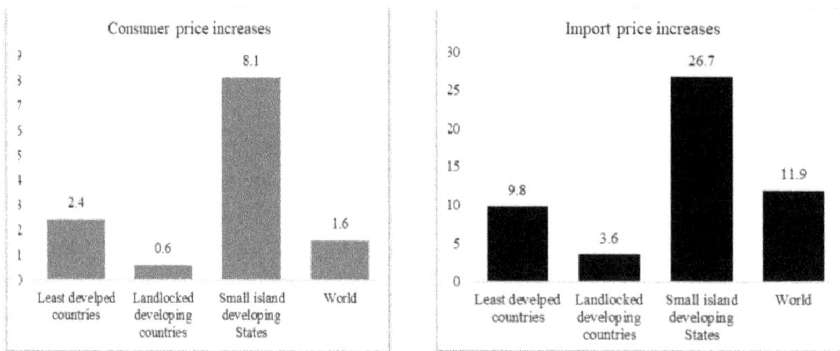

Fig. 7 Simulation of the effect of rising container freight rates on the levels of import prices and consumer prices (in percentage) (*Source* UNCTAD, 2022)

Global consumer prices are expected to be 1.6% higher in 2023 than they would have been without higher freight rates. The cumulative increase in consumer prices is expected to be 8.1% in small island developing States and 2.4% in least developed countries. The most recent data available for selected countries indicates import price increases of approximately 5% to 21% in 2021, with Grenada experiencing the highest increase (Fig. 8).

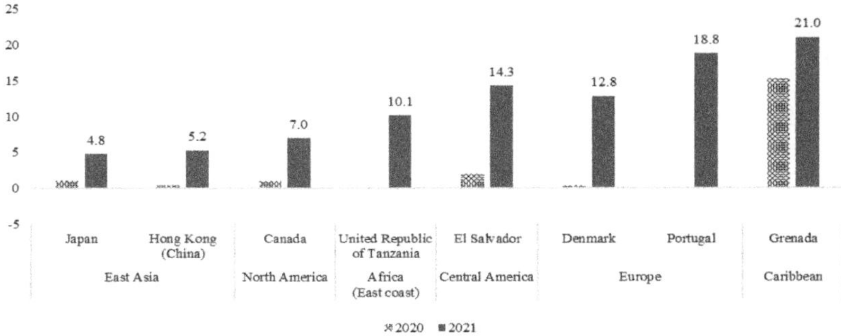

Fig. 8 Changes in import prices of containerized goods from China for selected economies (percentage) (*Source* UNCTAD, 2022)

8 The Future of Global Supply Chains in Post-COVID-19 World

Over the past few decades, much of global industrial production has been organized into global value chains. The COVID-19 pandemic has caused severe disruption to the manufacturing sector in many centers of global value chains, including China, the European Union, and the United States, resulting in an unprecedented combination of supply and demand shocks.

With the damage to operations in many cross-border supply chains, the pandemic will have some impact on production networks in the future, as the multi-step and multi-country supply chains that currently dominate production will likely have to adapt in order to build a more sustainable socio-economic system.

One lasting effect may be the acceleration of the automation of production systems. Less complex and more efficient supply chains are likely to emerge with new levels of resilience to business volatility in the face of crises and external shocks. For example, Nike has been talking for several years about digitizing its supply chain by running 1,200 automatic machines and moving production back to the United States, which would lead to lower shipping costs and import tariffs in the future (Wilding, 2020).

Supply chain disruptions in the aftermath of the pandemic have revealed the importance of the ability of supply chains to continue to function even when there are shocks. More recently, the Omicron variant spread and the war in Ukraine have increased the uncertainty surrounding supply chains. In the aftermath of all this, institutions and policymakers are currently discussing several options that would reshape supply chains, and this can be done through the following options:

8.1 Diversification

Countries can diversify their intermediate input suppliers internationally, by achieving greater equality in the quantities obtained from suppliers across different countries. Diversification here refers to an increase in the number of foreign suppliers for any input, even if this leads to an increase in costs. This allows producers to better weather supply shocks, unless the shock hits all supplying countries simultaneously (Dollar, 2019). In other words, diversification in this framework means diversification across countries, not across products; it also refers to the diversification of intermediate services, not the final goods and services; and the use of intermediate inputs, not their production or export. Diversification according to this concept leads to enhancing resilience by reducing dependence on one country or by establishing relationships in times of prosperity that can be benefited from during crises (IMF, 2022).

8.2 Localization

The localization of production is likely to increase in some sectors, which means separation from global supply chains by transferring foreign production to its country of origin, especially in the pharmaceutical sector. Prior to the pandemic, many countries were highly dependent on the active pharmaceutical ingredients trade, with 80% of the global supply of active pharmaceutical ingredients imported from China and India. In 2019, for example, China alone exported 10,12 million tons of pharmaceutical ingredients to 189 countries (UNCTAD, 2022). However, the economic evidence available so far is not in favor of resorting to the option of relocalization. The pursuit of self-reliance only would make production less efficient, and there is no evidence available to suggest that this would enhance resilience. It is estimated that the localization of global value chains could reduce global real GDP by more than 5%. Efforts to repatriate production systems will severely affect low- and middle-income countries, making it difficult for them to reach or move up the ladder of global value chain development (UNCTAD, 2020).

8.3 Substitution

Substitution refers to the ease with which a producer in the production process substitutes inputs from a supplier in one country for inputs from another country. While geographic diversification is concerned with establishing relationships with suppliers in different countries, substitution can be interpreted either as making firms' production technology more flexible, meaning that they can absorb slightly different inputs of the same type from different suppliers, or as standardizing intermediate inputs at the same time on international level (IMF, 2022). As an example of increased production flexibility, Tesla's response to the semiconductor shortage, the company made software bugs that enable it to use alternative semiconductors that were more readily available at the time. As an example of standardization, General Motors recently said it is working with a number of chip makers to cut the number of special-spec semiconductor chips it uses by 95% to just three sets of microcontrollers. In principle, each set of microcontrollers will be replaced by a set of chips, avoiding any replacement costs between them (New York Times, 2021).

The insights gained from this research on global supply chain disruptions in the context of the COVID-19 pandemic crisis hold significant practical implications for various stakeholders. Businesses operating within intricate supply chain networks can leverage the identified lessons to enhance their resilience and responsiveness to unforeseen disruptions. Adopting flexible and adaptive supply chain strategies, investing in digital technologies for real-time visibility, and diversifying sourcing and distribution channels emerge as practical measures. Policymakers can draw from these findings to formulate agile and proactive policies that foster a resilient economic infrastructure.

9 The Limitations of the Study

While our study provides valuable insights into the lessons learned from the COVID-19 pandemic's impact on global supply chains, several limitations should be acknowledged. Data limitations, including potential biases and gaps, may have affected the accuracy and comprehensiveness of our findings. The scope of our study focused on specific industries or regions, limiting the generalizability of our results. Additionally, the dynamic nature of the pandemic poses a challenge as the situation continues to evolve. Methodological constraints, such as the tools employed for analysis, and the influence of external factors like geopolitical events, further contribute to the nuanced understanding of supply chain disruptions. Recognizing these limitations, our study offers a foundation for future research to delve deeper into these complexities and refine strategies for enhancing supply chain resilience.

10 Conclusion

The coronavirus pandemic has revitalized the debate about global supply chains and trends toward re-establishing production networks. With the challenges posed by the global economic, trade, and geopolitical situation, the disruptions caused by the COVID-19 pandemic have highlighted and highlighted the weaknesses of global supply chains, including those related to the transportation networks that support them.

Among the conclusions reached by the chapter:

- Pandemic-related factors had an important role in determining supply chain patterns. Where the general lockdown policies applied to contain the pandemic had major international repercussions, and the international repercussions were greater in sectors that are heavily dependent on global value chains compared to sectors that are not highly dependent on global value chains, and were greater in sectors that implement complementary processes of production close to the end user compared to sectors which performs the main operations (inputs). These results related to the repercussions indicate two things, the first of which is that containing the pandemic locally is important not only for local activity, but also because future pandemics that lead to general lockdown may have negative repercussions on trading partners, including on commodities that are highly dependent on global value chains. Second, the reduction in the fallout from the pandemic over time indicates the resilience of global supply chains, including the commodities that are highly dependent on global value chains. This should sound like a cautionary sign for policies that seek to bring about permanent changes in the structure of global production and trade processes.
- Global supply chains have not been able to adapt to the asynchronous developments of the pandemic, and to strengthen and increase the resilience of global supply chains, there may be much

room for diversification away from local inputs. The chapter showed that resilience to shocks can be increased by increasing the diversification of inputs across countries and by increasing the substitution of inputs among different countries.

- While some of the imbalances between supply and demand and the direct effects of the pandemic on supply baskets and logistics may dissipate as global demand patterns return to normal. The structural factors, such as globalized versus regional trade and shipping networks, shifting consumption patterns, and increased e-commerce, and rapid digitization, are also currently shaping long-term expectations. These trends underscore the need to adopt a long-term vision through early mainstreaming of sustainability and resilience criteria in the context of transport logistics planning, trade, and investment decisions.
- Reforming global supply chains requires caution, given the impacts related to sustainability and social impacts (e.g., unsustainable resource exploitation, unemployment due to automation). Care should be taken to carefully assess the potential available options between resilience to shocks and the necessity of economic efficiency. Moreover, the strong localization or regionalization of supply chains risks reducing some countries' access to international markets and potentially hampering their social and economic development through export-led strategies. Accordingly, it is of paramount importance that multilateral approaches to policy development are strengthened so that countries can find the right balance between globalization and self-reliance.

Better redesigning of global supply baskets requires policies and initiatives that integrate risk, environmental sustainability, and technology as prerequisites for post-pandemic sustainable and resilient supply systems. Decision-makers and actors in the field of commercial logistics from governments, companies, and international organizations are invited to identify priority areas of action to help overcome various global concerns in the field of global supply chains and achieve lasting recovery, while building resilience and advancing the sustainability program. The recommendations that can be made in this regard include:

- Prepare for disruption, assess and manage risks, and build resilience in supply chains during crises.
- Utilizing technology and digitization to enhance sustainability and build resilience in the field of transportation and logistics.
- Addressing high freight rates, market concentration, and regulatory oversight, as well as setting up an emergency response mechanism to mitigate the direct impact of high transportation costs and prices on small developing countries in order to achieve food and energy security.
- Continuous cooperation to address the crisis of changing crews, and to protect the health and safety of seafarers.
- Develop procedures and requirements to expedite implementation of trade facilitation measures, particularly in view of experiences with recent disruptions in global supply chains.
- Expedite action to ensure and facilitate climate change impact assessments, and disaster risk reduction in ports and other critical transport infrastructure, particularly in vulnerable developing countries.
- Reducing carbon emissions from shipping, shifting toward smart and sustainable ports, as well as facilitating trade and transport in a climate-smart manner.

Bibliography

BBC News. (2019, June 29). A quick guide to the US-China trade war. Consulté le August 3, 2020, sur https://www.findevgateway.org/en/interview/2018/11/

China Briefing. (2019, July 29). *The US China trade war: A timeline.* Wiley Online Library.

CRSL. (2022, May 21). Clarkson Research Services Limited CRSL. Consulté le October 10, 2022, sur https://www.crsl.com/

Dollar, D. (2019, June). Invisible links: Value chains transform manufacturing—And distort the globalization debate. *Finance & Development*, 50.

IMF. (2022, April). *World Economic Outlook.* International Monetary Fund.

MarineTraffic, M. (2021). Ship tracking intelligence. Consulté le 10 05, 2021, sur www.marinetraffic.com

McKinsey & Company. (2022). Uncertainty returns—But this time, the cause is not COVID-19, COVID-19: Briefing Note No. 97. McKinsey and Company.

New York Times. (2021, November 18). Ford moves to ensure supply of chips and guide their design. Consulté le 07 8, 2022, sur https://www.nytimes.com; https://www.nytimes.com/2021/11/18/business/ford-globalfoundries-chip-shortage.html

UNCTAD. (2019). *Trade & Development report 2020*. United Nations.

UNCTAD. (2020). *World Investment Report 2020: International production beyond the pandemic*. United Nations publication.

UNCTAD. (2021a, May 21). *Global trade update*. Findexable Limited.

UNCTAD. (2021b). *Maritime transport review*. United Nations Publications.

UNCTAD. (2021c, September). *UNCTADstat*. Switzerland.

UNCTAD. (2021d). *World Investment Report 2021*. United Nations Publications.

UNCTAD. (2022). Sustainable and resilient transport and trade facilitation in times of pandemic and beyond: Key challenges and opportunities. UN Publications.

United Nations. (2019). *International trade and development report*. United Nations.

Wilding, R. (2020, April 19). Coronavirus is changing global supply chains in unexpected ways. *Brinknews*.

WTO. (2020a). *Overview of developments in the international trading environment: Annual report by the director-general*. World Trade Organisation.

WTO. (2020b). *World Trade Report 2020*. World Trade Organisation.

CHAPTER 8

Logistics Sector in Post-COVID-19: Challenges and Opportunities

Idris Al-Hsani and Zainab Al-Balushi

1 Introduction

The emergence of the coronavirus (COVID-19) pandemic in 2020 initiated an unprecedented global upheaval that severely disrupted the intricate web of logistics and transportation networks worldwide. This crisis generated a ripple effect across various sectors, but its impact on the transportation and logistics industry was particularly profound. The domino effect of trade restrictions, quarantines, and stringent border control measures significantly curtailed the smooth functioning of global supply chains. Governments worldwide grappled with the escalating crisis, responding with stringent measures that included imposing partial

I. Al-Hsani (✉)
Ministry of Commerce, Industry, and Investment Promotion, Muscat, Oman
e-mail: s46932@student.squ.edu.om

Z. Al-Balushi
College of Economics and Political Science, Sultan Qaboos University, Muscat, Oman
e-mail: zeinaba@squ.edu.om

A. Mishrif (ed.), *Business Resilience and Market Adaptability*, The Political Economy of the Middle East,
https://doi.org/10.1007/978-981-97-2962-3_8

or complete lockdowns. These restrictions substantially limited human mobility and disrupted the fluidity of transportation activities (Abdullah et al., 2021). The consequence was a cascade of challenges affecting logistics networks, such as disruptions in rail, trucking, maritime shipping, and air freight operations (Gray, 2020). Consequently, the flow of goods encountered hurdles, delays escalated, and unprecedented strains weighed on shipping and road freight, posing substantial obstacles to global trade (Deaton & Deaton, 2020; Sudan & Taggar, 2021).

However, amid the turbulence, there emerged a swift rebound from the initial decline in global commerce. The transportation and logistics industry responded to the pandemic's effects through multifaceted initiatives undertaken by both enterprises and governments, coupled with strategic investments in technological infrastructure. This chapter serves to delve into the manifold challenges and ensuing opportunities brought forth by the COVID-19 pandemic, both in the midst of the crisis and in the subsequent period. The overarching goal is to comprehensively explore the ramifications of the pandemic within the logistics and transportation industries on a global scale, with a focused lens on the Sultanate of Oman. This research not only underscores the vital role of the logistics sector as a pivotal economic driver in Oman but also aims to offer valuable insights to policymakers, aiding them in navigating organizational performance challenges in the aftermath of the pandemic. Moreover, this investigation seeks to illuminate the adaptation to the "new normal" post-COVID-19 and extract the pivotal lessons learned from this transformative period. The subsequent section within this chapter provides a detailed discussion on the effects of COVID-19 across various transportation modes, encompassing road, air, and sea transport systems.

2 Literature Review

The COVID-19 pandemic swiftly altered the landscape of the global transportation sector, necessitating an in-depth investigation into its adaptive responses and resilience strategies. This literature review serves as a comprehensive exploration into the dynamic capabilities that became the bedrock of the transportation industry's adaptability during this unprecedented crisis. Focusing on maritime, road, and air transport, this review elucidates the sector's remarkable resilience amid unparalleled challenges, examining the pivotal role of dynamic capabilities such as agility, flexibility, and innovation. It synthesizes insights from diverse studies that underscore the industry's swift adaptation, shedding light on how these capabilities were harnessed to not only withstand the pandemic's disruptions but also to emerge stronger, poised to navigate the uncertainties of the post-pandemic era. Within this context, distinct sections dedicated to each mode of transportation—road transport, air transport, and maritime transport—unveil both the challenges faced and the opportunities identified, presenting a compelling narrative of the sector's journey through the pandemic and into an evolving future.

2.1 Transportation Sector During the COVID-19 Pandemic

The COVID-19 pandemic has disrupted the global transportation sector in unprecedented ways, compelling a thorough examination of its response mechanisms. This literature review delves into the dynamic capabilities that have propelled the sector's resilience and adaptability during this crisis. It further explores the adaptive strategies employed across various transportation modes, including maritime, road, and air transport, shedding light on the sector's remarkable resilience in the face of unparalleled challenges.

2.1.1 Empowering Transportation: Dynamic Capabilities During the COVID-19 Pandemic

The COVID-19 pandemic has had a profound impact on the transportation sector, requiring a comprehensive examination of how dynamic capabilities have acted as the driving force behind its resilience and adaptability. Across various modes of transport, including maritime transport, road transport, and air transport, dynamic capabilities have emerged as a unifying factor, empowering these industries during this unprecedented crisis.

Dynamic capabilities, which encompass agility, flexibility, and innovation, have become the cornerstones of resilience in the transportation sector. This resilience was most evidently observed in the container shipping and ports industry (maritime sector), where demand experienced a significant drop (Notteboom et al., 2021). Companies in this sector swiftly adapted to the new normal by leveraging their dynamic capabilities. Agility allowed them to adjust their operations rapidly, ensuring the continued flow of goods while mitigating disruptions (Notteboom et al., 2021).

Innovation proved equally vital in container shipping and ports, where contactless cargo handling and digital documentation solutions reduced physical interactions and streamlined operations (Fusillo & Haralambides, 2020). The flexibility to reconfigure routes and adjust shipping frequencies helped maintain essential supply chains in the face of fluctuating demand and supply chain disruptions (Notteboom et al., 2021).

Similar patterns of resilience emerged in the road transport sector, which encountered challenges such as reduced demand and supply chain disruptions (Cui et al., 2021). Dynamic capabilities, particularly agility and flexibility, allowed companies to adapt their logistics networks rapidly, accommodating changes in demand and restrictions (Osinska & Zalewski, 2020).

This flexibility extended to the adoption of innovative technologies like route optimization software and electronic delivery options (Cui et al., 2021). These innovations not only improved operational efficiency but also ensured the safety of personnel and customers.

In the air transport sector, the pandemic led to a sharp decline in global travel (Bombelli, 2020). Dynamic capabilities once again took center stage, enabling airlines to adjust flight schedules, reroute planes, and repurpose passenger aircraft for cargo transport (Bombelli, 2020).

Innovation was critical for airlines as well, with the rapid adoption of digital platforms and remote work solutions to streamline operations and reduce costs (Calderon-Tellez & Herrera, 2021). These changes, initially pandemic responses, also opened the door to long-term sustainability by reducing the need for air travel and its associated emissions (Zambrano-Monserrate et al., 2020).

The synthesis of evidence from the container shipping, road transport, and air transport sectors strongly supports the proposition that dynamic capabilities, specifically agility, flexibility, and innovation, are pivotal in empowering the transportation sector to not only overcome future challenges but also thrive in a rapidly evolving landscape. As the transportation sector navigates the challenges of the post-pandemic world, the continued cultivation of dynamic capabilities is critical. Dynamic capabilities are not just responses to a crisis; they are strategic assets to be honed and developed continuously.

2.1.2 Adaptive Resilience: Transportation Sector's Strategies Amid COVID-19 Pandemic Challenges

The COVID-19 pandemic has presented unparalleled challenges to the transportation sector, necessitating rapid adaptation and strategic responses. This literature review explores the multifaceted response strategies deployed across various modes of transportation, including road, air, and maritime, highlighting the sector's adaptive resilience in the face of these challenges.

The container shipping and port sectors have faced unique challenges during the pandemic. Notteboom et al. (2021) have underscored a significant drop in demand for container shipping services, compelling the industry to respond with agility and innovation. Companies within this sector demonstrated their responsiveness through rapid operational adjustments, emphasizing the vital role of flexibility and adaptability. Moreover, Fusillo and Haralambides (2020) stressed the importance of responsive measures, advocating for a robust regulatory framework to bolster industry competitiveness and resilience.

In parallel, the maritime transport sector as a whole has had to confront substantial challenges, impacting cargo volumes, vessel operations, and operational costs (Carballo Piñeiro et al., 2021; Notteboom & Pallis, 2020; Oyenuga, 2021; Yazır et al., 2020). These studies have consistently highlighted the necessity for innovative strategies to mitigate disruptions. Strategic agility, exemplified by adaptability, innovation, and flexibility, played a pivotal role in effectively managing the pandemic's repercussions within the maritime industry (Notteboom et al., 2021).

The road transport sector faced unmatched challenges as well, requiring a focus on resilience (Wang et al., 2021). Resilience in this context was cultivated through response strategies, with investments in transportation infrastructure recognized as crucial for adapting to disruptions (Wang et al., 2021). Companies that exhibited agility, flexibility, and innovation could swiftly adapt their operations, making them better equipped to navigate reduced demand and supply chain disruptions (Osinska & Zalewski, 2020). Collaboration among stakeholders and innovative solutions played vital roles in enhancing resilience (Gonzalez et al., 2022).

Furthermore, the air transport sector experienced significant transformations during the pandemic, demanding effective response strategies. Bombelli's work (2020) highlighted the need for dynamic adaptability as companies adjusted their operations to a shifting landscape. Sustainability practices were emphasized as response strategies to address the decline in air travel and emissions, with measures such as the adoption of digital platforms and remote work instrumental in addressing challenges while aligning with sustainability objectives (Zambrano-Monserrate et al., 2020).

In synthesis, the literature underscores the supreme importance of tailored response strategies in the transportation sector during the COVID-19 pandemic. These strategies encompass adaptability, innovation, and swift responses to evolving circumstances, whether within the container shipping and port sectors, the broader maritime sector, the road transport industry, or the air transport sector. By embracing and integrating these responsive measures, the transportation sector has exhibited adaptive resilience, not only weathering the storms but also emerging more resilient and prepared for a future marked by uncertainty. This collective experience serves as a testament to the sector's ability to learn, adapt, and thrive amid unprecedented challenges.

In conclusion, this comprehensive exploration of the transportation sector's response to the COVID-19 pandemic reveals a consistent theme across all modes of transportation: the critical role of dynamic capabilities, strategic agility, and tailored response strategies in fostering resilience. The pandemic's unparalleled disruptions demanded adaptability, innovative solutions, collaborative efforts, and effective crisis management to ensure operational continuity.

As this review highlights, the transportation sector's ability to swiftly adapt, harnessing dynamic capabilities such as agility, flexibility, and innovation, is pivotal. These capabilities allowed it to not only weather the storm but also emerge stronger and more adaptable to future uncertainties. Embracing these strategies remains imperative as the sector navigates a post-pandemic world, ensuring its continued growth and resilience in the face of evolving challenges.

2.2 *Transportation Sector Post-COVID-19 Pandemic: Challenges and Opportunities*

The COVID-19 epidemic has had an impact on various means of transportation. As the world gradually emerges from the crisis, it becomes crucial to assess the challenges and opportunities that lie ahead for the transportation industry. This section of the literature review delves into three specific areas within the transportation sector in the post-COVID-19 pandemic era: the road transport industry, the air transport industry, and the maritime transport industry. By examining the literature surrounding these areas, we can gain valuable insights into the challenges faced by each sector and the potential opportunities for growth and adaptation in the evolving landscape.

2.2.1 *Resilient Road Transport: Post-Pandemic*

The road transport industry encountered substantial challenges during the COVID-19 pandemic. However, there are opportunities for resilience and growth through innovation, adaptation, and sustainable development strategies (Sudan & Taggar, 2021). This part of the literature review aims to present the argument that by leveraging technology, data-driven solutions, diversification, and supportive policy decisions, the road transport industry can build resilience in the post-COVID-19 era. The following discussion explores supporting evidence from various studies.

Sudan and Taggar (2021) laid the groundwork by examining transport intelligence and logistics systems' untapped potential in recovering from pandemic supply chain disruptions. Their work illuminates the fundamental role of technology and data-driven solutions. It asserts that by leveraging these tools, the road transport industry can enhance its supply chain resilience. This proposition gains further support from the findings of Gonzalez et al. (2022), who showcased the industry's adaptability by implementing safety protocols and exploring new business opportunities during the pandemic. Through these actions, the industry demonstrates its capacity for resilience, establishing a strong foundation for growth (Gonzalez et al., 2022; Sudan & Taggar, 2021).

Building upon this foundation, Fu et al. (2022) delve into the importance of diversification and innovation in fortifying resilience. Their chapter of highway freight transport in China reveals that multi-industry supply chains, characterized by diversified suppliers and high-value products, exhibited greater resilience during the pandemic. This finding emphasizes the interrelationship between diversification, innovation, and resilience, exposing them as interconnected forces that enable the industry to withstand disruptions and adapt to changing circumstances. It is through diversifying offerings and fostering innovation that the road transport industry can foster its ability to thrive (Fu et al., 2022).

Moreover, sustainable development strategies emerge as a pivotal component of the industry's journey toward resilience. Lee and Song

(2023) offer a compelling narrative that positions the Belt and Road Initiative as a catalyst for promoting sustainable and resilient road transport systems in the post-COVID-19 era. Their research highlights the potential of sustainable practices to enhance the industry's resilience, emphasizing the synergies between environmental responsibility and long-term viability. Sustainable development, when integrated with technology, diversification, and innovation, forms an organized framework that boosts the industry forward (Lee & Song, 2023).

As Mogaji et al. (2022) emphasize, the voices of policymakers are leading this transformative journey. Their work highlights the significance of policy recommendations in mitigating the pandemic's effects on transportation in Nigeria. Effective policies provide crucial support and guidance to the industry, enabling it to navigate the post-COVID-19 landscape with resilience and adaptability. The alignment of policy decisions with technology, diversification, innovation, and sustainable practices creates a harmonious narrative, strengthening the industry's capacity for growth and recovery (Mogaji et al., 2022).

Finally, technology, data-driven solutions, diversification, sustainable practices, and supporting regulations are combined to make the road transport sector resilient and prosperous after COVID-19. The information provided helps policymakers and industry practitioners build a resilient and sustainable future.

2.2.2 Navigating Air Transport's Post-Pandemic Future

Air transport has been hard hit by the COVID-19 epidemic. Despite the challenges, the sector is ready to adapt and innovate in the post-COVID-19 environment. Our exploration of this transformative journey reveals the vital role of adaptability, digital technologies, logistics improvements, and policy interventions as the keys to the industry's successful restoration. This review draws from an extensive body of scholarly writings, each of which sheds light on a different aspect of this incredible journey.

Research by Sun et al. (2021) reveals a surge in studies dedicated to vital areas like airline operations, airport management, and air cargo transportation, demonstrating the industry's solid spirit and adaptability. The industry has responded by swiftly implementing health and safety protocols, adjusting to changing demand patterns, and investing in digital technologies (Sun et al., 2021).

However, the pandemic has presented significant challenges. Decreased passenger demand, financial pressures on airlines, and changes in travel patterns have emerged as major issues (Troyer & Bidaisee, 2022). To mitigate these effects, policy interventions such as financial support for airlines have been proposed (Troyer & Bidaisee, 2022).

Amid the challenges lie opportunities for growth and innovation. Li (2020) identifies areas of potential growth in China's air cargo sector, such as increased demand for medical supplies and e-commerce shipments. The adoption of blockchain technology is suggested as a means to enhance supply chain transparency and efficiency (Tijan et al., 2019). Furthermore, measures to restore passenger confidence are recommended to support the recovery of the Turkish civil aviation industry (Deveci et al., 2022).

In summary, by embracing adaptability, leveraging digital technologies, improving logistics, and implementing supportive policies, the industry can overcome its challenges. The evidence from scholarly works guides policymakers and industry practitioners toward a future filled with growth and innovation in the post-pandemic era (Deveci et al., 2022; Li, 2020; Sun et al., 2021; Tijan et al., 2019; Troyer & Bidaisee, 2022). Let this narrative of resilience and revival inspire a new dawn for the air transport industry.

2.2.3 Maritime Sector's Post-COVID-19 Challenges and Opportunities

The maritime transport business must be resilient, agile, and adaptable to overcome difficulties and grasp possibilities after the COVID-19 pandemic. A range of literature supports this argument, highlighting key factors that contribute to the industry's resilience and sustainable development.

However, one crucial aspect was emphasized by Merk et al. (2022) is the role of digitalization, sustainability, and decarbonisation as drivers of change in the maritime transport industry. These factors enable the industry to enhance operational efficiency, reduce environmental impact, and embrace innovative practices.

Carballo Piñeiro et al. (2021), who highlight the potential for improving efficiency, transparency, and sustainability, emphasize the significance of digital technologies even more. Collaboration among stakeholders is also recognized as vital for fostering resilience and driving positive change in the industry.

Supporting the argument for resilience, Sun and Zhang (2022) highlight the successful adaptation of leading shipping lines to changing demand patterns and the implementation of health and safety protocols. Their findings emphasize the significance of digital transformation, innovation, and collaboration in enhancing the industry's competitiveness and ability to tolerate future disruptions.

Additionally, Yazır et al. (2020) shed light on the challenges faced by the maritime transport industry, including decreased demand, supply chain disruptions, and crew welfare concerns. They stress the value of digitalization, automation, and innovation in addressing these challenges and enabling the industry to respond effectively to changing circumstances.

Yet, examining the economic impacts of the pandemic, Zhou et al. (2022) reveal a decline in cargo throughput and port revenue. They propose policy interventions, such as financial support, to mitigate these effects and promote industry recovery and resilience.

Turning to governance, Dong et al. (2023) emphasize the importance of adaptive, responsive, and inclusive port governance in enhancing the industry's resilience and sustainability. Their findings underscore the need for effective governance structures that can adapt to changing circumstances and foster collaboration among relevant stakeholders.

Lastly, Gu and Liu (2023) explore the pandemic's impact on port congestion and air quality. Their research demonstrates reduced port activity but improved air quality, presenting an opportunity to prioritize sustainable development through initiatives such as green ports.

In conclusion, the literature presents a robust argument for resilience, agility, and adaptability as essential attributes for the maritime transport industry in the post-COVID-19 era. The supportive evidence highlights the importance of digitalization, sustainability, collaboration, and policy interventions in driving positive changes, enhancing the industry's competitiveness, and ensuring its long-term sustainability. By embracing these factors, the maritime transport industry can overcome challenges, capitalize on opportunities, and build a resilient future.

3 Research Methodology

The global logistics and transportation sector faced an unparalleled crisis with the onset of the COVID-19 pandemic in spring 2020. This dynamic situation presented a blend of challenges and opportunities, particularly in the Sultanate of Oman's logistics landscape. Given the absence of established theories or tested hypotheses in Oman regarding the pandemic's impact on this sector, a qualitative research method employing a case study approach was deemed most suitable.

3.1 *Embracing Qualitative Research*

3.1.1 *Rationale for Case Study Approach*

The choice of a case study approach was necessitated by the absence of existing comprehensive theories that specifically addressed the repercussions of the pandemic on Oman's logistics and transportation industry. A case study methodology offered a unique advantage in allowing an in-depth analysis of real-world scenarios within their natural contexts. This facilitated a detailed exploration of the multifaceted impacts, responses, and adaptations of logistics and transportation firms in Oman during the COVID-19 pandemic.

3.2 *Exploring Unexplored Territories:*

The research methodology adopted was inherently exploratory, seeking to navigate unexplored dimensions within Oman's logistics sector amid the pandemic's upheaval. By employing exploratory research, the study aimed to uncover nuanced details and underlying factors influencing the industry's response to this unprecedented external shock. This approach aimed at developing a comprehensive understanding of the complex effects and strategic adaptations implemented by senior management.

3.3 *Comprehensive Data Collection:*

3.3.1 *Qualitative Data Sources*

Primary data collection predominantly involved qualitative methods such as in-depth interviews, semi-structured interviews, and focus group discussions. These approaches facilitated obtaining rich insights from key stakeholders, including senior executives, managers, and employees within Oman's logistics and transportation firms.

However, supplementing primary data sources, document analysis involved scrutinizing official reports, industry publications, government policies, and organizational documents. This complementary process enriched qualitative insights obtained through interviews and provided a broader perspective.

3.4 *Thematic Data Analysis:*

3.4.1 Unveiling Patterns and Trends

The qualitative data collected underwent rigorous thematic analysis, involving the identification, coding, and interpretation of recurring themes, patterns, and narratives. This method allowed for the extraction of significant trends, challenges, and adaptive strategies adopted by logistics firms amid the COVID-19 crisis.

To conclude, the qualitative research methodology, particularly the case study approach, facilitated a profound exploration of the nuanced impacts and responses within Oman's logistics and transportation sector during the unprecedented COVID-19 pandemic. This research aspired to offer critical insights into the dynamic interplay of challenges and opportunities faced by logistics firms, thereby contributing to the existing knowledge base and guiding future strategies for resilience and adaptability in the sector.

4 Analysis and Discussion

The strategic importance of logistics in Oman's economic development has been underscored in various governmental initiatives and strategic plans. Benayoune (2018) highlights the Omani government's recognition of logistics as a pivotal element in diversifying the economy, aiming to reduce dependence on oil and gas while fostering economic diversity. Central to this vision is the Sultanate of Oman Logistics Strategy 2040, which sets a grand ambition for Oman to establish itself as one of the top 10 global logistics hubs by 2040. This strategy outlines a comprehensive blueprint aimed at augmenting the logistics sector's contribution to the country's Gross Domestic Product (GDP).

The analytical investigation undertaken herein focused on the operations and strategic responses of two prominent logistics and transportation entities operating in Oman, labeled here as "Firm I" and "Firm II" to maintain confidentiality. These case study companies were chosen for their prominence and representativeness within the sector. For an extensive analysis, interviews were conducted with key personnel—specifically, the cargo service manager from Firm I and the asset performance manager from Firm II. The managerial perspectives provided by these individuals offered deep insights into the financial landscape of their respective businesses and the resultant strategic adaptations necessitated by the protracted pandemic crisis.

Delving into the specifics, our engagement with Firm I primarily emphasized air and cargo transportation dynamics, while our interaction with Firm II delved into maritime and door-to-door transportation services. The decision to concentrate on these domains was guided by the expertise and operational focal points of the interviewed managers. These individuals, possessing a profound understanding of their companies' financial standing and strategic trajectories, provided invaluable insights that formed the bedrock of our investigative analysis. Given the prolonged duration and unpredictability of the epidemic, there was a pressing need for meticulous data collection to comprehensively capture the challenges and adaptive strategies deployed by these industry leaders. The selection process for participants in this analysis was meticulous, engaging top-tier management representatives from leading logistics and transportation firms in Oman. Augmenting primary insights, a broad spectrum of secondary data was collated from various sources, including the companies' official websites, news articles, research reports, and annual reports.

This meticulous and multifaceted approach to data collection and analysis aimed to encapsulate the intricate operational nuances and strategic maneuvers deployed by these key players within Oman's logistics landscape. Through this comprehensive investigation, we aimed to distill valuable insights that underscore the sector's resilience, adaptive measures, and the broader implications of the pandemic on the logistics and transportation domain.

5 Findings

We discussed our observations with two high-level industry practitioners intending to assess the results and devise a viable course of action to handle the logistics and transportation sector challenges as well as the new opportunities associated with the post-pandemic era "The New Normal."

In regard to the challenges and threats that faced the logistics and transportation sector (globally, nationally, and internally within the organization) post-COVID-19 pandemic, the cargo service manager from "Firm I" clarified that the main challenge that is facing air cargo transportation is the stability of passenger flights. As passenger aircraft are back in service now, there is an increase in capacity and a drop in demand. This means that the flight operators are struggling to fill their flights. Likewise, the asset performance manager from "Firm II" stated that today's most challenging factor in the shipping industry is oil prices. As oil prices are going up, the same applies to shipping freight rates. As a result, this has resulted in a higher cost of shipping today. Another challenge facing the shipping sector is the limited availability of empty containers. When combined with other issues resulting from COVID-19, such as an increase in the supply–demand imbalance in global trade, a decline in the workforce, and country-imposed restrictions, the shortage of empty containers has become a worldwide crisis with a more disastrous impact than during previous periods. The lack of empty containers in areas where they are required slows down industrial activity and blocks the world's supply networks, forcing the use of ineffective alternative techniques. The asset performance manager from "Firm II" added that they noticed that China was behind such disruptions as they stayed open longer than other countries after the pandemic. Fortunately, this problem is resolved now, and the supply chains are back to normal. In addition, there was the challenge of establishing new warehouses to cope with the high demand in the post-pandemic era. However, there are many initiatives that have been considered and adopted to overcome these challenges. The cargo service manager from "Firm I" said that their company has established what is called "route rationalization," which is done by the commercial flight planning team. Route rationalization means that there is a debate and negotiation of flight rights and routes between two or more parties to maximize efficiency. To maximize efficiency, route rationalization may also be defined as the administration of a company following scientific principles. For example, they used to have three daily flights to Bangkok, but now they have only one single flight a day. They consider this as rational and logical, as if you are not making a huge profit, then you don't need to incur huge losses.

In regard to the new opportunities that resulted from the COVID-19 pandemic, the asset performance manager from "Firm II" specified that there is a huge demand in the shipping industry for the sake of going back to normal, but this takes time as there is a need to establish factories and warehouses. So, it is a challenge and an opportunity at the same time. Moreover, to meet the increased demand for importing and exporting goods into Oman, the company is now making significant investments. Examples of these investments are the purchase of new ships and containers to cope with the higher demand. These ships are not serving the Sultanate of Oman only as they are working in international waters and all over the world to serve different countries like the USA, Japan, and European countries. More new shipping lines are established to link Oman with the global network. Furthermore, there are employment plans going on in the shipping and maritime transportation sectors in Oman to take care of the higher demand taking place after the pandemic. Similarly, the cargo service manager of "Firm I" specified that the cargo shipments are doubled nowadays due to the high demand. They continue shipping cargo using passenger aircraft, which was not the case before the pandemic. He mentioned that they used to carry around 20 tons of cargo, but now they are carrying more than 45 tons using passenger aircraft, as they removed the seats from some of these aircraft to load cargo instead. Another key opportunity is that they opened new routes like Vietnam, Hong Kong, and different destinations in China. The cargo business demand is higher in the post-pandemic and "Firm II" is making every effort to take advantage of this opportunity.

5.1 Theoretical Contributions and Managerial Implications

In this section, we delve into the theoretical implications and practical applications emerging from our study. Our research not only deepens comprehension of crisis management within the logistics sector but also furnishes actionable insights for industry professionals and policymakers. We explore how our discoveries enrich prevailing theoretical frameworks and offer practical guidance for making strategic decisions within the logistics industry. This segment illuminates the significance of our study's contributions across academic and practical landscapes.

5.2 Theoretical Contributions

Our study makes several noteworthy theoretical contributions to the realm of logistics management and crisis response:

1. Enhanced Understanding of Mitigation Strategies: Through qualitative analysis of logistics companies' reactions to the pandemic, our study contributes to comprehending crisis mitigation strategies. By scrutinizing real-world instances, we provide insights into the application and effectiveness of these strategies within the logistics

sector during crises, augmenting the evolving knowledge base on crisis management within specific industry contexts.

2. Insights into Dynamic Capabilities and Strategic Agility: Our research extends the theoretical framework of dynamic capabilities and strategic agility by investigating their operation within the logistics sector during the COVID-19 pandemic. By furnishing practical examples and accounts from industry experts, we bridge the gap between theory and practice, enriching the literature on dynamic capabilities and strategic management.

5.3 *Managerial Implications*

Our findings carry substantial implications for industry practitioners, policymakers, and logistics stakeholders:

Strategic Decision-Making: For logistics companies, our study furnishes actionable insights into crisis management and strategic decision-making. By sharing experiences and strategies of logistics firms amid the pandemic, we offer guidance on mitigating risks, enhancing dynamic capabilities, and making informed choices during crises.

Policy Recommendations: Policymakers will find our research pertinent in formulating strategies to support the logistics sector. We provide recommendations on government interventions and policies that can fortify supply chain resilience, ensure business continuity, and promote sustainability. These insights can shape policies fostering the sector's ability to respond effectively to future crises.

6 Conclusion

To conclude, every crisis exposes a system's weaknesses and tests its resilience. The COVID-19 pandemic has caused the second major worldwide crisis since the financial crisis of 2008/2009. The approximately three-year-old COVID-19 epidemic has become a worldwide pandemic and continues to have an undesirable effect on all of civilization. While regions and countries have experienced the virus's fury, the logistics and transportation sectors have experienced many challenges and figured out many new opportunities. There were concerns raised about the reliance on a few countries as major importers and the extensive just-in-time operations and deliveries (Notteboom et al., 2021). Choi (2021) argued that the "new normal" is a phenomenon brought about by COVID-19. This chapter examines the opportunities and challenges that the COVID-19 pandemic offered for the logistics and transportation sector both during and post-pandemic. A case chapter approach was conducted as a data collection tool with two leading logistics and transportation companies operating in Oman to investigate the challenges and opportunities associated with the COVID-19 pandemic in the logistics and transportation sector around the globe and more precisely in the Sultanate of Oman.

The evolving dynamics of crises often unveil inherent vulnerabilities while fortifying resilience within systems. In the annals of global upheavals, the COVID-19 pandemic stands as a significant inflection point, marking the second profound global crisis since the financial turbulence of 2008/2009. Spanning over three tumultuous years, this pervasive pandemic has etched its profound impact across the fabric of global civilization. Amid the throes of this unprecedented challenge, the logistics and transportation sectors have borne the weight of multifaceted trials while unveiling novel pathways toward unprecedented growth and adaptation. Notteboom et al. (2021) have adeptly underscored the perilous dependence on a select few nations as primary importers, raising concerns over the vulnerability posed by an overreliance on just-in-time operations and deliveries. Choi (2021) posits that the pandemic's aftermath has delineated a "new normal," birthing transformative paradigms across industries. This chapter embarks on a comprehensive exploration, delving into the rich tapestry of opportunities and adversities unfurled by the COVID-19 pandemic, meticulously charting its impact on the logistics and transportation domains. Employing a strategic case chapter approach, this inquiry peered into the crucible of challenges and innovations, traversing the corridors of two distinguished logistics and transportation entities within Oman. Beyond the Sultanate's borders, this study extrapolates nuanced insights, unraveling the broader contours and repercussions of the pandemic's vicissitudes on the global logistics and transportation milieu. As a testament to resilience, this examination navigates the turbulences, gleaning invaluable lessons, and illuminating the path forward for a redefined, adaptable, and fortified logistics and transportation sector in a post-pandemic world.

6.1 Limitations and Suggestions for Future Research

Despite offering substantial insights into how logistics companies responded to the challenges and opportunities presented by the COVID-19 pandemic, this study has certain constraints that prompt further research directions. Focusing primarily on Oman as the geographical context, while beneficial in generating region-specific findings, might not directly apply to diverse socio-economic and cultural settings. Future research endeavors should consider conducting comparative analyses across multiple countries to better comprehend the industry's response to crises in various contexts.

Moreover, the sample size and participant selection in this study's interviews may not fully represent the entire spectrum of experiences and perspectives within the logistics sector. Conducting research with a larger, more diversified sample could provide a broader understanding of the industry and validate the current findings.

Furthermore, this study predominantly relied on qualitative data obtained from interviews. While these qualitative insights were valuable, future research could benefit from incorporating quantitative analysis. Integrating quantitative data on financial metrics, key performance indicators, and operational efficiency could offer a more robust evaluation of the pandemic's impact on the sector.

Additionally, this study primarily focused on immediate responses to the pandemic. Future research could delve into the long-term effects and sustainability of the implemented strategies. Tracking the performance and adaptation of companies over an extended period could elucidate how lessons learned during the pandemic continue to shape their strategies in the post-pandemic era.

Exploring the role of government policies and regulations in shaping logistics companies' responses to the pandemic is another avenue for future research. Understanding how government interventions influence the industry's resilience and adaptability would provide significant insights.

While recognizing the limitations of this study in terms of scope and focus on logistics firms, it is important to underscore that these findings contribute valuable insights into the sector's response to the pandemic. These insights could serve as a foundation for future research projects aiming to investigate the reactions of additional stakeholders within the industry during crises. Despite the limitations, the study's outcomes offer meaningful contributions and pave the way for broader research.

References

Abdullah, M., Ali, N., Hussain, S. A., Aslam, A. B., & Javid, M. A. (2021). Measuring changes in travel behavior pattern due to COVID-19 in a developing country: A case study of Pakistan. *Transport Policy, 108*, 21–33. https://doi.org/10.1016/j.tranpol.2021.04.023

Benayoune, A. (2018). Towards effective human capital development for the logistics industry. *International Journal of Trade, Economics and Finance*, *9*(4), 153–158. https://doi.org/10.18178/ijtef.2018.9.4.606

Bombelli, A. (2020). Integrators' global networks: A topology analysis with insights into the effect of the COVID-19 pandemic. *Journal of Transport Geography, 87*,. https://doi.org/10.1016/j.jtrangeo.2020.102815

Calderon-Tellez, J. A., & Herrera, M. M. (2021). Appraising the impact of air transport on the environment: Lessons from the COVID-19 pandemic. *Transportation Research Interdisciplinary Perspectives, 10*,. https://doi.org/10.1016/j.trip.2021.100351

Carballo Piñeiro, L., Mejia, M. Q., & Ballini, F. (2021, June 1). Beyond COVID-19: The future of maritime transport. *WMU Journal of Maritime Affairs*. Springer Science and Business Media Deutschland GmbH. https://doi.org/10.1007/s13437-021-00243-1

Cui, Q., He, L., Liu, Y., Zheng, Y., Wei, W., Yang, B., & Zhou, M. (2021). The impacts of COVID-19 pandemic on China's transport sectors based on the CGE model coupled with a decomposition analysis approach. *Transport Policy, 103*, 103–115. https://doi.org/10.1016/j.tranpol.2021.01.017

Deaton, B. J., & Deaton, B. J. (2020). Food security and Canada's agricultural system challenged by COVID-19. *Canadian Journal of Agricultural Economics, 68*(2), 143–149. https://doi.org/10.1111/cjag.12227

Deveci, M., Çiftçi, M. E., Akyurt, İZ., & Gonzalez, E. D. R. S. (2022). Impact of COVID-19 pandemic on the Turkish civil aviation industry. *Sustainable Operations and Computers, 3*, 93–102. https://doi.org/10.1016/j.susoc.2021.11.002

Dong, G., Liu, Z., Tae-Woo Lee, P., Chi, X., & Ye, J. (2023). Port governance in the post COVID-19 pandemic era: Heterogeneous service and collusive incentive. *Ocean and Coastal Management, 232*,. https://doi.org/10.1016/j.ocecoaman.2022.106427

Fu, X., Qiang, Y., Liu, X., Jiang, Y. Z., Zhang, D., & Wang, J. (2022). Will multi-industry supply chains' resilience under the impact of COVID-19 pandemic be different? A perspective from China's highway freight transport. *Transport Policy, 118*, 165–178.

Fusillo, M., & Haralambides, H. (2020). Do carrier expectations indicate industry structure in container shipping? An econometric analysis. *Journal of Shipping and Trade*, *5*(1). https://doi.org/10.1186/s41072-019-0057-2

Gonzalez, J. N., Camarero-Orive, A., González-Cancelas, N., & Guzman, A. F. (2022). Impact of the COVID-19 pandemic on road freight transportation—A Colombian case study. *Research in Transportation Business and Management, 43*,. https://doi.org/10.1016/j.rtbm.2022.100802

Gray, R. S. (2020). Agriculture, transportation, and the COVID-19 crisis. *Canadian Journal of Agricultural Economics, 68*(2), 239–243. https://doi.org/10.1111/cjag.12235

Gu, B., & Liu, J. (2023). COVID-19 pandemic, port congestion, and air quality: Evidence from China. *Ocean and Coastal Management, 235*,. https://doi.org/10.1016/j.ocecoaman.2023.106497

Lee, P. T. W., & Song, Z. (2023). Exploring a new development direction of the Belt and Road Initiative in the transitional period towards the post-COVID-19 era. *Transportation Research Part e: Logistics and Transportation Review, 172*,. https://doi.org/10.1016/j.tre.2023.103082

Li, T. (2020). A SWOT analysis of China's air cargo sector in the context of COVID-19 pandemic. *Journal of Air Transport Management, 88*,. https://doi.org/10.1016/j.jairtraman.2020.101875

Merk, O., Hoffmann, J., & Haralambides, H. (2022). Post-COVID-19 scenarios for the governance of maritime transport and ports. *Maritime Economics & Logistics*. https://doi.org/10.1057/s41278-022-00228-8

Mogaji, E., Adekunle, I., Aririguzoh, S., & Oginni, A. (2022). Dealing with impact of COVID-19 on transportation in a developing country: Insights and policy recommendations. *Transport Policy, 116*, 304–314. https://doi.org/10.1016/j.tranpol.2021.12.002

Notteboom, T., & Pallis, T. (2020). IAPH-WPSP port economic impact barometer. *IAPH-WPSP Port Economic Impact Barometer*, July 6. https://sustainableworldports.org/wp-content/uploads/WPSP-Port-Economic-Impact-Barometer-09-April-2020.pdf

Notteboom, T., Pallis, T., & Rodrigue, J. P. (2021). Disruptions and resilience in global container shipping and ports: The COVID-19 pandemic versus the 2008–2009 financial crisis. *Maritime Economics and Logistics, 23*(2), 179–210. https://doi.org/10.1057/s41278-020-00180-5

Osinska, M., & Zalewski, W. (2020). Effectiveness of the anti-crisis policy in the period of COVID-19 pandemic in the road transport industry. *European Research Studies Journal*, *XXIII*(Special Issue 2), 40–57. https://doi.org/10.35808/ersj/1807

Sudan, T., & Taggar, R. (2021). Recovering supply chain disruptions in post-COVID-19 pandemic through transport intelligence and logistics systems:

India's experiences and policy options. *Frontiers in Future Transportation, 2*,. https://doi.org/10.3389/ffutr.2021.660116

Sun, X., Wandelt, S., Zheng, C., & Zhang, A. (2021). COVID-19 pandemic and air transportation: Successfully navigating the paper hurricane. *Journal of Air Transport Management, 94*,. https://doi.org/10.1016/j.jairtraman.2021.102062

Sun, Z., & Zhang, Y. (2022). Strategic crisis response of shipping industry in the post COVID-19 era: A case of the top 10 shipping lines. *Journal of Marine Science and Engineering, 10*(5), 635. https://doi.org/10.3390/jmse10050635

Tijan, E., Aksentijević, S., Ivanić, K., & Jardas, M. (2019, February 1). Blockchain technology implementation in logistics. *Sustainability (Switzerland)*. MDPI. https://doi.org/10.3390/su11041185

Troyer, H. L., & Bidaisee, S. (2022). The impact of COVID-19 on the aviation industry: A literature review. *International Public Health Journal, 14*(1), 13–21. https://www.proquest.com/scholarly-journals/impact-covid-19-on-aviation-industry-literature/docview/2679856351/se-2

Wang, H., Han, J., Su, M., Wan, S., & Zhang, Z. (2021). The relationship between freight transport and economic development: A case study of China. *Research in Transportation Economics, 85*,. https://doi.org/10.1016/j.retrec.2020.100885

Yazır, D., Şahin, B., Yip, T. L., & Tseng, P. H. (2020). Effects of COVID-19 on maritime industry: A review. *International Maritime Health, 71*(4), 253–264. https://doi.org/10.5603/IMH.2020.0044

Zambrano-Monserrate, M. A., Ruano, M. A., & Sanchez-Alcalde, L. (2020). Indirect effects of COVID-19 on the environment. *Science of the Total Environment, 728*,. https://doi.org/10.1016/j.scitotenv.2020.138813

Zhou, X., Jing, D., Dai, L., Wang, Y., Guo, S., & Hu, H. (2022). Evaluating the economic impacts of COVID-19 pandemic on shipping and port industry: A case study of the port of Shanghai. *Ocean and Coastal Management, 230*,. https://doi.org/10.1016/j.ocecoaman.2022.106339

CHAPTER 9

Assessing the Pandemic's Impact: Ensuring Adequate Food Supply in the MENA Area

Rasha Osman and Sufian Abdel-Gadir

1 Introduction

The global challenge of food insecurity has reached critical proportions. The repercussions of persistent conflict in Ukraine and the persistent effects of the COVID-19 pandemic have exacerbated the worldwide condition of food insecurity in the midst of the worldwide financial stoppage. Food frameworks have been shaken and enormous quantities of individuals have been left without admittance to sufficient nourishment. Food and Agriculture Organization of the United Nations (FAO) gauges that 222 million individuals (2.8% of the total populace) are as of now seriously uncertain in their food (WFP & FAO, 2022).

R. Osman
University of Juba, Juba, Sudan

S. Abdel-Gadir (✉)
Sultan Qaboos University, Muscat, Oman
e-mail: sufian@squ.edu.om

A. Mishrif (ed.), *Business Resilience and Market Adaptability*, The Political Economy of the Middle East,
https://doi.org/10.1007/978-981-97-2962-3_9

Food insecurity has emerged as a significant concern on a global scale, with particularly pronounced challenges observed in the Middle East and North Africa (MENA) region. This region is grappling with an escalating food security crisis. Before the development of COVID-19, UN organizations detailed that in excess of 55 million individuals among its populace of 456.7 million were wrestling with lack of healthy sustenance. The pandemic, delayed clashes, and different variables have exacerbated the pervasiveness of appetite. Amazingly, in 2020, MENA represented 20% of the world's seriously food-uncertain populace, a strikingly lopsided figure considering its portion of the worldwide populace is just 6% (Belhaj & Solima, 2021).

The appearance of the COVID-19 pandemic has acquainted new weaknesses with an all-around delicate food security circumstance in the MENA locale, which is portrayed by dry scenes, political shakiness, and provincial contentions. The pandemic has disturbed each part of the food store network, from agrarian creation to circulation and access, compounding existing food security issues and uncovering new weaknesses (Abu Nahleh et al., 2023; Gaba, 2021a, b; Fei & Ni, 2020; Woertz, 2020). The effects of the pandemic remember diminished venture for agrarian exploration, absence of framework in rustic regions, expanding water shortage, and disturbances in worldwide food supply chains (Carlos et al., 2023; Devendra et al., 2023). Furthermore, the pandemic has prompted low efficiency, restricted market openness, loss of business, expanded wellbeing costs, expanded neediness levels, hunger, and passings (Hasan, 2023). These difficulties require cautious assessment and vital intercessions to address the perplexing interaction between the pandemic, climate change, clashes, and food security (Denis, 2023, Oladipo & Oyinloye, 2022).

This chapter seeks a few interconnected goals. It highlights a significant gap in the existing literature, specifically the lack of a comprehensive evaluation of the direct correlation between COVID-19 outbreak and food scarcity in the MENA nations. It highlights the requirement for a more careful and nuanced comprehension of what the pandemic has meant for food security around here. Thus, the essential objective of this chapter is to connect this current examination hole and deal significant bits of knowledge into this basic relationship. Besides, by digging into key factors, for example, climate change, agrarian land, populace development, and expansion rates, this exploration attempts to add to the ongoing group of information by revealing insight into the variables straightforwardly affecting food availability during COVID-19 era.

This chapter follows a structured organization beyond this introduction. Segment 2 gives a hypothetical establishment, joined by a broad survey of pertinent writing relating to COVID-19 and food security. Segment 3 carefully frames our strategy, explaining our examination plan, information assortment methodology, and scientific techniques. Our discoveries and examination are introduced in Segment 4, offering nuanced experiences into the particular impact of Coronavirus on food security in the MENA district. At last, in Area 5, we compactly sum up our key discoveries and commitments and give suggestions emerging from our review. Basically, this part plans to convey a strong and savvy investigation of the exchange between Coronavirus and food security in MENA nations during the pandemic.

2 Literature Review

The impacts of the Coronavirus pandemic on food security are perplexing and unusual. Laborde et al. (2020) feature the pandemic's expansive repercussions on the transparency, availability, and quality of food. Moreover, Daniel Gebeyehu et al. (2022) verifies that Coronavirus meaningfully affects food security in MENA nations, influencing both the stockpile and utilization of food. Moreover, the aggravations in the food supply chains brought about by the virus, like lockdowns, conclusion of boundaries, and work deficiencies, have harmed the accessibility, openness, usage, and solidness of food and nourishment security (Du, 2022). The pandemic affects work, pay creating exercises, and buying power, further adding to food insecurity (Tonnang et al., 2023).

The adverse influence of the Coronavirus pandemic on food security in the MENA area has been surveyed in a few examinations. One investigation discovered that Jordanian, Lebanese, Saudi Middle Eastern, and Palestinian respondents nitty–gritty were the most vital speeds of food weakness in the locale, while Oman and Bahrain revealed the least rates (El Shikieri, 2023). One more review zeroed in on the Gulf Collaboration Committee (GCC) locale, which comprises major league salary and food-secure nations. It was discovered that the virus only limitedly impacted food-related practices in GCC locale, because of the great buying force of the populace (Abu Nahleh et al., 2023). A review led in Saudi Arabia analyzed the commonness of food insecurity among COVID-19 patients and its relationship with lack of healthy sustenance risk. It observed that food insecurity was related with an expanded gamble of hunger among COVID-19 patients (Bilan et al., 2023). Furthermore, a reasonable structure was proposed for the Unified Bedouin Emirates (UAE) to work on the strength of agri-food supply chains and accomplish food security even with the pandemic (Adesoji et al., 2023).

Notwithstanding, the hypothetical foundation for understanding the impact of Coronavirus on food security in the MENA locale is a complex system that thinks about a few key variables. These variables incorporate climate change, arable land accessibility, populace development, expansion, genuine per capita pay development, and the immediate impacts of the Coronavirus pandemic itself. A careful assessment of these variables is fundamental for getting a handle on the intricacy of the circumstance in the MENA locale.

2.1 *Climate Change and Food Security*

Climate change is a basic driver of food security issues on the planet. The MENA regions are especially helpless against its belongings because of expanding temperatures, water shortages, and changing precipitation designs. These environmental shifts can disrupt agricultural practices and reduce crop yields, affecting food availability and access (Namdar et al., 2021; Tekce & Deniz, 2016).

2.2 *Agricultural Productivity*

In MENA countries, the interplay between agricultural productivity and value added significantly influences food security. An eminent productive impact on various food security metrics, such as per capita total food availability and per capita nutrient supply, is observed when agricultural productivity is on the rise. Notwithstanding, taking note of that regardless of its importance is significant, the agricultural sector in these countries remains predominantly traditional and highly susceptible to climate change. Rainfed agriculture is the prevailing practice in most nations, and the consequences of rising temperatures and shifting rainfall patterns have led to notable reductions in crop and livestock output. Consequently, this has adversely affected food distribution, as highlighted in the IPCC's Climate Change report from 2007.

2.3 *Population Growth*

Populace development has been found to fundamentally affect food security in MENA countries. Studies have shown that as the population grows, the predominance of undernourishment also increases, especially in low-paying and middle-paying nations (Goran, 2023). The expansion in population puts weight on the generally delicate regular asset base, leading to food insecurity (Yimer, 2016). Additionally, the study found that steady population growth is strongly correlated with food insecurity in the study area (Bengana et al., 2022). The connection between population development and food security is perplexing, with both provincial and metropolitan population development influencing the predominance of undernourishment (Collomb, 2003). It has been observed that food shortages are one of the main driving factors of political instability in the MENA region, highlighting the importance of ensuring food security for governments in the region (Subramaniam et al., 2023).

2.4 *Inflation*

The quick ascent of food costs, especially in emerging nations, has raised worries about food security (Ali Koc et al., 2017). The effect of expansion on food security in MENA nations has been analyzed in several studies. One study found that price increases have a harmful effect on food security in the region (Khorshed & Shahiduzzaman, 2008). Another study focused on the reaction of customer value expansion to world food value shocks and found that taking off food costs prompted an ascent in inflation, reducing consumers' purchasing power (Abd El Rahman, 2023; Marga &Albers, 2013). These findings suggest that inflation can have negative consequences for food security in MENA countries, as it reduces affordability and access to food.

2.5 *Actual Capita Income Growth*

Actual capita income growth can enhance food security by boosting individuals' purchasing power. Nevertheless, it is crucial to take into account income distribution disparities (Abdul Manap & Ismail, 2019). Notwithstanding, in regions wrestling with food insecurity, there are difficulties accomplishing genuine Gross domestic product per capita development, as demonstrated by the FAO in 2019.

2.6 COVID-19

The pandemic acquainted exceptional disturbances with the food inventory network, influencing creation, circulation, and admittance to food. The impacts of lockdowns, exchange limitations, and disturbances in labor markets have been especially articulated (Laborde et al., 2020).

By considering these elements and their transaction, we can foster an all-encompassing comprehension of the difficulties looked by the MENA district in ensuring food security during and past the Coronavirus pandemic. This hypothetical establishment gives the premise to exact investigation and strategy suggestions pointed toward resolving these perplexing issues.

3 Coronavirus and Food Security in MENA: Key Difficulties

MENA region wrestles with a bunch of considerable difficulties that profoundly influence its food security. These difficulties incorporate water shortage, monetary unpredictability, and a weighty dependence on food imports, delivering the locale powerless to elevated food insecurity. Also, MENA faces the developing impact of climate change, appearing in delayed dry seasons and heatwaves that straightforwardly upset agrarian creation. Beneath, we portray these key difficulties:

3.1 Overreliance on Food Imports

MENA nations vigorously rest on other worldwide districts to fulfill their food necessities because of restricted neighborhood food creation abilities and quick populace development. This dependence opens them to worldwide vacillations in food costs and disturbances in supply chains, as exemplified during the COVID-19 pandemic. MENA, in general, imports roughly 50% of its food from a modest bunch of key providers, with specific countries like Algeria, Iraq, Lebanon, Tunisia, and Bay states outperforming this limit (Profound Information Examination, July 2022). A relevant model is Lebanon, which brought in 81% of wheat from Ukraine and 15% from Russia in 2020 (Tazrouti, 2022). Egypt likewise relied upon these two nations for 80% of its wheat imports (Kandeel, 2022).

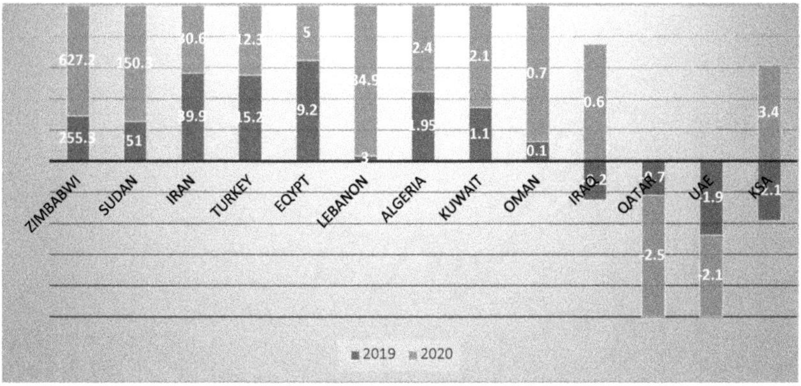

Fig. 1 Inflation, % change in consumer price index (2019–2020) (*Source* World Bank, World Development Indicator [WDI])

3.2 Value Instability

The pandemic likewise set off changes in food costs. Disturbances in supply affixes prompted cost increments for specific food things because of deficiencies, while others encountered cost drops as request lessened. This unpredictability represented a critical test for buyers in Oman, making it hard to anticipate and deal with their food costs (see Fig. 1).

3.3 Limited Arable Land

The shortage of arable land presents a particular and squeezing challenge inside the MENA region. The region is restricted limit with regard to economical homegrown food creation compels it to intensely depend on imports to meet its food needs. This dependence intertwines food security with the stability of its import capacity.

Figure 2 offers a compelling perspective by comparing the percentages of agricultural land and GDP value added across selected MENA countries, with additional analysis involving China and the USA. Notably, China and the USA, despite possessing considerable agricultural land, exhibit a relatively modest contribution of agriculture to their GDP. This suggests highly mechanized and efficient agricultural sectors that may not serve as primary drivers of overall economic output. Saudi Arabia and Sudan stand out for their agricultural land percentages in the MENA

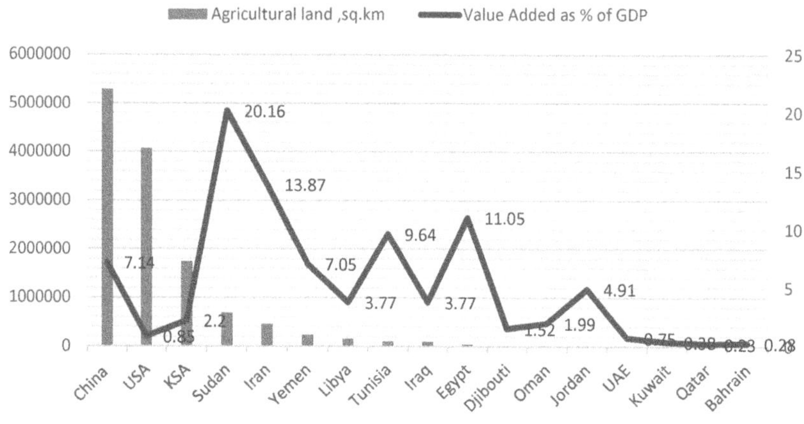

Fig. 2 Agricultural land vs. value added as % of GDP (*Source* Agricultural land by country, around the world | TheGlobalEconomy.com)

region. However, it's vital to acknowledge that Saudi Arabia, along with other Gulf Cooperation Council (GCC) countries, typically registers a lower GDP contribution from agriculture due to their focus on oil-based economies, which overshadow the agricultural sector in terms of economic significance.

Addressing these challenges within the MENA region necessitates strategic considerations that encompass enhancing domestic food production while recognizing the varying economic priorities among MENA nations, particularly the GCC countries with their emphasis on oil-based industries.

3.4 *Effect on Global Food Security Index (GFSI)*

The Global Food Security Index (GFSI) is an exhaustive apparatus created by The Economist Intelligence Unit (EIU) to survey and quantify the condition of food security in nations all over the planet. The GFSI assesses food security in light of a bunch of pointers and sub-markers gathered into three center aspects: reasonableness, accessibility, and quality and wellbeing.

While thinking about the presentation of MENA nations in Global Food Security Index (GFSI), it becomes clear that their standings change fundamentally. Prominently, the gathering of GCC (Gulf Cooperation

Council) nations sticks out, with Emirates getting the 26th position and Qatar following intently at 29th among the 170 nations assessed for food security. This momentous presentation can be ascribed to their significant monetary limit, generally got from oil and gas incomes, empowering them to obtain the fundamental food assets from global business sectors.

As an unmistakable difference, Syria and Yemen wind up at the lower end of the food security range, possessing the 111th and 113th positions, individually, on the GFSI. The continuous contentions in both of these countries have created a long-shaded area over their food security circumstances, contributing essentially to their lower rankings in the index. These contentions have disturbed food creation, dissemination, and access, fueling food security challenges and highlighting the staggering effect of such emergencies on a country's capacity to guarantee its populace's admittance to protected and nutritious food (Fig. 3).

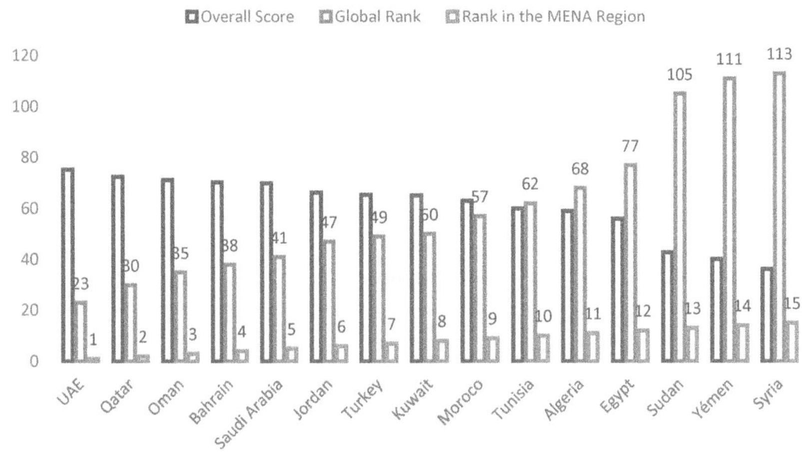

Fig. 3 Positioning of the MENA nations in the Global Food Security Index in 2022 (*Source* The Economist Intelligence Unit)

4 Methodology

4.1 Model Specification

The Model:

$$GFSI = f(CO_2, \text{Agric}, \text{GDPPC}, \text{POPG}, \text{INF}, \text{DUMV})$$

The egression: equation is:

$$\text{LnGFSI}_{it} = c + \alpha \text{LnCO}_{2it} + \beta \text{Ln Agric}_{it} + \delta \text{LnGDPPC}_{it} + £\text{LnPOPG}_{it} + \gamma \text{LnINF}_{it} + \eta\prime \text{DUM}_{it} + \varepsilon_{it}$$

where

- $GFSI_{it}$ is an intermediary of in general food security and it is a dependent variable,
- CO_{2it} represents the carbon dioxide emissions metric ton per capita,
- $Agric_{it}$ is agricultural land (% of land area),
- $GDPPC_{it}$ is genuine GDP per capita (constant 2015 US $),
- $POPG_{it}$ is the population growth rate,
- INF_{it} is the inflation rate (annual %),
- DUM_{it} is the spurious variable that expects a value of 0 for the pre-COVID-19 period (for example 2012–2018) and 1 for the COVID-19-time frame (for example 2019–2022),
- c is the intercept, α, β, δ, £, π, γ, and η' are the regression coefficients, and $\varepsilon t.$ is the error term.

4.2 Data Sources

All data were gathered from World Development Indicators database except for food security (GFSI) variable which was obtained from the Global Food Security Index database.

5 Results and Discussion

5.1 Panel Unit Root Test

The results of the panel unit root test, as presented in Table 1, indicate that all variables are non-stationary at their levels. However, after taking the first difference of the variables, they all become stationary. This

Table 1 Panel unit root test

Variables	*Levin, Lin & Chu t*		*Im, Pesaran and Shin W-stat*		*ADF—Fisher Chi-square*		*PP—Fisher Chi-square*	
	Level p-value	*First Difference p-value*	*Level p-value*	*First Difference p-value*	*Level p-value*	*First Difference p-value*	*Level p-value*	*First Difference p-value*
LnGFSI	0.6746	0.0625	0.6498	0.0001	0.5321	0.0003	0.2351	0.0000
LnPOPG	0.0488	0.6782	0.0222	0.0000	0.0654	0.0001	0.1234	0.0010
LnAgric	0.0178	0.0893	0.0867	0.0001	0.0432	0.000	0.5642	0.000
LnINF	0.5678	0.0646	0.0789	0.0000	0.6541	0.0000	0.15642	0.0000
InGDPP$_C$	0.0002	0.0015	0.0000	0.0002	0.0320	0.0000	0.0032	0.0000
LnDUM	0.8976	0.8965	0.9020	0.0000	0.6754	0.0000	0.3421	0.0000

suggests that the variables have achieved stationarity after differencing, which is a crucial step in time series analysis and econometrics.

The way that the variables are fixed after differencing is a positive result as it considers a more dependable analysis, particularly while managing board information. Stationarity is fundamental for leading cointegration tests and investigating long-run harmony connections between variables. The subsequent stage, as referenced in the conversation, is to continue with the board cointegration test to decide in the event that there exists a long-run concordance relationship among the factors in the board data. These outcomes establish the groundwork for additional analysis and conversations regarding the connections between the variables and their suggestions for the review's targets.

5.2 *Cointegration Test*

The consequences of the Johansen Fisher Cointegration Test, as introduced in Table 2, are demonstrative of the presence of a long-run association between the factors in the panel data. The test surveys the amount of cointegrating conditions, which address the quantity of genuinely huge long-haul connections among the variables.

The trace test in Table 2 suggests the existence of five cointegrating equations at the 0.05 level. This result indicates that there are five statistically significant long-term relationships among the variables under

Table 2 Johansen fisher panel cointegration test

Hypothesized No. of CE(s)	*Fisher Stat.* * *(from trace test)*	*Prob*	*Fisher Stat.* * *(from max-eigen test)*	*Prob*
None	172.3	0.0000	69.71	0.0000
At most 1	89.95	0.0000	27.74	0.0000
At most 2	56.04	0.0000	15.16	0.0051
At most 3	29.27	0.0008	30.31	0.0322
At most 4	17.51	0.0469	27.82	0.0670
At most 5	11.36	0.2618	22.36	0.8001

* MacKinnon-Haug-Michelis *p*-values
Source Results based on E-Views 12 output

investigation. The *p*-values associated with these statistics are all very close to zero, suggesting a high level of confidence in the cointegration results.

Overall, these findings are significant as they show that the factors in the board information are not just fixed but also exhibit meaningful long-term relationships. This makes way for additional analysis and understanding of these connections with regard to the research objectives. The cointegration results recommend that the variables are interconnected over the long haul, and changes in a single variable are probably going to impact the others in a genuinely critical way.

5.3 Error Correction Model Results

The outcomes introduced in Table 3, which depend on the Vector Error Correction Model (VECM), provide significant insights into the connections among the variables being scrutinized.

The Error Correction Term (ECT) coefficient is a critical boundary in the VECM, and it is prominent that it has a negative and significant value of roughly—0.272. This coefficient indicates the speed at which disequilibrium in the growth rate of MENA is corrected each year.

In this context, a negative ECT coefficient suggests that there is a tendency for the system to correct any deviations from long-term equilibrium in the growth rate of MENA countries. Specifically, the coefficient of −0.272 indicates that roughly 0.27% of the total disequilibrium in the MENA growth rate will be corrected annually. This implies that if there are deviations from the long-run equilibrium, the system will adjust over time to bring the growth rate of MENA closer to its equilibrium level.

Table 3 Vector error correction model (VECM)

Error Correction:	*D(LnGFSI)*	*D(LnCO2)*	*D(LnAgric)*	$D(LnGDPP_C)$	*D(INF)*	*D(LnPOPG)*
CointEq1	−0.272379	0.466280	0.061234)	−0.98769	21.7865	−2.54321
	(0.05541)	(0.24278)	(0.02345)	(24.8976)	(15.0889)	(0.45678)
	[−4.91495]	[1.92058]	[2.61125]	[−0.03967]	[0.00262]	[−5.56761]

Additionally, the coefficient estimates for the lagged contrasts in the factors (D(LnGFSI), D(LnCO_2), D(LnAgric), D(LnGDPPC), D(INF), D(LnPOPG)) provide information about the short-term dynamics and relationships among these variables.

Overall, these results are important for grasping the elements of the factors and their change toward long-haul balance with regard to the model. The negative and significant ECT coefficient suggests a tendency for the system to self-correct over time, which is a crucial finding in the analysis of the variables' interplay.

5.4 *Fully Modified OLS (FMOLS)*

The results of the Fully Modified OLS (FMOLS) estimation in Table 4 provide valuable insights into the long-run relationships between the dependent variable, GFSI (Global Food Security Index), and the independent variables.

FMOLS is an appropriate method to estimate long-run parameters when dealing with cointegrated panels. It considers cross-sectional heterogeneity, endogeneity, and sequential connection issues, which are crucial considerations when analyzing panel data with potential cointegration.

Here are some key observations from the FMOLS results:

Table 4 FMOL results

Dependent Variable: GFSI				
Method: Panel Fully Modified Least Squares (FMOLS)				
Variable	*Coefficient*	*Std. Error*	*t-Statistic*	*Prob*
LnCO_2	−46.59351	20.69357	−2.251594	0.0284
LnDUM	−8.830755	1.659417	−5.321600	0.0000
Ln$GDPP_C$	3.001568	1.003862	−0.406145	0.6862
LnINF	−6.003690	2.611580	−2.298872	0.0001
LnPOPG	−0.720319	1.515525	−0.475293	0.6365
LnAGRI	−2.759672	3.037968	−0.908394	0.3676
R-squared	0.923487	Mean dependent var		49.42025
Adjusted *R*-squared	0.891491	S.D. dependent var		11.67233
S.E. of regression	3.844953	Sum squared resid		813.1015
Long-run variance	24.39005			

1. **Significant Variables**: The coefficients of $LnCO_2$, LnDUM, and LnINF have *t*-statistics that are measurably huge at ordinary importance levels (with *p*-values less than 0.05). This suggests that these factors essentially affect GFSI over the long haul.
2. **Insignificant Variables**: The coefficients of LnGDPPC, LnAGRI, and LnPOPG do not appear to be statistically significant as their *t*-statistics are not significantly different from zero. This indicates that these variables may not have a substantial long-term effect on GFSI in the context of the model.
3. ***R*-squared and Adjusted *R*-squared**: The *R*-squared and adjusted *R*-squared values are generally high, showing that the model makes sense of a critical part of the variety in GFSI. This recommends that the included variables on the whole have areas of strength for power over the long haul.
4. **S.E. of Regression and Long-run Variance**: The standard error of regression and the long-run variance provide proportions of the model's integrity of fit and the stability of long-term relationships. These values can be useful for assessing the model's reliability and precision.

In outline, the FMOLS results show that specific variables, like $LnCO_2$, LnDUM, and LnINF, are significant determinants of GFSI over the long haul. These discoveries can be important for policymakers and scientists keen on understanding the elements impacting global food security. In any case, it's fundamental to decipher the outcomes inside the particular setting of the review and think about their pragmatic ramifications.

6 Conclusion and Policy Recommendations

Food security and the flexibility of food supply chains are central for supporting the global economy, upgrading the prosperity of residents, and cultivating impartial turn of events. This part presents a thorough report that offers canny proof on the essential issue of food security in MENA locale. Utilizing data from overall reports, it coordinates a short evaluation of the contemporary effect of the Coronavirus pandemic on food security inside the MENA area.

In this chapter, we have dissected the repercussions of the Coronavirus pandemic on food security in the MENA area. To explore the presence of an excessively involved acquaintance among the variables, we utilize Cointegration technique, with Johansen Cointegration tests applied to affirm cointegration. Furthermore, we utilize the Fully Modified Least Squares (FMOLS) technique to gauge the magnitude of the long-term relationships among these variables. The information utilized for this study is obtained from the World Bank, 2022 and the Global Food Security Index data set.

The essential discoveries of this exploration highlight the presence of a co-coordinating connection between the variables and food security in MENA nations, as laid out by Johansen Cointegration tests. To evaluate the strength of these connections, the FMOLS strategy is utilized. Prominently, the outcomes uncover that the Coronavirus pandemic antagonistically influences food security in the MENA area. Moreover, the review recognizes that per capita pay has a positive and genuinely huge impact on the food security index. Interestingly, factors, for example, climate change (CO_2 levels), expansion rates, and the accessibility of farming area affect food security.

In light of these discoveries, a few strategy suggestions and proposals arise:

1. Strategy Audit: States in the MENA locale ought to basically survey their approaches connected with food security. This incorporates techniques for guaranteeing a steady and strong food store network, particularly amid crises like the Coronavirus pandemic.
2. Interest in Food Creation: MENA nations ought to focus on significant interests in food creation. Lessening dependence on food imports by helping homegrown creation can improve food security and diminish weakness to outer shocks.

In conclusion, this study uncovers understanding into the confounded components of food security despite the Coronavirus pandemic inside the MENA area.

6.1 Research Limitation

One of the constraints of this study is the accessibility of data, especially with respect to food security. The information for the food security record is only accessible from the year 2012 onwards, limiting the historical scope of the analysis.

References

Abdul Manap, N., & Ismail, N. (2019). Food security and economic growth. *International Journal of Modern Trends in Social Sciences, 2*(8), 108–118.

Abd El Rahman, S. E. D. D. (2023). *The food security dynamic in MENA countries: How should policies be distinctive?* (Security Policy Paper). https://doi.org/10.26735/wbuf6491

Abu Nahleh, Y., Al Ali, B., Al Ali, H., Alzarooni, S., Almulla, S., & Alteneiji, F. (2023). The impact of COVID-19 on supply chain in UAE food sector. *Sustainability, 15*(11), 8859. https://doi.org/10.3390/su15118859

Adesoji, F., Ilham, H., Trinh, H. H., & Akadiri, S. S. (2023). Economic growth, social, and welfare development during COVID-19 pandemic: Do country-specific characters matter in the MENA region?. *Environmental Science and Pollution Research, 30*, 60552–60573. https://doi.org/10.1007/s11356-023-26678-y

Ali Koç, A., Ozdamar, O., & Uysal, P. (2017). The economic determinants of food security in the MENA region. *International Journal of Food and Beverage Manufacturing and Business Models, 2*(1), 1–19. https://doi.org/10.4018/IJFBMBM.2017010101

Belhaj, F., & Solima, A. (2021). https://www.worldbank.org/en/news/opinion/2021/09/24/mena-has-a-food-security-problem-but-there-are-ways-to-address-it. Accessed 10 December 2023.

Bengana, I. M., Adeleye, B. N., Boukhelkhal, A. A., Isioma Okafor, V., Hamoud Alnefaie, A., & Salim, E. I. E. (2022). Evaluating the nonlinear population-economic growth nexus in MENA countries. https://doi.org/10.21203/rs.3.rs-2255332/v1

Bilan, Y., Vysochyna, A., Vasylieva, T., Grytsyshen, D., & Smutka, L. (2023). Impact of coronavirus disease (COVID-19) on food security: Bibliometric analysis and empirical evidence. *Frontiers in Sustainable Food Systems, 7*. https://doi.org/10.3389/fsufs.2023.1126454

Carlos, C., Ribeiro, S., & Vitorio, D. (2023). The impacts arising from the COVID-19 pandemic on supply chains. *GeSec*. https://doi.org/10.7769/gesec.v14i4.1943

Collomb, P. (2003). Population growth and food security in the countries of the middle east and north Africa. In H. G. Brauch, P. H. Liotta, A. Marquina, P. F. Rogers, & M. El-Sayed Selim (Eds.), *Security and environment in the mediterranean* (pp. 777–811). Springer. https://doi.org/10.1007/978-3-642-55854-2_49

Daniel, G., Leah, E., Stuart, W., & Shahidul, I, Md. (2022). Impact of COVID-19 on the food security and identifying the compromised food security dimension: A systematic review protocol. *PLoS One*. https://doi.org/10.1371/journal.pone.0272859

Devendra, P., Neupane, R. C., Sigdel, S., Poudel, P. R., & Khanal, A. R. (2023). COVID-19 pandemic, climate change, and conflicts on agriculture: A trio of challenges to global food security. *Sustainability, 15*(10), 8280. https://doi.org/10.3390/su15108280

Denis, D. (2023). The Russia-Ukraine war: Implications for global and regional food security and potential policy responses. *Global Food Security, 36*, 100675. https://doi.org/10.1016/j.gfs.2023.100675

Du, X. (2022). The impact of COVID-19 and associated policy responses on global food security. *Agricultural Economics*. https://doi.org/10.1111/agec.12749

El Shikieri, A. B. (2023). Impact of food insecurity and its influencing factors on the risk of malnutrition among COVID-19 patients. *PLoS One, 18*(6), e0287311. https://doi.org/10.1371/journal.pone.0287311

Fei, S., & Ni, J. (2020). Local food systems and COVID-19: A look into China's response. *FAO*. https://www.fao.org/in-action/food-for-cities-programme/news/detail/en/c/1270350/. Accessed 9 December 2023.

Gaba, U. (2021a). Impact of the coronavirus pandemic on the global economy. https://countercurrents.org/2021/02/impact-of-the-coronavirus-pandemic-on-the-global-economy/. Accessed 8 December 2023.

Gaba, U. (2021b). Impact of the coronavirus pandemic on the global economy. https://countercurrents.org/2021/02/impact-of-the-coronavirus-pandemic-on-the-global-economy/. Accessed 18 November 2023.

Goran, M. (2023). Impacts of population growth and economic development on food security in low-income and middle-income countries. *Frontiers in Human Dynamics, 5*. https://doi.org/10.3389/fhumd.2023.1121662

Hasan, Y. (2023). The future of food systems and food security in context of lessons learned from covid-19 pandemic as a global challenge: Insights from a qualitative perspective. *AgroLife Scientific Journal, 12*(1), 143–157. https://doi.org/10.17930/agl2023117

IPCC. (2007). *Climate change 2007, impacts, adaptation and vulnerability; contribution of working group II to the fourth assessment report of the inter-governmental panel on climate change*. Cambridge University Press.

Kandeel, A. (2022, August 31). Climate vulnerability and food insecurity in MENA should be priorities for US policymakers. *Atlantic Council MENA Source (blog)*. https://www.atlanticcouncil.org/blogs/menasource/climate-vulnerability-and-food-insecurity-in-mena-should-be-priorities-for-us-policy maker

Khorshed, A., & Shahiduzzaman, M. (2008). Inflation and food security: Some emerging issues in developing countries.

Laborde, D., Martin, W., & Swinnen, J. (2020, July 31). COVID-19 risks to global food security. *Science, 369*(6503), 500–502. https://doi.org/10.1126/science.abc4765

Marga, P., & Albers, R. (2013). Food prices, government subsidies and fiscal balances in south mediterranean countries. *Development Policy Review, 31*(3), 273–290. https://doi.org/10.1111/DPR.12007

Namdar, R., Karami, E., & Keshavarz, M. (2021). Climate change and vulnerability: The case of MENA countries. *ISPRS International Journal of Geo-information, 10*(11), 794. https://doi.org/10.3390/IJGI10110794

Oladipo, I. E., & Oyinloye, O. B. (2022). Food insecurity and conflict dynamics: A theoretical perspective. *American Journal of Social and Management Sciences, 3*(1), 30–46. https://doi.org/10.53982/ajsms.2022.0301.03-j

Subramaniam, Y., Loganathan, N., & Masron, T. A. (2023). Food security and political instability-foreign divestment analysis. *Journal of Chinese Economic and Foreign Trade Studies, 16*(1). https://doi.org/10.1108/jcefts-04-2022-0025

Tazrouti, M. (2022, April 12). The invasion of Ukraine is supercharging food insecurity in the Middle East and North Africa. *Greenpeace*. https://www.greenpeace.org/international/story/53163/russia-invasion-of-ukraine-supercharging-food-insecurity-middle-east-north-africa

Tekce, M., & Deniz, P. (2016). The impacts of climate change on agricultural trade in the MENA region. *Research in World Economy, 7*(2). https://doi.org/10.5430/RWE.V7N2P1

Tonnang, H. E. Z., Sokame, B. M., Wamalwa, M., Niassy, S., & Muriithi, B. (2023). System dynamics modeling for assessing the impact of COVID-19 on food supply chains: A case study of Kenya and Rwanda. *Sustainability, 15*(6), 4717. https://doi.org/10.3390/su15064717

Woertz, E. (2020). Wither the self-sufficiency illusion? Food security in Arab Gulf States and the impact of COVID-19. *Food Security, 12*(4), 757–760.

World Food Programme (WFP) and the Food and Agriculture Organization (FAO). (2022, September 21). *Hunger hotspots: FAO-WFP early warnings on acute food insecurity: October 2022 to January 2023 outlook* (Report). WFP/FAO, p. vii. https://www.fao.org/3/cc2134en/cc2134en.pdf

Yimer, M. (2016). The impact of population growth on food security: Case study of Tehuledere woreda, northern Ethiopia. *Journal of Ecology and the Natural Environment, 8*(11), 184–191. https://doi.org/10.5897/JENE2016.0595

CHAPTER 10

COVID-19 and Food Security: A Short Bibliometric Analysis of Countries with Different Income Levels

Maryam Al Maqbali and Behnaz Saboori

1 Introduction

Food security is a fundamental human right that must be accessible for all individuals despite their economic status, ethnicity, or background. Based on the OCED (2020), food security is defined as, "when all individuals have the physical, social and economic access to sufficient, safe and nutritious food that meets their dietary needs and food preferences

M. Al Maqbali (✉)
Department of Clinical Nutrition and Dietetics, Sultan Qaboos Comprehensive Cancer Care and Research Centre (SQCCCRC), Muscat, Oman
e-mail: m.almaqbali@cccrc.gov.om

B. Saboori
Department of Natural Resource Economics, College of Agricultural and Marine Sciences, Sultan Qaboos University, Muscat, Oman
e-mail: b.saboori1@squ.edu.om

A. Mishrif (ed.), *Business Resilience and Market Adaptability*, The Political Economy of the Middle East,
https://doi.org/10.1007/978-981-97-2962-3_10

for an active and healthy life." It's considered one of the major determinants of health since it can directly affect individuals' productivity. In fact, food insecurity is associated with malnutrition, growth retardation, poor immunity, increased incidence of chronic disease, and overall poor quality of life and low productivity (Friedman, 2021). Governments around the globe are making extreme efforts to reduce the incidence of food insecurity. However, in December 2019, COVID-19 raised in China and spread to all over the world and was considered as global pandemic by the world health organization in March 2020 (WHO, 2020). Because of the vast spread of the disease, the fact that no cure has been identified, and its unknown long-term complications, many restrictions were introduced by governments in the hope of controlling or at least limiting its expansion. These restrictions include transposition restrictions, quarantine, social distancing, wearing masks, lockdowns, and more. Thus, global trade, food access, income, economy, and food security, all were negatively affected.

Whether people got infected by COVID-19 or not, they must have suffered from one or more of its other consequences. Food security is a major determinant of health, and due to COVID-19-related trade restrictions, agricultural labor loss, and food chain disruption, food insecurity increased significantly (Béné, 2020). It was estimated by the World Food Program that over 250 million people and almost 100 million people all over the world suffered from acute and chronic food insecurity respectively in 2020 (Singh et al., 2021). Based on the data released by the Food and Agriculture Organization (FAO) in 2021, over 650 million individuals could still be starving until 2030 because of COVID-19 on the world's food security in the long-term (Jiang et al., 2021). FAO (2023a, b) have estimated that over 750 million faced hunger in 2022, which is 122 million more individuals compared to the pre-pandemic. It's crucial to mention that the sharp increase in the world's food insecurity due to the pandemic has stalled and almost 3.8 million less individuals suffered from hunger in 2022 compared to 2021. This was mainly a result of the economic recovery as the number of confirmed COVID-19 cases are decreasing significantly. However, there is no doubt that food insecurity levels are still far above its levels before the onset of the pandemic since its affecting over 9% of the global population in 2022 compared to 7.9% in 2019.

These alarming rates of food security show that the issues caused by COVID-19 in relation to food security are not on a country or a national level, rather, it's more of a global crisis that affected people's life all over the world. Furthermore, many scholars have empathized with the food security challenges caused by COVID-19. However, most of these papers are focused on a specific country. Essentially, the aim of this chapter is to review the respected studies on COVID-19 and food security in countries with different income levels, such as low-income countries, middle-income countries, and high-income countries. Following are the sections of the chapter. The next part of the chapter explains the methodology followed by the results and discussion section for low, middle, and high-income countries and ended with the last section that concludes the chapter.

2 Methodology

This chapter, however, is a holistic collection of what has been found in the previously published papers and reviews the impact of COVID-19 on food security all around the world. It aims to identify the impact of the pandemic on food security in different countries based on their income levels. We reviewed previous studies on the effect of COVID-19 on food security in this chapter. A literature review was conducted on the impact and challenges of COVID-19 on the world's food security, using the keywords food security and COVID-19, data was collected from Google Scholar and Scopus databases. The second step involved screening the reviewed articles to ensure they had the necessary information and data. This stage focused on criteria such as COVID-19's impact on food security, the mechanism by which COVID-19 affected food security, and its effect on food production and food supply chain in different countries and nations. The third round of screening was conducted based on the abstract and title of the articles to ensure they met the eligibility criteria. Lastly, we excluded articles that didn't meet our criteria, and we presented the rest in a table to simplify data extraction and analysis.

A total of 200 papers have been reviewed. We excluded 149 papers from the study because they did not meet the inclusion criteria of having the keywords COVID-19 and food security in the title, conducting the study in a low, middle, or high-income country, using primary and secondary data, and providing comprehensive results regarding COVID-19 and food security status in a particular country. For the remaining 51 papers that met the inclusion criteria, detailed data extraction was performed. These data included study design, methodology, type of data used (primary or secondary), the country in which the study was performed and the key findings. Finally, the findings were arranged to provide a comprehensive overview of the pandemic's impact on food security. The findings were categorized based on the countries income levels to meet the goal of this chapter.

3 Results and Discussion

The key findings of the studies that have been reviewed in this chapter are that there is an increase in food insecurity because of COVID-19 pandemic. The summarized results are presented in Tables 1, 2, and 3. The following sections provide a detailed explanation on the pandemic's impact on food security in different countries based on their income level.

Food security can only be achieved when food security determinants are met which are food access (individuals obtain a sufficient amount of food/nutrient from their income), food availability (food is physically available and people do not starve), food utilization (contributing to physiological requirement by providing sufficient food and adequate hygienic practices), and food stability (having access to adequate food

Table 1 The impact of COVID-19 on food security in low-income countries

Author/s	*Country*	*Income level*	*Results & key findings*
Singh et al. (2021)	Nepal	Low	Increase in food insecurity
Habtewold (2021)	Ethiopia	Low	Increase in food insecurity
Madzorera et al. (2021)	Ethiopia & Nigeria	Low & Upper middle	Increase in food insecurity
Adjognon et al. (2021)	Mali	Low	Higher increase in food insecurity in urban areas
Aggarwal (2021)	Malawi	Low	No evidence for an increase in food insecurity
Kansiime et al. (2021)	Kenya & Uganda	Low middle and low-income	Increase in food insecurity
Hirvonen et al. (2021)	Addis Ababa, Ethiopia	Low	No change in food security

Source Authors' own work

Table 2 The impact of COVID-19 on food security in middle-income countries

Author/s	*Country*	*Income level*	*Results & key findings*
Abay et al. (2021)	Nigeria	Middle	Increase in food insecurity
Kharroubi et al. (2021)	Lebanon	Upper middle	Steady increase in food insecurity
Rodrigues et al. (2022)	Brazil	Upper middle	Increase in food insecurity
Jaacks et al. (2021)	India	Lower middle	Increase in food insecurity
Rabbi et al. (2021)	Bangladesh	Lower middle	Increase in food insecurity
Folayan et al. (2021)	Nigeria	Lower middle	Increase in food insecurity
Jayatissa et al. (2021)	Sri Lanka	Upper middle	Increase in food insecurity
Houessou et al. (2021)	Benin	Lower middle	Increase in food insecurity
Shahzad et al. (2021)	Pakistan	Lower middle	Increase in food insecurity
Mandal et al. (2021)	Bangladesh	Lower middle	Increase in food insecurity
Ceballos et al. (2021)	Haryana & Odisha, India	Lower middle	No change in food security
Yazdanpanah et al. (2021)	Iran	Upper middle	Increase in food insecurity
Amare et al. (2021)	Nigeria	Lower middle	Increase in food insecurity
Ceballos et al. (2021)	Guatemala	Upper middle	Increase in food insecurity
Ahmed et al. (2021)	Bangladesh	Lower middle	Increase in food insecurity
Rocha et al. (2021)	Brazil	Upper middle	Increase in food insecurity
Nguyen et al. (2021)	India	Lower middle	Increase in food insecurity
Ruszczyk et al. (2021)	Bangladesh	Lower middle	Increase in food insecurity
Ibukun and Adebayo (2021)	Nigeria	Lower middle	Increase in food insecurity
Alam and Khatun (2021)	Bangladesh	Lower middle	Increase in the likelihood of food insecurity

(continued)

Table 2 (continued)

Author/s	*Country*	*Income level*	*Results & key findings*
Gaitán-Rossi et al. (2021)	Mexico	Upper middle	Increase in food security
Kalantari et al. (2021)	Iran	Upper middle	Higher Household Food Insecurity Access Scale in people infected by COVID-19
Sohel et al. (2021)	Bangladesh	Lower middle	Increase in food insecurity
Büyüksoy et al. (2021)	Turkey	Upper middle	Increase in food security
Hammond et al. (2022)	Burundi; Kenya; Rwanda; Tanzania; Uganda; Zambia; and Vietnam	Low- & middle-income countries	Increase in food insecurity
Suresh et al. (2022)	India	Lower middle	Increase in food insecurity
Headey et al. (2022)	Myanmar	Lower middle	Increase in food insecurity
Murdad et al. (2022)	Malaysia	Upper middle	Increase in food insecurity

Source Authors' Own work

over time) (Bloem & Farris, 2021). Having food insecurity means that there is a disruption in one or more of these determinants resulting from the pandemic or any other disturbances. This pandemic affected different countries in different ways based on their income level. Being said so, in the following sections, explanations of the possible mechanisms by which COVID-19 leads to disrupted food security in different countries based on their income level will be provided.

3.1 Low-Income Countries

COVID-19 impact on low-income countries is higher compared to other countries because many individuals and families from these countries are from poor socioeconomic backgrounds; those individuals ended up in a worse financial situation, especially after COVID-19-related restrictions were introduced since it affected their lives in many ways. The noted

Table 3 The impact of COVID-19 on food security in high-income countries

Author/s	*Country*	*Income level*	*Results & key findings*
Kleve et al. (2021)	Australia	High	Increase in food insecurity
Morales et al. (2021)	USA	High	Increase in food insecurity
Cardarelli et al. (2021)	USA	High	Increase in food insecurity
Reimold et al. (2021)	USA	High	Increase in food insecurity
Clay and Rogus (2021)	New York (USA)	High	Increase in food insecurity
Lauren et al. (2021)	USA	High	Increase in food insecurity
Brown and Reid (2021)	USA	High	Increase in food insecurity
Davitt et al., (2021)	USA	High	Increase food insecurity rates among student who lives alone
Lamarche et al. (2021)	Canada	High	Decrease in food insecurity
Hanbazaza (2021)	KSA	High	28.4% of participants were food insecure
Soldavini et al., (2021)	USA	High	Increase in food insecurity
Mialki et al. (2021)	USA	High	Significant changes in food security (mostly increase in food insecurity)
Larson et al. (2021)	USA	High	Increase in food insecurity
Ostolaza et al. (2021)	Puerto Rico	High	Increase in food insecurity

Source Authors' own work

impact from previously published papers is that there is an association between COVID-19 and food insecurity as can be seen in Table 1.

3.1.1 Food Production

During the COVID-19 pandemic, food production was affected in different ways in low-income countries. However, the main mechanism that leads to this disruption is its impact on farmers and farming in general. As it's commonly known, most low-income countries depend on agriculture as a main source of both food and income. As a matter of fact, restrictions that are related to COVID-19 have significantly affected farmers in low-income countries. For instance, in countries like Nepal with its high reliance on other countries for importing seeds and fertilizers, many farmers, mainly in Nepal's Terai area, were unable to get fertilizers when needed and they had labor scarcity, both of which directly influenced local food production (Kansiime et al., 2021).

One of the countries that Nepal relies on for food production is India, and rice is one of the main crops being imported. As a result of border closure, it was reported that most households ended up having food shortages during the period of rice plantation and had to buy rice and other food from the local mill at a higher cost. On top of that, due to the internal movement restrictions, many Ugandan farmers reported that all these restrictions hold back their farming activities and pose challenges in terms of getting customers, having access to agricultural inputs, or getting feed for their animals (Kansiime et al., 2021). Additionally, many farmers reported that they were forced to destroy their food crops in the frame because they were unable to sell them in the market due to the pandemic-related market closure and movement restrictions (Singh et al., 2021). Crop production plays an essential role in ensuring a diverse diet. As a result of the pandemic restrictions, Indian farmers, for example, experienced disruptions in production, sales, and pricing, along with a decrease in agricultural revenues, according to a survey, households reported having unfavorable dietary changes, including a decrease in fruit and animal-based food intake (Madzorera et al., 2021).

It's crucial to mention that these consequences are not as severe on farmers as other non-farmers households, farmers are not as likely as other individuals to have their food security deteriorate. One explanation is that while others, non-farmers, depend on the market to purchase food, farmers were able to rely on self-planted food during these difficult times (Kansiime et al., 2021).

3.1.2 Job and Income Loss

Another way COVID-19 affected individuals' food security is through its indirect impact on household income. Based on the World Bank, the pandemic would have driven almost 50 million people into severe poverty by 2020. Based on the WHO (2022), the number of people suffering from hunger grew to over 780 million in 2020 compared to 678 million in 2019, and it increased even more in 2021 to reach 828 million. The estimated number of food insecure individuals in 2021 was over 2 billion people around the world, which is 359 million higher than 2019; this is mostly attributable to income loss as well as food chain disturbance. In addition, the pandemic has had many consequences on business activities as well as employment rates, knowing that these sectors' productivity has dropped substantially since the beginning of COVID-19. A study found that one of the major consequences of COVID-19 is job loss, showing that over 80% of Ethiopian households who participated in the study lost their jobs due to the pandemic, which would probably lead to income loss and negatively affect food security (Habtewold, 2021).

Furthermore, the majority of households in these countries work as employees in the private sector, and people rely on daily wages, knowing that social security and insurance systems are limited. Over the first year of the pandemic, low-income countries witnessed a significant decrease in GDP, wage, employment in formal sector, which was estimated as 16–20%, at the same time unemployment rate have increased from 6% to almost 7% (Buffie et al., 2023). The ILO (2023) reported that job gap in low-income countries is the highest compared to middle-income (11%) and high-income (8.2%) countries at over 21% in 2023. Singh et al. (2021) stated that the most affected individuals are those coming from poor socioeconomic backgrounds because the closure of the market and business leads to those individuals losing their job as well as their daily wages which is their main source of income, thus, increasing their risk of having food insecurity. Also, based on a study in Malawi and Liberia, it has found that market activity declined significantly, leading to a monthly income decrease by over 40% and 50% in Malawi and Liberia respectively (Aggarwal et al., 2020). Kansiime et al. (2021) have found that over 50% of respondents in an online questionnaire in Uganda reported losing their regular source of income, payment delay or reduction due to COVID-19 restrictions that lead to disruption in business activities.

Even interior movement has been prohibited by the Ugandan government, which has an impact on commercial activity and business owners' abilities to pay their employees on time. This led to an increase in layoff and unemployment rates. A study has found that small and medium enterprises in Kampala in Uganda kept reducing the number of workers and over 80% of them reduced their workforce by more than 50%. Furthermore, some individuals are found to be more likely than others to experience income shocks, such as farmers and self-employed respondents; one possible explanation that is given for this is that due to COVID-19-induced lockdown, farmers may have difficulty getting to their farms, accessing inputs, or transporting their goods to markets. The social distance regulations also limit the number of people who can attend a market at a given time and shorten the hours of operation for food markets. Salaried employees were able to work from home based on the type of job they are having, unlike farmers who have been severely affected as a result of these regulations, even a minor disruption in their income-generating activities might have severe impacts on their food security (Kansiime et al., 2021).

A coping mechanism for income reduction that was commonly used among most respondents was depending on savings for living and altering eating patterns by skipping meals, reducing portion size, and consuming a less diversified diet; this coping mechanism was found to be used by many households not only in Uganda but also in other developing countries to reduce the effect of an income shock. Comparing eating patterns during the pandemic to the eating pattern before COVID-19 in Uganda showed that there was a 30% and 40%increase in the number of those who lowered their food intake and those who had less diversified diets respectively. Also, there was over 30% and 40% increase in the number of people who were unable to get nutritious food and households who were more food insecure compared to the pre-pandemic period, knowing that roughly half the respondents reported being concerned about running out of food. All these alterations in food security could be strongly associated with income shocks (Naicker et al., 2021).

As mentioned earlier, farmers are at a higher risk of experiencing income shock. However, it was found that when it comes to food security, those people are unlikely to experience a decrease in food security compared to employed and wage workers who lost their work or income. A possible explanation is that although wage workers and self-employed individuals were unable to get food due to income reduction and food prices increase, farmers were able to maintain their diet by relying on self-produced food when alternative ways of food availability failed (Kansiime et al., 2021).

3.1.3 Food Prices

Just like other countries, COVID-19 caused food supply disruptions in low-income countries due to its related restrictions and global inflation, it led to trade flows and supply chains disruption, economic depression, and income shock. Reduced food availability and higher food prices have negative consequences leading to a reduction to food access by reducing impoverished households' purchasing power and forcing them to lower the quantity of their typical family food requirements (Madzorera et al., 2021). Those from low socioeconomic backgrounds are among the most affected individuals by this increase in food prices. Singh et al. (2021) have found that most participants in the study stated that the increase in food costs are one of the primary causes of food insecurity, especially owing to food's limited affordability. For instance, many participants reported being unable to buy food even when it is available in the market due to the significant increase in prices. According to a recent United Nations study, food costs in cities throughout the world have risen suddenly owing to interruptions in food supplies, particularly from rural farming regions, as a result of the COVID-related lockdown.

Further, a study that was conducted on households in Addis Ababa has found that there is a rise in calorie consumption of stable food and fruits. However, there is a decrease in calories per capita from legumes, nuts, and vegetables, all of which are considered healthy, nutritious food. However, the total food budget has remained the same and there is only one change in the type of food being purchased. For instance, an increase in fruit and legume costs leads households to reduce their intake of those items in favor of cheaper staples. Vegetable costs, for example, have risen by over 50% since March 2020. As a result of the recent rise in vegetable costs, many households shifted their food intake from vegetables to starchy staples (Hirvonen et al., 2021).

As of 2023, with the recedes of the pandemic and the fact that almost all nations and countries have transitioned into the semblance of normalcy, shipping cost have decreased and agricultural inputs such as fertilizers, seeds, and energy became more affordable, as a result, food prices gradually decreased (see Fig. 1). However, acute food insecurity and food price inflation are still a challenge in low-income countries. As

Fig. 1 FAO food price index (*Source* FAO, 2023a, b)

of mid-2023, almost one fourth of low-income countries experienced a 15% inflation in annual domestic food prices. These are believed to be consequences of the pandemic along with logistic challenges, socioeconomic fragility, and the limited storage capacity for food in these countries compared to their high food insecurity risk (Rother et al., 2023).

3.1.4 Stay Home Restriction

COVID-19-related stay-home restriction was found to be associated with an over 8% rise in running out of food and an over 9% increase in spending a day without eating a meal in the last month among Ethiopian households. Also, the consequences were more severe on those that have "restricted social gatherings" and "no traveling" restrictions (Madzorera et al., 2021). Based on the World Bank statistics, it is expected that poverty rates will start to decline by 2021 by 21 million. It could be because, in 2020, several countries implemented many restrictions and lockdowns to control the pandemics spread. However, in 2021, countries seem to be indifferent to applying these restrictions (World Bank Blogs, 2021).

3.2 *Middle-Income Countries:*

Middle-income countries are no better than low-income countries in the aspect of COVID-19 impacts on food security. Even the mechanisms by which COVID-19 affected food security were like those seen in low-income countries. It can be seen in Table 2 that almost all reviewed papers that have been conducted in middle-income countries found that COVID-19 was associated with the increase in food insecurity. In the following section, a detailed explanation of the impact of COVID-19 on food security in middle-income countries will be provided.

3.2.1 Food Production, Agriculture, and Farming

Smallholder farmers play an imperative role in the food production chain, providing the most food in low-/middle-income countries. In some parts of Africa, Asia, and China, small farms produce over 70% of all food products; individuals in these nations are at a higher risk of food insecurity and poverty in general. Despite food availability, many households face a scarcity of healthy foods as well as a lack of purchasing power. Furthermore, access to food, whether from self-produced or from farming or non-farming activity income, was already inadequate, and it got even worse due to pandemic-related restrictions imposed to prevent disease spread (Hammond et al., 2022).

From farmers' standpoints, it is already known that even before COVID-19 hit the globe, farmers' income in most middle-income countries was considered as low and many governments were working hard to increase their income. For example, the average income of farmers in India was found to be less than $150 and the government was aiming to double it by 2022, as a simple disruption in their source of income can lead to significant consequences. Besides, it was found that due to the lockdown, out of 331 farmers, around 122 and 50 farmers were unable to harvest and sell their crops, respectively. Also, findings from a survey that was conducted in 2020 indicated that many Indian farmers experienced a loss in sales, a drop in farm revenue, and a change in their usual food intakes to a less nutritious diet (Jaacks et al., 2021).

Moreover, smallholder farmers in India experienced different challenges running their farms as a result of the pandemic's restrictions. First, they had to adjust their harvest timing to minimize the losses; however, over one-third of farmers were found to be affected more severely because they could not manage to sell and harvest their crops as early as they should be and some farmers were not able to harvest at all, and most of those farmers reported that this is a result of the restriction caused by COVID-19 pandemic. Second, during the lockdown, a large number of workers returned to their hometowns. In order to get back to their work, farmers had to pay more money for labor, transportation, accommodation, and food, which increased labor costs. It was found in Haryana, India that over 40% of farmers reported spending more on harvest than they typically do. Furthermore, many farmers point out that the increase in labor and machinery costs is the main reason behind the increase in harvest costs. Additionally, many farmers were not able to prepare for the upcoming season as a result of labor shortages and high labor costs. Third, the lockdown included market closure, and many farmers had limited or no access to the market, leading them to store their harvest. To add, a study has found that more than 50% of farmers were unable to sell their crops, instead, they have stored these crops to be sold or consumed later. Regions with good storage facilities had no issues with storage and crop maintenance; unlike other regions that could not properly store their harvested crops, which led to a significant loss, especially in crops like pulses that are highly perishable. To avoid further losses, many farmers ended up selling their crops at a very low price and some of them could not sell all of their crops despite price reduction (Ceballos et al., 2020; Jaacks et al., 2021). Farmers in Bangladesh have lost approximately 600 million dollars since the outbreak of COVID-19. Due to the loss of 12–15 million liters of milk, the Bangladesh poultry and dairy industry lost more than 130 and 6 million dollars/day, respectively. A major reason behind this loss are market closure and the lack of a good storage system (Rabbi et al., 2021).

Also, due to this disruption in farming activity, many farmers were at an elevated risk of being food insecure, since they faced financial challenges because of the falling demand, supply interruptions, and having to sell at low prices. Furthermore, studies have found that about one-third of farmers were worried about getting food and many of them were at risk of spending a whole day without eating. Alam and Khatun (2021) reported that in Bangladesh, farmers had to sell their crops with over 50% reduction in their price. Thus, farmers' food insecurity keeps increasing as their revenue decreases, which makes production even harder and increases the risk of food shortage at the same time. Knowing that this reduction in output price was not only in farming activities but also in livestock and fishing activities.

All these findings show the impact of COVID-19 on food production through its disruption of agriculture and farming activities. This is strongly linked to the reduction in food security among farmers, individuals, and communities in general. If the COVID-19 scenario persists, it will have a detrimental effect on farmers, consumers, and food production as a whole.

3.2.2 Food Price

Just like other countries, many governments in middle-income countries apply strict lockdown precautions, even in areas where infection rates are low. Trade interruptions caused by such policies caused an increase in food prices in some areas, especially food insecure areas. This is especially concerning since a relatively small increase in food prices could have a significant impact on the welfare of disadvantaged groups. Based on statistics from China's Bureau of Statistics, there was over 10% increase in food prices from August 2020 to August 2021. With that being said, according to recent studies, a 2% rise in food costs would result in a 0.24% increase in malnourishment (Dietrich et al., 2022; Sohel et al., 2021).

It should be noted that the increase in food prices was primarily due to imported food rather than locally produced foods that saw a decrease. As stated earlier, many farmers had to sell their crops at lower prices due to COVID-19 restrictions. This is definitely negative for farmers; however, from a consumer's standpoint, this can be beneficial and help moderate restrictions' impact on food prices. A study has found that in Bangladesh, the majority of people rely on consuming vegetables and backyard vegetables in some cases. This is because it was the only thing they could afford since the prices of most other food, including meat and fish, were significantly high for those people. However, depending only on a diet that consists of vegetables might lead to malnutrition since it lacks too many macro- and micro-nutrients. In addition, some people cannot afford the purchase of locally produced food due to transportation restrictions, which limit the transport of locally produced food from villages to the city. Consequently, traders hike up the already high food prices as a result of the shortage (Sohel et al., 2021).

Also, imported food items are still extremely important, especially for countries that rely on imports. For example, in comparison with the pre-lockdown period, in Turkey, the consumer price index grew by over 2% in August. As a result, even if households purchased the same food products with the same amount, the money spent on food might have grown.

Thus, it can be said that consumers who live in countries that rely on imports would be at an elevated food insecurity risk (Büyüksoy et al., 2021).

Nevertheless, it can be understood that prices of both locally produced and imported food have increased due to the pandemic. A study reported that nine out of every ten households who participated in the study reported that food availability has decreased. When it comes to food prices, most households report that since the beginning of the lockdown, there has been an increase in prices among all food groups. According to these data, there was a considerable rise in the percentage of families experiencing food insecurity in the after the lockdown compared to the before lockdown period. After the lockdown, 91%, 87%, and 20% of households reported eating a few types of meal, eating less, and not eating even when hungry, respectively. Additionally, nutritional diversity was also altered since it is found that there is a decrease in household dietary diversity score from 6.8 to 6.4 which is found to be mainly due to a decrease in the diversity of animal-based food from 1.3 to 0.8, and an increase in vegetables and fruit diversity from 2.1 to 2.5. This increase in fruit and vegetables consumption can be due to the fact that some food like fruits and vegetables are available around the year in these countries, making people consume more of it since it is locally produced (Ceballos et al., 2021). This proves what was stated earlier, households tend to increase their consumption of locally produced food that is usually available and sold at a price that most households can afford.

Additionally, a study that was conducted in Dhaka city, Bangladesh, has shown that during the lockdown period, many people reduced their fish intake, which is an invaluable protein source in their diet; hence it is a major component of food security maintenance in Bangladesh. The study has found that over 70% of participants reported an increase in fish price by up to 0.48$/kg. As a coping mechanism, households reduce their food intake and try to replace it with eggs, lentils, and dried fish. In contrast, the prices of vegetables and fruits have decreased, and their consumption has increased. However, the increase in fruit and vegetable consumption was not only related to its price but also due to other factors, such as trying to improve immunity by increasing vitamin C intake (Mandal et al., 2021). Thus, it can be said that even if households were able to afford some locally produced food, they would still have shortages of other necessary food items due to high prices.

3.2.3 Employment and Income

To make things even more difficult, COVID-19 restrictions and sanitary regulations led to job loss, being absent from work, or working for a few hours; all these factors led to income loss among affected individuals and indirectly affected food access. As a result, people ended up eating food that was cheaper and usually had lower nutritional value.

Jayatissa et al. (2021) have reported that approximately 90% of families reported a decrease in monthly incomes because of the pandemic. The main contributing causes to lower income were loss of work, wage reduction, and alternative income loss. To add, in Malaysia, most businesses made the conscious decision to have their staff work remotely, and some had to lay off a lot of employees. The number of workers in several food retail industries has declined, affecting food production quantity, food supply constraints, and food security. Also, many participants reported a decline in their income by up to 50%, and over 37% of participants reported even higher reductions in income. For instance, households that are very poor end up losing an even larger proportion of their income, and some of them have lost their income completely. It is estimated that low-income households lost between 25% and up to 100% of their income. The reason behind this significant reduction in income is the fact that job opportunities for these individuals are usually the ones that require movement. During the lockdown and movement restriction, those individuals were not able to continue their work and ended up losing their only source of income (Mandal et al., 2021).

As stated earlier, many individuals in middle-income countries work in the agriculture sector and during COVID-19 lockdown, farmers could not sell their crops. It was reported that in Malaysia almost 68% of farmers lost their income, especially during strict movement control orders. Also, in India, tomato farmers' income reduced by 50% during the period of lockdown compared to a typical year (Ceballos et al., 2021; Murdad et al., 2022). Households who depend on farm activity or those relying on their own business were found to be significantly more food insecure compared to households who depend on wage jobs, remittances, and aid incomes. This is not unexpected given that certain wage-related tasks may still be conducted online, or those engaged in wage-related activities could have longer-term contracts or funds that they may draw on during such situations (Amare et al., 2021).

Informal workers were found to be severely affected by the COVID-19 pandemic, particularly in food security. It was reported that during the lockdown period, many informal workers in Bangladesh ended up having no source of income at all, resulting in severe food insecurity during and after the lockdown period, which was mainly related to stay-home restrictions. For example, people who sell on the street could not run their job. Besides, some informal workers reported that they could not follow stay-home regulations because they need to earn money and get income since it is the only way by which they could ensure food security. For those individuals, following these restrictions means consuming less food, consuming less fish and meat, relying mainly on consuming vegetables, suffering from cravings, and consuming unhealthy or poor nutritional food (Sohel et al., 2021).

Also, low income has been found to be strongly linked with food insecurity. Individuals who lost their jobs during the pandemic reported being food insecure and gaining fewer calories due to financial reasons. In the same vein, individuals whose income stayed unchanged were at a lower likelihood of suffering from food insecurity, unlike individuals with reduced income who are at a higher risk of food insecurity. Participants in a study that was conducted in Bangladesh reported that they used to eat 3 full meals/day before the lockdown and ended up aiming for eating only one meal per day after the lockdown and usually this one meal is composed of starchy food like potato and rice, meat, and fish are usually reduced to the lowest due to its high cost (Ahmed et al., 2021; Gaitán-Rossi et al., 2021; Ibukun & Adebayo, 2021; Ruszczyk et al., 2021). Also, another study that was conducted on Turkish households found that over 60% of households had an income that was below the poverty line. This income has decreased further among almost half of the participants through the pandemic. As a result, food insecurity rose three times when household monthly income dropped and increased twice when household total monthly income was below the poverty level. An explanation for this decrease in income is that at least one person was fired from employment in one out of every six households (Büyüksoy et al., 2021).

All these findings prove that income reduction is associated with food security since it can lead to poor diet quality and substituting healthy food with unhealthy food choices which can lead to short- and long-term consequences such as malnutrition, poor health and immunity, and poor productivity (Ceballos et al., 2021).

3.2.4 Rural Versus Urban Area

The pandemic's impact on rural vs urban areas is not significantly different. Generally, households with a low economic status have been affected more severely compared to households with higher economic status (Amare et al., 2021). However, it was found that poor people living in urban areas are more affected compared to those living in rural areas, especially during the lockdown period. Even though food production and distribution are considered "essential," many governments allow only formal retailers, such as supermarkets, and put more restrictions on informal food retailers, who usually sell food at lower prices, that poor people often rely on them. Also, based on a study that was conducted in Myanmar, the number of households reported going hungry was not significantly high; however, urban households reporting going hungry (9%) were significantly higher compared to rural households (1%) which meant that rural households were rarely in extreme food insecurity. One explanation for this is that, unlike rural households, urban households usually have no access to farming activity.

Also, urban areas witnessed more income reduction than rural areas. Although it is uncommon for urban households to be income poor, by early 2020 there was a significant increase in income-poor among urban individuals from 8 to 28%. To add, based on a phone survey, it was reported that there is a 49% and 41% decrease in income in urban and rural areas respectively. Besides income reduction, living costs in urban areas are much higher compared to rural areas. Home rental, for instance, accounts for 40% of income expenditures in urban areas and only 4% in rural areas. This will probably put more financial stress on households and will make them more food insecure.

However, these findings do not mean that COVID-19's impact on rural household's food security was not significant. It was found that during COVID-19 restrictions, Indian households end up consuming more stable food such as rice and wheat and consume less nutritious food such as fish, eggs, and milk. This alteration in eating habits leads to significant health consequences such as malnutrition and poor immunity. Also, it was found that 80% and 40% of urban non-farmers and rural producers respectively were severely food insecure due to a disruption in food access, distribution, availability, and safety indicating food instability. Thus, it can be said that COVID-19 left no one unaffected (Headey et al., 2022; Houessou et al., 2021; Suresh et al., 2022).

3.3 High-Income Countries

Unlike low- and middle-income countries, the impact of COVID-19 on high-income countries has not been very well reviewed. For this reason, the pandemic's consequences on food security in these countries are not clear. However, although studies that were conducted in high-income countries reported a decrease in food security, as can be seen in Table 3, the consequences might not be as severe as those in low- and middle-income countries.

3.3.1 Consumer Purchasing Behavior and Supply Chain Disruptions

One of the mechanisms by which COVID-19 affected food security is through its impact on consumers' purchasing behavior, which in many cases led to food supply chain disruption. As a result of movement restrictions and lockdown, many households were unable to go out and depended on online ordering to get the needed food items from restaurants and groceries. For instance, in some countries such as the United Kingdom, one of the actions that have been made to maintain food security is prioritizing online food shopping all around the country (Morales et al., 2021). The rates of online shopping and food delivery have increased significantly since the onset of the pandemic. It has been found that in April 2022, over 50% of people in KSA use online shopping compared to less than 10% before the pandemic. Also, statistics from an online shopping app in the UAE showed that there was an increase in the times of downloads and daily orders by 70% and 50% respectively. Generally, all the Gulf countries have witnessed a significant increase in online shopping since the outbreak. However, due to the sudden order overload, many online stores ended up failing to fulfill this high demand. Despite this, many people, to be more precise, the uneducated ones and the elderly, were unable to shop online due to their lack of knowledge and skills (Ben Hassen & El Bilali, 2022; Brown and Reid, 2021).

Furthermore, Cardarelli et al. (2021) stated that because of the lockdown and limited time for groceries, as well as the high food demand, many people became frustrated with the food supply disruption and changed their purchasing habits. For example, consumers began purchasing shelf-stable food products, and if possible, they will purchase significantly more food than they would under normal circumstances. Food shortages in supermarkets and other food outlets resulted from these purchasing habits, the significant increase in food purchasing during this period resulted in an inflexible food supply chain that could not cope with the pandemic. Purchasing a large amount of food, more than what is required, would almost certainly put other people in a position of food insecurity. Having said that, Reimold (2021) discovered that by the time people start buying in bulk, many others are struggling to get food. The most common barriers that have been faced by those people include failing to find the type of food they are preferring\looking for, being unable to make it to the store at a convenient time due to work or distance. Introducing policies to control purchasing behaviors during similar situations will help in limiting the consequences of these behaviors.

On the positive side, some studies have shown that COVID-19 leads to some desirable behaviors. Due to the fear of being infected, many people started taking extra care of their health by shifting their diet toward more healthful food choices, especially among those reporting testing positive for COVID-19. For instance, women, in particular, have been found to shift their eating behavior into a more healthful diet, such as spending more time on cooking and eating less processed food cooked away from home. Some people, however, were found to shift their diet to a less healthful diet such as individuals with low income, the elderly, people with anxiety and depression, and university students (Acton et al., 2022; Davitt et al., 2021; Mialki et al., 2021; Soldavini et al., 2021).

3.3.2 University Students

A major group of individuals who have been affected by the pandemic are universities and colleges students. Before the beginning of the pandemic, university students had higher food security scores. Many universities provide campus food pantries and others provide reduced-price meals for their students that help in keeping their food secure. However, due to remote classes and university closure, students had no access to these services which negatively affected their food security status. During the online class period, students either return back home and live with their families or stay by themselves and a few of them stay at the university accommodation. Those who live with their family were found to be at a lower risk of being food insecure. In fact, many of them had an improved food security status since they relied on their family to get food access. Contrary, students who lived by themselves and those who stayed on campus were found to be more food insecure (Soldavini et al., 2021).

One reason behind this is employment loss. It was found that during the COVID-19 period, the highest unemployment rate was among those aged between 19 and 24 years old. It was found that most of the students ended up being unemployed, were laid off, or started working for fewer hours. Those students in particular had a higher food insecurity rate compared to the students whose employment status stayed unchanged. Losing their source of income, students were no longer capable of acquiring sufficient nutritious food. One additional thing that should be considered is that some students are supporting their families financially and due to these changes in employment, their food security status has worsened significantly. Also, many of the students who live by themselves were unable to make their own food either due to lack of time or because they did not have the needed skills (Davitt et al., 2021).

Also, international students were found to be among the highest students whose food security has been negatively affected. Perhaps this is primarily due to the closed border and the necessity of staying in a foreign country during these difficult times. A study that was conducted in the US has reported that residential status has an impact on food security. More than 35% of international students were more food insecure compared to students who are in the US (22.2%) and out of the US (19.1). Finally, food insecurity among students was found to be associated with many complications, such as poor sleep, low academic functionality, weight gain, anxiety, eating disorders, and poor overall psychological status (Davitt et al., 2021; Mialki et al., 2021).

3.3.3 *Worries, Anxiety, and Mental Health.*

Because of the sudden spread of COVID-19 and the unknown complications of the disease, it is not surprising that the pandemic was associated with many psychological complications, such as depression, anxiety, and poor overall mental health. As a result of fear of infection, many people isolated themselves and avoided going out even for food. Asians, in particular, were at higher food insecurity due to discrimination and racist practice against them which further worsened their food insecurity and mental health deterioration (Larson et al., 2021; Lauren et al., 2021; Morales et al., 2021).

3.3.4 *Race and Ethnicity*

It is well known that high-income countries have a diverse population of people of various races and ethnicities. According to Morales et al.

(2021), overall food insecurity have increased across all races and ethnicities. The only difference is the mechanism by which their food security has been compromised. It was discovered that black households could not afford to buy food; this was explained as being since most African Americans lives in the regions where the pandemic is most severe; Hispanic and Asian households were afraid to go out to get food (Morales et al., 2021).

One explanation for this fear is discrimination against Asians, that increased significantly during the pandemic, many people called COVID-19 "Chinese flu," which has discrimination against Asians, or what is called "anti-Asian xenophobia." Over 1800 cases of Asian-American targeted harassment and violence have been reported only during the first 6 month of the pandemic (Morales et al., 2021). The fear of going out was observed in all racial and ethnic groups; however, Asians have an added fear and anxiety as a result of this discrimination.

In addition, Hispanic households face transportation challenges when going out to get food, while white households cannot find the food they seek. Hispanics, on the other hand, faced another issue that was heavily targeted by the enforced immigration restrictions. This created a fear of being separated from their family, making it difficult for them to leave their home (Morales et al., 2021). In general, the impact of COVID-19 on food insecurity in high-income countries has not been well documented, but it appears that many factors contributed to it.

4 COVID-19, Malnutrition and Nutritional Intervention

Maintaining good health and immunity requires a well-balanced, nutritious diet. The human immune system is activated constantly; however, during disease or infection, its activity is typically increased in order to defend the body against any invader. To do so, the body needs more immune cells to defend itself, which requires more DNA, RNA, glucose, amino acids, and other substrates to help support this process. In addition to the roles that folate, iron, magnesium, and zinc play in the synthesis of nucleic acid and nucleotide synthesis, various micro-nutrients typically act as cofactors for energy production and biosynthesis (Calder, 2020).

Furthermore, vitamins A and D, as well as their metabolites, are critical regulators of immune cell gene expression. In addition, they play a role in immune cell maturation, differentiation, and responsiveness. It can be stated that nutrition plays a large and diverse role in enhancing immunity;

thus, providing the body with sufficient nutritious food is necessary to support the body's immune system so that it can respond appropriately to any challenge (Calder, 2020). Having said that, it has been discovered that malnourished COVID-19 patients are over 70% more likely to die and over 100% more likely to stay in the hospital than individuals who are not malnourished and/or have no history of malnutrition (Vong et al., 2022).

5 Conclusion

This chapter examined the impact of COVID-19 on food security in various income-level countries. COVID-19 caused many complications for almost all people all over the world; one of these complications is food insecurity; rates of food insecurity have risen dramatically since the onset of the pandemic. It had the greatest impact on low- and middle-income countries because these countries rely primarily on agricultural activities, and food supply chains that have been significantly disrupted as a result of border and market closures, thus, limiting people's access to food. Furthermore, COVID-19 restrictions result in job and income loss, exacerbating the situation. High-income countries, on the other hand, have received scant attention, but it appears that COVID-19-induced fear and anxiety play a crucial role in the resulting food insecurity in these countries. More research is needed to understand COVID-19's impact on high-income countries. Governments should work on developing more policies to help people in difficult times, such as providing food or money to people who are facing food insecurity. They should also consider loosening restrictions on movement and trade, particularly for self-employed individuals, salaries workers, and informal workers.

6 Limitation of the Study

A major limitation of this chapter is the limited data availability. The literature is lacking comprehensive and reliable statistics regarding COVID-19 impact of food security, and the available data are usually on a country or nation level. Also, the impact of COVID-19 pandemic on food security might be affected by many confounding factors such as the Russian-Ukraine war, and separating the pandemics impact on food security form these factors can be extremely challenging.

References

Abay, K. A., Amare, M., Tiberti, L., & Andam, K. S. (2021). COVID-19-induced disruptions of school feeding services exacerbate food insecurity in Nigeria. *The Journal of Nutrition, 151*(8), 2245–2254.

Acton, R. B., Vanderlee, L., Cameron, A. J., Goodman, S., Jáuregui, A., Sacks, G., White, C. M., White, M., & Hammond, D. (2022). Self-reported impacts of the COVID-19 pandemic on diet-related behaviours and food security in five countries: Results from the International Food Policy Study 2020. *The Journal of Nutrition, 152*, 35S–46S.

Adjognon, G. S., Bloem, J. R., & Sanoh, A. (2021). The coronavirus pandemic and food security: Evidence from Mali. *Food Policy, 101*, 102050.

Aggarwal, B. (2021). Livelihoods in COVID times: Gendered perils and new pathways in India. *World Development, 139*, 105312. https://doi.org/10.1016/j.worlddev.2020.105312

Aggarwal, S., Jeong, D., Kumar, N., Park, D. S., Robinson, J., & Spearot, A. (2020). *Did COVID-19 market disruptions disrupt food security? Evidence from households in rural Liberia and Malawi* (No. w27932). National Bureau of Economic Research.

Ahmed, F., Islam, A., Pakrashi, D., Rahman, T., & Siddique, A. (2021). Determinants and dynamics of food insecurity during COVID-19 in rural Bangladesh. *Food Policy, 101*, 102066.

Alam, G. M., & Khatun, M. N. (2021). Impact of COVID-19 on vegetable supply chain and food security: Empirical evidence from Bangladesh. *PLoS ONE, 16*(3), e0248120.

Amare, M., Abay, K. A., Tiberti, L., & Chamberlin, J. (2021). COVID-19 and food security: Panel data evidence from Nigeria. *Food Policy, 101*, 102099.

Ben Hassen, T., & El Bilali, H. (2022). Impacts of the COVID-19 pandemic on food security and food consumption: Preliminary insights from the gulf cooperation council region. *Cogent Social Sciences, 8*(1), 2064608.

Béné, C. (2020). Resilience of local food systems and links to food security—A review of some important concepts in the context of COVID-19 and other shocks. *Food Security, 12*(4), 805–822.

Bloem, J. R., & Farris, J. (2021). COVID-19 working paper: The COVID-19 pandemic and food security in low-and middle-income countries: A review of the emerging microeconomic literature. *Agriculture & Food Security, 11*(1).

Brown, H., & Reid, K. (2021). Navigating infodemics, unlocking social capital and maintaining food security during the COVID-19 first wave in the UK: Older adults' experiences. *International Journal of Environmental Research and Public Health, 18*(14), 7220. https://doi.org/10.3390/ijerph18147220

Buffie, E. F., Adam, C., Zanna, L. F., & Kpodar, K. (2023). Loss-of-learning and the post-Covid recovery in low-income countries. *Journal of Macroeconomics, 75*, 103492.

Büyüksoy, G. D. B., Çatıker, A., & Özdil, K. (2021). Food insecurity and affecting factors in households with children during the COVID-19 pandemic: A cross-sectional study. *Disaster Medicine and Public Health Preparedness, 16*(6), 1–6. https://doi.org/10.1017/dmp.2021.172

Calder, P. C. (2020). Nutrition, immunity and COVID-19. *BMJ Nutrition, Prevention & Health, 3*(1), 74.

Cardarelli, K. M., DeWitt, E., Gillespie, R., Graham, R. H., Norman-Burgdolf, H., & Mullins, J. T. (2021). Policy implications of the COVID-19 pandemic on food insecurity in rural America: Evidence from Appalachia. *International Journal of Environmental Research and Public Health, 18*(23), 12792.

Ceballos, F., Hernandez, M. A., & Paz, C. (2021). Short-term impacts of COVID-19 on food security and nutrition in rural Guatemala: Phone-based farm household survey evidence. *Agricultural Economics, 52*(3), 477–494.

Ceballos, F., Kannan, S., & Kramer, B. (2020). Impacts of a national lockdown on smallholder farmers' income and food security: Empirical evidence from two states in India. *World Development, 136*, 105069.

Clay, L. A., & Rogus, S. (2021). Food access worries, food assistance use, purchasing behavior, and food insecurity among New Yorkers during COVID-19. *Frontiers in Nutrition*, 539.

Davitt, E. D., Heer, M. M., Winham, D. M., Knoblauch, S. T., & Shelley, M. C. (2021). Effects of COVID-19 on university student food security. *Nutrients, 13*(6), 1932.

Dietrich, S., Giuffrida, V., Martorano, B., & Schmerzeck, G. (2022). COVID-19 policy responses, mobility, and food prices. *American Journal of Agricultural Economics, 104*(2), 569–588.

FAO. (2023a). FAO food price index. https://www.fao.org/worldfoodsituation/foodpricesindex/en/

FAO. (2023b). The state of food security and nutrition in the world. https://www.fao.org/3/cc3017en/cc3017en.pdf

Folayan, M. O., Ibigbami, O., El Tantawi, M., Brown, B., Aly, N. M., Ezechi, O., Abeldaño, G. F., Ara, E., Ayanore, M. A., Ellakany, P., Gaffar, B., Al-Khanati, N. M., Idigbe, I., Ishabiyi, A. O., Jafer, M., Tu-Allah Khan, A., Khalid, Z., Lawal, F. B., Lusher, J.,... & Nguyen, A. L. (2021). Factors associated with financial security, food security and quality of daily lives of residents in Nigeria during the first wave of the COVID-19 pandemic. *International Journal of Environmental Research and Public Health, 18*(15), 7925.

Friedman, C. (2021). Food insecurity of people with disabilities who were Medicare beneficiaries during the COVID-19 pandemic. *Disability and Health Journal, 14*(4), 101166. https://doi.org/10.1016/j.dhjo.2021.101166

Gaitán-Rossi, P., Vilar-Compte, M., Teruel, G., & Pérez-Escamilla, R. (2021). Food insecurity measurement and prevalence estimates during the COVID-19 pandemic in a repeated cross-sectional survey in Mexico. *Public Health Nutrition, 24*(3), 412–421.

Habtewold, T. M. (2021). Impacts of COVID-19 on food security, employment and education: An empirical assessment during the early phase of the pandemic. *Clinical Nutrition Open Science, 38*, 59–72. https://doi.org/10.1016/j.nutos.2021.06.002

Hammond, J., Siegal, K., Milner, D., Elimu, E., Vail, T., Cathala, P., Gatera, A., Karim, A., Lee, J.-E., Douxchamps, S., Tu, M. T., Ouma, E., Lukuyu, B., Lutakome, P., Leitner, S., Wanyama, I., Thi, T. P., Phuc, P. T. H., Herrero, M., & van Wijk, M. (2022). Perceived effects of COVID-19 restrictions on smallholder farmers: Evidence from seven lower-and middle-income countries. *Agricultural Systems, 198*, 103367.

Hanbazaza, M. A. (2021). The impact of COVID-19 curfew on food security status, eating habits, and health among adults living in Saudi Arabia. *Progress in Nutrition.*

Headey, D., Goudet, S., Isabel, L., Maffioli, E. M., Oo, T. Z., & Russell, T. (2022). Poverty and food insecurity during COVID-19: Phone-survey evidence from rural and urban Myanmar in 2020. *Global Food Security, 33*, 100626.

Hirvonen, K., De Brauw, A., & Abate, G. T. (2021). Food consumption and food security during the COVID-19 pandemic in Addis Ababa. *American Journal of Agricultural Economics, 103*(3), 772–789.

Houessou, M. D., Cassee, A., & Sonneveld, B. G. (2021). The effects of the COVID-19 pandemic on food security in rural and urban settlements in Benin: Do allotment gardens soften the blow? *Sustainability, 13*(13), 7313.

Ibukun, C. O., & Adebayo, A. A. (2021). Household food security and the COVID-19 pandemic in Nigeria. *African Development Review, 33*, S75–S87.

ILO. (2023). X ILO monitor on the world of work. Eleventh edition A global employment divide: Low-income countries will be left further behind without action on jobs and social protection. https://www.ilo.org/wcmsp5/groups/public/---dgreports/---dcomm/---publ/documents/briefingnote/wcms_883341.pdf

Jaacks, L. M., Veluguri, D., Serupally, R., Roy, A., Prabhakaran, P., & Ramanjaneyulu, G. V. (2021). Impact of the COVID-19 pandemic on agricultural production, livelihoods, and food security in India: Baseline results of a phone survey. *Food Security, 13*(5), 1323–1339.

Jayatissa, R., Herath, H. P., Perera, A. G., Dayaratne, T. T., De Alwis, N. D., & Nanayakkara, H. P. L. K. (2021). Impact of COVID-19 on child malnutrition, obesity in women and household food insecurity in underserved urban settlements in Sri Lanka: A prospective follow-up study. *Public Health Nutrition, 24*(11), 3233–3241.

Jiang, X., Chen, Y., & Wang, J. (2021). Global food security under COVID-19: Comparison and enlightenment of policy responses in different countries. *Foods, 10*(11), 2850.

Kalantari, N., Eini-Zinab, H., Ezzeddin, N., & Miri, N. (2021). Household food insecurity scores are higher among adults infected with COVID-19: A cross-sectional online study among an Iranian. *Population Journal of Environmental Health and Sustainable Development*. https://doi.org/10.18502/jehsd.v6i4.8151

Kansiime, M. K., Tambo, J. A., Mugambi, I., Bundi, M., Kara, A., & Owuor, C. (2021). COVID-19 implications on household income and food security in Kenya and Uganda: Findings from a rapid assessment. *World Development, 137*, 105199.

Kharroubi, S., Naja, F., Diab-El-Harake, M., & Jomaa, L. (2021). Food insecurity pre-and post the COVID-19 pandemic and economic crisis in Lebanon: Prevalence and projections. *Nutrients, 13*(9), 2976.

Kleve, S., Bennett, C. J., Davidson, Z. E., Kellow, N. J., McCaffrey, T. A., O'Reilly, S., Enticott, J., Moran, L. J., Harrison, C. L., Teede, H., & Lim, S. (2021). Food Insecurity Prevalence, Severity and Determinants in Australian Households during the COVID-19 Pandemic from the Perspective of Women. *Nutrients, 13*(12), 4262.

Lamarche, B., Brassard, D., Lapointe, A., Laramée, C., Kearney, M., Côté, M., Bélanger-Gravel, A., Desroches, S., Lemieux, S., & Plante, C. (2021). Changes in diet quality and food security among adults during the COVID-19–related early lockdown: Results from NutriQuébec. *The American Journal of Clinical Nutrition, 113*(4), 984–992.

Larson, N., Slaughter-Acey, J., Alexander, T., Berge, J., Harnack, L., & Neumark-Sztainer, D. (2021). Emerging adults' intersecting experiences of food insecurity, unsafe neighbourhoods and discrimination during the coronavirus disease 2019 (COVID-19) outbreak. *Public Health Nutrition, 24*(3), 519–530.

Lauren, B. N., Silver, E. R., Faye, A. S., Rogers, A. M., Woo-Baidal, J. A., Ozanne, E. M., & Hur, C. (2021). Predictors of households at risk for food insecurity in the United States during the COVID-19 pandemic. *Public Health Nutrition, 24*(12), 3929–3936.

Madzorera, I., Ismail, A., Hemler, E., Korte, M., Olufemi, A., Wang, D., Assefa, N., Workneh, F., Lankoande, B., Chukwu, A., Ourohire, M., Mattei, J., Soura, A., Berhane, Y., Sie, A., Oduola, A., & Fawzi, W. (2021). Impact of COVID-19 on nutrition, food security and dietary diversity and quality in Burkina Faso, Ethiopia and Nigeria. *Current Developments in Nutrition, 5*(Supplement_2), 234.

Mandal, S. C., Boidya, P., Haque, M. I. M., Hossain, A., Shams, Z., & Mamun, A. A. (2021). The impact of the COVID-19 pandemic on fish consumption and household food security in Dhaka city Bangladesh. *Global Food Security, 29*, 100526.

Mialki, K., House, L. A., Mathews, A. E., & Shelnutt, K. P. (2021). Covid-19 and college students: Food security status before and after the onset of a pandemic. *Nutrients, 13*(2), 628.

Morales, D. X., Morales, S. A., & Beltran, T. F. (2021). Racial/ethnic disparities in household food insecurity during the COVID-19 pandemic: A nationally representative study. *Journal of Racial and Ethnic Health Disparities, 8*(5), 1300–1314.

Murdad, R., Muhiddin, M., Osman, W. H., Tajidin, N. E., Haida, Z., Awang, A., & Jalloh, M. B. (2022). Ensuring urban food security in malaysia during the COVID-19 pandemic—Is urban farming the answer? A review. *Sustainability, 14*(7), 4155.

Naicker, A., Palmer, K., Makanjana, O., & Nzama, P. F. (2021). The impact of the COVID-19 pandemic on food consumption habits, food purchasing behaviours, and food security status among South Africans. *African Journal of Inter/multidisciplinary Studies, 3*(1), 131–143.

Nguyen, P. H., Kachwaha, S., Pant, A., Tran, L. M., Ghosh, S., Sharma, P. K., Shastri, V. D., Escobar-Alegria, J., Avula, R., & Menon, P. (2021). Impact of COVID-19 on household food insecurity and interlinkages with child feeding practices and coping strategies in Uttar Pradesh, India: A longitudinal community-based study. *BMJ open, 11*(4), e048738.

OCED. (2020). Food security and Nutrition. https://www.oecd.org/agriculture/topics/food-security/

Ostolaza, C., Rosas, C., García-Blanco, A. M., Gittelsohn, J., & Colón-Ramos, U. (2021). Impact of the COVID-19 pandemic on food insecurity in Puerto Rico. *Journal of Hunger & Environmental Nutrition*, 1–16.

Rabbi, M. F., Oláh, J., Popp, J., Máté, D., & Kovács, S. (2021). Food security and the COVID-19 crisis from a consumer buying behavior perspective—The case of Bangladesh. *Foods, 10*(12), 3073.

Reimold, A. E., Grummon, A. H., Taillie, L. S., Brewer, N. T., Rimm, E. B., & Hall, M. G. (2021). Barriers and facilitators to achieving food security during the COVID-19 pandemic. *Preventive Medicine Reports, 23*, 101500. https://doi.org/10.1016/j.pmedr.2021.101500

Rocha, H. A., Sudfeld, C. R., Leite, Á. J., Rocha, S. G., Machado, M. M., Campos, J. S., Ce Silva, A., & Correia, L. L. (2021). Coronavirus disease 2019, food security and maternal mental health in Ceará, Brazil: A repeated cross-sectional survey. *Public Health Nutrition, 24*(7), 1836–1840.

Rodrigues, E. C., de Deus Mendonça, R., Camargo, P. P., de Menezes, M. C., de Carvalho, N. C., & Meireles, A. L. (2022). Home food insecurity during the suspension of classes in Brazilian public schools due to the COVID-19 pandemic. *Nutrition, 93*, 111448.

Rother, B., Sosa, S., Debbich, M., Castrovillari, C., & Prifti, E. (2023). Global food crisis update: Recent developments, outlook, and IMF Engagement. *IMF Notes*, *2023*(002).

Ruszczyk, H. A., RaHMan, M. F., Bracken, L. J., & Sudha, S. (2021). Contextualizing the COVID-19 pandemic's impact on food security in two small cities in Bangladesh. *Environment and Urbanization, 33*(1), 239–254.

Santos, L. P., Schäfer, A. A., Meller, F. O., Crochemore-Silva, I., Nunes, B. P., Harter, J., Pellegrini, D. C. P., & de Mola, C. L. (2022). Association between food insecurity and major depressive episodes amid Covid-19 pandemic: Results of four consecutive epidemiological surveys from southern Brazil. *Public Health Nutrition, 25*(4), 944–953. https://doi.org/10.1017/S1368980021004626

Shahzad, M. A., Qing, P., Rizwan, M., Razzaq, A., & Faisal, M. (2021, June). COVID-19 pandemic, determinants of food insecurity, and household mitigation measures: A case study of Punjab, Pakistan. In *Healthcare* (Vol. 9, No. 6, p. 621). Multidisciplinary Digital Publishing Institute.

Singh, D. R., Sunuwar, D. R., Shah, S. K., Sah, L. K., Karki, K., & Sah, R. K. (2021). Food insecurity during COVID-19 pandemic: A genuine concern for people from disadvantaged community and low-income families in Province 2 of Nepal. *PLoS ONE, 16*(7), e0254954.

Sohel, M. S., Hossain, B., Sarker, M. N. I., Horaira, G. A., Sifullah, M. K., & Rahman, M. A. (2021). Impacts of COVID-19 induced food insecurity among informal migrants: Insight from Dhaka, Bangladesh. *Journal of Public Affairs*, e2770.

Soldavini, J., Andrew, H., & Berner, M. (2021). Characteristics associated with changes in food security status among college students during the COVID-19 pandemic. *Translational Behavioral Medicine, 11*(2), 295–304.

Suresh, V., Fishman, R., von Lieres, J. S., & Rao, B. R. (2022). Impact of the COVID-19 lockdown on the economic situation and food security of rural households in India. *Journal of Agribusiness in Developing and Emerging Economies, 12*(3), 497–509.

Updated estimates of the impact of covid-19 on global poverty: Turning the corner on the pandemic in 2021? World Bank Blogs. (2021, June 24). Retrieved April 12, 2022, from https://blogs.worldbank.org/opendata/updated-estimates-impact-covid-19-global-poverty-turning-corner-pandemic-2021

Vong, T., Yanek, L. R., Wang, L., Yu, H., Fan, C., Zhou, E., Oh, S. J., Szvarca, D., Kim, A., Potter, J. J., Mullin, G. E. (2022). Malnutrition increases

hospital length of stay and mortality among adult inpatients with COVID-19. *Nutrients, 14*(6), 1310.
WHO. (2022). N report: Global hunger numbers rose to as many as 828 million in 2021. https://www.who.int/news/item/06-07-2022-un-report--global-hunger-numbers-rose-to-as-many-as-828-million-in-2021
World Health Organisation. (2020, March 11). WHO director-general's opening remarks at the media briefing on COVID-19. https://www.who.int/director-general/speeches/detail/who-director-general-s-opening-remarks-at-the-media-briefing-on-covid-19---11-march-2020
Yazdanpanah, M., Tajeri Moghadam, M., Savari, M., Zobeidi, T., Sieber, S., & Löhr, K. (2021). The impact of livelihood assets on the food security of farmers in Southern Iran during the COVID-19 pandemic. *International Journal of Environmental Research and Public Health, 18*(10), 5310.

PART IV

The Impact of COVID-19 on Labor Market

CHAPTER 11

Assessing COVID-19's Economic Impact on Future Prospects of Indian Workers in GCC

Muskan Mustaqeem

1 Introduction

Since the expansion of the oil industry, the Gulf countries have become the most popular destinations for migrant workers due to their structural requirements for importing unskilled and skilled foreign labour. These emigrant workers make up a disproportionately large share, which makes them a preeminent labour force throughout a wide range of sectors, from construction, maintenance, hospitality, and domestic care sectors to public sectors. A vast majority of these labourers originate from South Asian countries like India. In GCC countries, migrant workers are primarily referred to as "expatriate" (or "ex-pat") workers (Richardson & McKenna, 2003) due to the nature of their temporary contract for employment (Ward et al., 2001, as cited by McGinley, 2008), governed

M. Mustaqeem (✉)
Jamia Millia Islamia, Central University, New Delhi, India
e-mail: muskan188145@st.jmi.ac.in

A. Mishrif (ed.), *Business Resilience and Market Adaptability*, The Political Economy of the Middle East,
https://doi.org/10.1007/978-981-97-2962-3_11

under the "kafala system". It is a system of structural reliance between a local employer and a foreign labour (Khan & Harroff-Tavel, 2011). As a result, an emigrant worker (low-skilled i.e., blue-collar, or domestic worker; retailers; and high-skilled workers, or white collar) requires an in-country employer (a local individual or company) (see more on this in Sect. 3).

Prior to the spread of the coronavirus in the GCC, emigrant workers were already struggling with the exploitative and abusive aspects of the kafala system, leading to widespread condemnation of the practice worldwide. On the other hand, workers have also borne the socio-economic implications of the workforce nationalisation programme (as a part of a diversification strategy), oil declines in major periods, the implementation of various taxes, and the recent COVID-19 crisis in the GCC countries. Since the gulf economies are highly dependent on oil revenues, any downward movement in prices implicates budget deficits and government spending, on the employment-generating sectors like infrastructure and construction that absorb most of the low- or unskilled expatriate community. The massive oil revenues post-1970 triggered two parallel developments: one was the subsidisation of social living for nationals, including education, health, monthly allowances, etc., and another was the expansion of the non-oil industry, i.e., the construction sector, to develop modern infrastructure, which required a tremendous workforce. In the beginning of the 1990s, the investment in infrastructure development gained more pace, making the construction industry the major employment sector, which has seen remarkable growth in the following decades. However, since 2008, the oil price has been steadily falling, with a steep decline in 2014–2015, reducing the GDP of Gulf countries and their capacity to regulate market volatility with rising inflation. These nations also saw a halt in their GDP, substantial drops in export income, rising budget deficits, and contracting current accounts (Vohra, 2017). In the meantime, there has been a growing demand for job creation from the unemployed young population, which was shielded by generous subsidies and assistance for a long time. Once there was a budget deficit, the Gulf governments slashed these subsidies while invoking tax regimes to sustain essential state infrastructure.

In addition to diversifying their markets, Gulf countries, especially Saudi Arabia, are worried about their growing reliance on foreign workers, which is draining huge amounts of remittances and creating a workforce imbalance in the private sector. And there have been calls from locals to address this parity given the fact that the expatriate communities cannot be a reliable social unit. To address these concerning issues, the Gulf States have brought in the policy of nationalisation of the workforce, which addresses twin objectives: (a) employment generation and job security for the nationals; and (b) reducing the dependence on expatriate workers. Another measure to address the labour imbalance was the decision by many GCC countries to tax outgoing remittances, as well as the implementation of an age limit for the renewal of visas for emigrants sixty years of age or older during COVID-19. These shifts in GCC employment sectors have direct implications for both skilled and low-skilled expat workers. The diversification drive is driven by the desire to become sustainable in a growingly interdependent world; therefore, GCC states embarked on structural reforms along with building a sustainable support system based on a competitive market strategy.

The desire for such reforms has been worked on in these governments for a long time. Before the Gulf States could streamline initiative to stabilise their economies, the COVID-19 pandemic brought a vehement disaster, buckling the drive for diversification, which was being represented by path-breaking initiatives like Vision 2030 in Saudi Arabia and other GCC countries. These countries also realised that economic recovery will be sluggish in post-COVID-19 period, therefore the nationalisation of workforce was implemented as an alternative measure. As a result, this exercise jeopardised the future of expatriates, as many were laid off, left jobless and stranded without the procurement of their proper wages, compensations, or other benefits. The economic and social circumstances of expat employees, particularly the low-skilled, and their long-term commitment to remain in the GCC have been impacted by these developments or events. Therefore, this chapter discusses the perceptions of Indian emigrant workers who have spent a significant amount of time working, living, and retiring in the Gulf. This chapter looks at the shifting perceptions of job security and employment stability among Bihari expatriate employees in the GCC. Future employment of expat employees is said to be negatively impacted by factors such as the Kafala system, economic diversification policy, workforce nationalisation, oil price decreases, taxation regime changes, a contracting construction industry, and the economic ramifications of COVID-19.

2 Research Methodology

Around 8.9 million Indian expatriates contribute to the labour force in the GCC (MEA, 2020) a significant portion of whom are employed in the construction and maintenance sectors in low-skilled positions. These low-skilled workers come from the lower strata of society, with less education and poor socio-economic conditions. Emigration from India to the GCC, particularly from Kerala state, remained high until 2015. However, in subsequent year, Bihar emerged as India's second-largest state after Uttar Pradesh, sender unskilled workers, surpassing skilled workers (e-migrate, 2021). The chapter scrutinises the economic repercussions of COVID-19 on Indian emigrant, especially those from the state of Bihar, residing and working in the GCC during the pandemic. It aims to evaluate the emigrants' perception on their employment in the context of ongoing events in the GCC post-COVID-19. Employing a quantitative research design, the chapter utilises a sample survey approach for data collection. Respondents, originating from the Indian state of Bihar, were identified using online snowball technique (through digital channels), overcoming COVID-19-related restrictions.

The author selected few initial participants those who fulfilled the research objectives and research criteria and were asked to participate in the study. The author shared the research information and purpose with them, like survey questionnaire online link/form, and invitation with their network through digital channels. As the initial participants shared the questionnaire with their contacts, the participant pool expands through a cascade effect. Those who received the invitations were encouraged to participate online and through telephone conversation and further shared the interview questionnaire among their networks. The process continued, leading to the continuous expansion of the sample size, and reached 133 samples.

The survey, titled 'Bihari Emigrants in the GCC and the COVID-19 Pandemic', was conducted in English. Data collection involved distributing questionnaires via email and various social networking sites for educated emigrants, while telephonic interviews were conducted for illiterate emigrants. The surveyed was conducted in the GCC during May and June 2021 which includes 109 low-skilled workers (blue collars) and 24 skilled workers (white collars). The author employed a three-point Likert scale to determine differences in perceptions between low-skilled and skilled workers regarding COVID-19 management and post-COVID-19 employment prospects. Chi-square tests were utilised to assess the disparities in perception, with a significance level set at $p < 0.05$. Statistical analyses were conducted using the Statistical Package for the Social Sciences (SPSS) version 24.0 (IBM).

3 Research Gap and Limitation

The economic implications on emigrants living in the destination country and emigrants' impressions of the destination government's COVID-19 management have not been addressed in the many studies that have looked at the socio-economic effects of the COVID-19 on the national population. The effects of coronavirus on people's mental health and emotional well-being have also been studied extensively. This chapter seeks to address these gaps by analysing the repercussions of the COVID-19 economic crisis on emigrants, encompassing both low- and high-skilled workers. The focus is on the consequences of employment loss and reduced working hours, along with exploring emigrants' perceptions of the future employment market in the Gulf region post-COVID-19. The sample comprises of male emigrants, as there is no migration of females from Bihar to the GCC. Furthermore, the inclusion criteria involve emigrants who were employed for more than a year before the COVID-19-related lockdown and were either still present in the GCC or awaiting repatriation during the interview. Lastly, the study does not incorporate any returned emigrants of GCC.

4 The Shaping of the Factors

4.1 The Kafala System

In the 1960s, the oil industry began booming and gained momentum in the 1970s, which led to a new and rapid expansion of wealth. The increasing influx of capital and the presence of a crude oil market inspired the dream of economic development and modification for GCC countries. This in turn, becomes the primary driver for international labour migration supply and remittances (Snudden, 2018). To attract the regular rotational supply of cheap-skilled and unskilled labour on a non-permanent contractual basis (Diop et al., 2018), GCC countries established a legal framework known as the Kafala (Sponsorship) or labour immigration management system. In kafala, a local citizen acts as a legal kafeel or employer who provides contractual sponsorship to migrant labour on their entry/exist into the country, work visa, and place of residency. Their relationship is based on unequal power dynamics where a sponsor assumes full responsibility for the worker in terms of immigration status and employment-related mobility (Robinson, 2021) and continues to dominate the contract without connecting labour into the formal system, keeping them out of the social safety net (Diop et al., 2018).

This systemic practice constructs an environment where workers are required to surrender their legal documents, their right to change employment, agree to work under unfair wages, unfavourable working and living conditions and becomes the victims of exploitation, and mistreatment. The inability to change employment without the consent of their employer is one of the most abusive pressure and violations of human rights. Expatriates are constantly at the mercy of their sponsors, whose permission to keep workers in the country can be revoked at any time or become undocumented or irregular migrant worker, if they try to leave job, disobey employer, or engage in forming a union or protesting against state/sponsor. Therefore, the labour regulation system becomes one of the most exploitive features of the GCC labour market, which has left expat labour, particularly unskilled workers vulnerable to exploitation. Many experts argue that the system encourages modern-day slavery through a never-ending cycle of abuse and violations of numerous human rights, gradually weakening labour standards (MFA, 2012). Under the kafala system, expatriates' precarious nature of their living situation, and their inability to switch jobs, compel them to actively cultivate in reevaluating their employment status in the GCC countries.

4.2 *Oil Plunge, Economic Diversification and Workforce Nationalisation*

The governments of the GCC states have reaped huge benefits from oil exports since the early 1990s. However, the GCC authorities were compelled to continue their structural reform policies in response to financial pressure and the realisation of the need for economic diversification after oil prices dropped dramatically in 1998–1999. The GCC countries have been attempting to find a solution that would help lessen their reliance on oil and gas, increase their national workforce participation rate in labour markets, and secure their high and sustainable income for the future. According to Mishrif (2018), there are three key drivers that contributed to the realisation of economic diversification: the development of the public sector; the private sector (due to its minor role and high dependency on expatriates); the development of human resources (which would increase the number of national citizens in the private sector and improve their skills); and the third driving force of diversification is sovereign wealth funds (SWFs), which have invested in key economic sectors such as infrastructure, finance, banking, Islamic finance, technology, transportation, education, construction. In the current economic conditions, economic diversification has become a necessity, not a policy option in the GCC countries, as the economic structure is unsustainable and all GCC countries have suffered from the negative effects of the fluctuation in international oil prices and the declining demand of oil and gas.

Since 1995, GCC countries implemented several development plans including Oman Vision 2020, Bahrain vision 2030, Saudi Vision 2030, UAE Vision 2021, Qatar National Vision 2030, and Abu Dhabi Economic Vision 2030. Economic diversification has been a consistent goal in these visions or development plans, with an emphasis on the private sector in some countries (such as Bahrain) and the public sector in others (such as the UAE). On the flip side the survival of these economic model is depends on government expenditure and revenues generated from oil (Obeid, 2020). During the years 2009 onwards, when oil prices were above US$100 per barrel, the GCC countries amassed most of their wealth. The oil earnings contributed to a combined budget surplus and once again reminded them to build robust and diversified economies that can weather the consequences of oil price shocks (Mishrif, 2018) on the future. When oil prices reached $100 per barrel in 2009 and beyond, the GCC countries amassed the majority of their wealth in the form of a surplus budget. These earnings were also a reminder to reduce oil dependence and build robust and diversified economies that can weather the consequences of oil shocks in the future (Mishrif, 2018), despite high revenues. During this period, the private sector continued to remain weaker than the public sector and relied heavily on oil and gas revenues. Therefore, the private sector became the priority area in the development strategy to attract foreign development investment and make it more attractive through upgradation in key sectors like digital infrastructure, education, banking and finance, etc., which can generate more employment for nationals (as the public sector can no longer absorb more nationals).

With the oil price dropping by more than 70% since 2014, as well as socio-demographic and political shifts (Mishrif, 2018), they have stressed the importance of nationalisation policies and diversification plans for GCC economies. The long-term focus on infrastructure development made the construction industry the only employment sector for unskilled workers due to the increasing demand for cheap foreign workers, who later emerged as an indispensable workforce. This huge influx created a workforce disparity, mainly in the private sector, which gradually became a concern for the GCC governments. To overcome the workforce disparity (Fasano & Iqbal, 2003), among citizens and foreigners, the GCC government adopted human resource development strategies known as the "localization" programme, aimed at integrating locals into the job market, especially in the private sector, where companies were instructed to hire more than 30 per cent of their employees from amongst the nationals (Randeree, 2009).

The economic development models or plans were in their nascent stage when the oil slump placed an enormous strain on revenues and brought the countries near to recession in 2016. Imperiling these new economic models at risk, prompting GCC governments to expedite the localization and diversification process. As part of the government's plan to deal with budget pressures and diversify the economy, thousands of expatriate workers were fired. Emigrant workers, as a result, became social losers (Migrant-Rights.Org, 2015). As these workers neither enjoy any organisational power nor any legal protection or social security (MFA, 2013), they can easily be laid off. The GCC states tried to ride two horses at once: they continued to "hire" low-wage, semi-skilled, or unskilled labour for their infrastructure and construction projects and 'fired' many skilled expats to create employment for their citizens to make the employment market accessible at their convenience with the localisation initiative, which was called 'hiring nationals and firing non-nationals'. These domestic policy shifts and economic strategies have adversely impacted the employability of expatriates because certain sectors like construction have shrunk and squeezed the jobs of low-skilled expatriate workers to a greater extent, besides turning these labourers into 'social losers' (Beck & Richter, 2021).

Nearly two-thirds of all GCC construction and infrastructure projects are located in Saudi Arabia and the UAE. Many large-scale projects in infrastructure, construction, and the business sector were highly impacted. The number of contracts awarded for construction projects was obstructed and eventually discontinued by GCC governments (Line-sight, n.d.). Conversely, unskilled workers in construction and maintenance jobs bore the brunt of this volatility and consequently were placed in a disadvantageous position (Bloomer, 2017). After the 2014 oil plunge, one of the leading construction companies in Saudi Arabia (due to subsequent reductions in state contracts) laid off more than 77,000 foreign workers and delayed the payment of their salaries for months (Rashad, 2016). In Qatar, many migrants in the hospitality, construction, and shipping industries were forced to leave and sent on long unpaid leaves (Migrant-Rights.Org, 2017), resulting in job loss. Pre- and post-2014, the construction boom has experienced both times of rapid expansion and periods of stagnation. After many decades, GCC governments are still on the road to fulfilling their growing appetite for high-profile mega projects, like the Neom business futuristic city in Saudi Arabia, the Burj Khalifa, and the construction of large-scale events like World Expo 2020 in Dubai and FIFA World Cup 2022 in Qatar (Gulf Construction Trends in 2018 and 2019), Oman's special economic zone at Duqm, and the GCC rail project, which would connect all the Persian Gulf countries together (Ulrichsen, 2014). When oil prices fall, the future robust construction demand becomes uncertain, as does the employability of unskilled migrant workers in the GCC (A.-R. Abdul-Aziz et al., 2018).

4.3 Budget Deficits and Tax Implementations

In their drive to deal with the fluctuations in oil and gas prices, the GCC nations instrumentalised tax policy to overcome budget and economic deficiencies. It was a strategy to increase non-oil revenues and halt the outflow of corporate budgets. During the mid-twentieth century, GCC countries implemented few taxes on corporate and trade activities with extremely low rates and small tax bases (IMF, 2015), which were meant for non-national businessmen generating a limited amount of revenue. In recent years, the GCC embarked on implementing a modern tax system in an attempt to stabilise the budget and diversify revenues, which included remittances. This new taxation includes VAT (Value Added Taxes at 5%), indirect taxes (cost of visas, rent, and recruitment fees), gasoline tax (Stark & Budzinski, 2018), family tax (in Saudi Arabia), and recently proposed taxing of expatriate income or wages (remittances) (Malit & Naufal, 2016). The rationale behind taxing the remittance is to redirect the remittance outflow, generate non-oil revenues from it, and invest it in the domestic economy. The GCC states are the greatest source of remittance outflows to countries like India and other Asian countries as well. Because expatriates in these countries cannot obtain citizenship or sponsor their immediate families, a large portion of their income is sent back home.

The imposition of taxes on the earnings of the workers will result in a rise in the cost of remittances. To avoid the high cost of sending money through formal channels, expatriates often opt for unrecognised channels of fund transfer (Ratha et al., 2017). Similarly, in the World Bank's 2022 report, KNOMAD predicted a $100 billion outflow of remittances to India by the end of the year. The use of informal channels for remittance transfer was one of the reasons cited by the World Bank for this huge increment in the annual remittance. Taxes on remittances will grease the wheels of unrecorded and unregulated remittance transfer channels. On the other hand, the repercussion of the proposed tax is that it will not only increase the cost of living in the GCC region but also make it less appealing to potential skilled and low-skilled expat workers. Shah (2012) and Stark and Budzinski (2018) have suggested that the tax reform would have detrimental effects on the socio-economic well-being of low- and unskilled migrant workers in the long run.

4.4 *Shrinking Construction and COVID-19*

The construction sector in the GCC countries employs millions of expatriates, both skilled and unskilled. After the 2014 oil fluctuation petered out, the construction sector went through a period of uncertainty as many countries were already experiencing delays in projects. The 2014 fall in oil revenues has led to a realignment of GCC government priorities, which resulted in a reduction in expenditure on infrastructure and construction projects. The ongoing and planned projects have been affected, leading to delays, disruptions in the supply chain, and cancellations of projects, and a decline in new project starts. The decline in oil prices also led to a decline in economic activity and a decrease in investment in the region. This, in turn, affected the demand for construction services and reduced the amount of work available for construction companies.

Many construction companies in the GCC region were forced to cut costs by reducing their workforce, and some companies went out of business. This had a negative impact on emigrant workers, many of whom were employed in the construction sector. The decline in oil prices also led to a decline in government spending on housing and infrastructure, which further reduced employment opportunities in the construction sector. However, the GCC governments' determination to pursue their diversification strategy did help them drive the construction sector forward in 2019 (Business and Human Rights Resource Centre. (n.d.). With the 2022 FIFA World Cup and the 2020 World Expo on the horizon, construction ramped up in Qatar and the United Arab Emirates. As well as in accordance with Saudi Arabia's Vision 2030 strategic plan, construction picked up pace, particularly in the areas of housing, infrastructure, and transportation.

The COVID-19 pandemic once again caused a collapse in energy demand and an oil price war that hampered both the private and public sectors, particularly infrastructure projects, with limited investment in the construction sector and raising questions about future development opportunities. The health and economic crisis of 2020 also disrupted sizeable construction projects due to delays in the material and labour supply chains owing to international border closures and a reduction in manpower and intensified the pre-existing situation of expatriate labourers, who are typically sheltered in highly substantial numbers in labour camp facilities in the GCC. During the pandemic, these workers struggled to survive amidst racism and xenophobic activities, unequal access to health care, wage theft, forced deportation, and detentions. Furthermore, the changing employment conditions for expatriate workers gained a boost from the crisis, which prompted greater impetus in the drive for nationalisation. Countries like Kuwait and Oman, decided to discontinue extending visas for expats aged sixty and above. On the other hand, the UAE gave a warning of strict actions against countries of labour origin if they failed to repatriate their nationals. These occurrences caused alarm concerning the existing employment status and future job prospects of expatriates in the GCC.

However, the COVID-19 outbreak has had a significant impact on the construction sector in the GCC countries. The decline in oil prices and the economic downturn have led to reduced government expenditure on construction projects. The repatriation of labour to their home countries and disruptions in supply chains have also had a negative impact on construction projects that were underway.[1] In addition, the government's priorities was shifted during COVID-19 towards addressing the immediate economic and health crisis caused by the pandemic, which has led to delays in finalising contracts for projects that were in the planning stage. One the other hand, hundreds of thousands of expats continue to remain outstanding where they are working under the strain of a heightened workload and a diminished workforce while waiting to be repatriated. This situation has placed worker in a difficult position, forcing them to re-evaluate future prospects of continuing working in the GCC.

5 Analysis, Findings, and Discussion

5.1 *Demographic Characteristics of the Survey Respondents*

Table 32 displays the survey population of GCC migrant workers. The majority, 36.8% of the total population surveyed, was recorded as working in Saudi Arabia. A total of 26.3% were working in the UAE, followed by 13.5% in Kuwait, 9.8% in Qatar, and 7% and 7.5% in Bahrain and Oman, respectively. In comparison with 44.4% of migrants who fall into the age category of 41 or older, most migrant respondents (55.6%) are between the ages of 20 and 40. Younger emigrants were found in Saudi Arabia and the United Arab Emirates, which further supports the GCC countries' significantly younger emigrant populations. The total of 81.95% of respondents recorded working as low-skilled workers, with the highest number working in Saudi Arabia (33.83%) and the UAE (16.54%), followed by Kuwait (12.03%), Qatar (8.27%), and Bahrain and Oman with 5.26% and 6.03%, respectively. On the other hand, a total of 24 respondents recorded working as skilled employees, which represents 18% of the total sample interviewed. Out of which, the highest number of skilled emigrants recorded working in the UAE (9.77%) was followed by Saudi Arabia (3.0%; see supplementary material Table 32). Most respondents (42.8%) are from the Siwan district, followed by the Gopalganj district (30.8%) and other districts (26.2%). Siwan and Gopalganj emerge as the highest low-skilled labour sending districts from Bihar, as per data from the Ministry of External Affairs and the e-migrate portal. In terms of the educational qualification of these respondents, 73.6% either belong to the illiterate category or have completed primary and high schooling, and 26.3% have completed education beyond a diploma or post-graduation. In terms of the marital status of migrant respondents, the data recorded

19.5% unmarried and 80.5% married. Together, in all the GCC countries, only 7.5% of emigrant respondents were recorded as living with their families, with the highest number of respondents living in Saudi Arabia (see the supplementary material, Table 32) (Table 1).

These respondents working in the GCC were largely recorded to fulfil their economic situation since they couldn't find employment in their home country. When prompted about decisions related to emigration to the GCC, nearly all the respondents stated they did so for a better income and financial opportunity. The economic potential was singled out as a major factor in their desire to relocate to the Gulf region. Emigrant respondents admitted that they took help from recruitment agents or agencies (94%) to facilitate their migration to the Gulf countries prior to COVID-19 (see supplementary material, Table 32). This is because, most of the time, an individual from Bihar state who is seeking a job in the GCC (mainly as a low-skilled worker) has no choice but to go through a recruiting agent. For this, largely, a recruiting agent would charge between fifty thousand and one lakh rupees (or more) in exchange for finding them a job in the GCC. (The high charges by recruitment agents don't guarantee job seekers a good job or earning opportunity in the GCC.) Those from Bihar seeking (or already working) in the GCC may find it difficult to find work without a strong social network. Bihari labourers rarely have time to build networks or relationships with their employers or co-workers due to their low-skilled profession or long working hours (lasting more than 9–12 hours; see supplementary material, Table 34).

5.2 *Migrants, Employment, and Remittances*

Table 33 presents the status of employment among migrant workers and remittances earned by Bihari migrant labourers in the GCC (see supplementary material, Table 33). Migration from Bihar to the Gulf States consists mostly of unskilled, low-skilled, or semi-skilled workers. The majority of survey respondents (72.1%) were engaged in construction and maintenance; 1.5% were sales workers; 1.5% were drivers; and 6.7% were foremen and safety managers or officers. However, 17.2% were managers or professional workers (skilled workers), and only one respondent reported owning a small business. More than 50% of the survey emigrants (58.6%) earned less than $500 (US dollars) in a month, and

Table 1 Demographic profile of the migrants

Age of emigrant workers	*UAE*	*KSA*	*Kuwait*	*Qatar*	*Bahrain*	*Oman*
Below 30 years	7 (5.26%)	17 (12.78%)	4 (3.0%)	5 (3.75%)	2 (1.50%)	2 (1.50%)
Between 31 to 40 years,	7 (5.26%)	16 (12.03%)	5 (3.75%)	3 (2.25%)	3 (2.25%)	3 (2.25%)
Between 41 to 50,	9 (6.76%)	9 (6.76%)	4 (3.0%)	3 (2.25%)	2 (1.50%)	3 (2.25%)
Above 51	12 (9.0%)	7 (5.26%)	5 (3.75%)	2 (1.50%)	1 (0.75%)	2 (1.50%)
Total (N = 133)	35 (26.31%)	49 (36.84%)	18 (13.53%)	13 (9.77%)	8 (6.01%)	10 (7.51%)

Age		*Below 30 years*	*Between 31 and 40 years*	*Between 41 and 50 years*	*Above 51*	*Total*
Occupation	Low skilled (Blue collar)	31 (23.30%)	34 (25.56%)	24 (18.04%)	20 (15.03%)	109 (81.98%)
	Skilled (white collar)	6 (4.51%)	3 (2.25%)	6 (4.51%)	9 (6.76%)	24 (18%)
Total		37 (27.81%)	37 (27.81%)	30 (22.55%)	29 (21.80%)	133 (100%)

Countries of destination		*UAE*	*KSA*	*Kuwait*	*Qatar*	*Bahrain*	*Oman*	*Total*
Occupation	Low skilled (Blue collar)	22 (16.54%)	45 (33.83%)	16 (12.03%)	11 (8.27%)	7 (5.26%)	8 (6.01)	109 (81.98%)
	Skilled (white collar)	13 (9.77%)	4 (3.0%)	2 (1.50%)	2 (1.50%)	1 (0.75%)	2 (1.50%)	24 (18%)

Countries of destination	*UAE*	*KSA*	*Kuwait*	*Qatar*	*Bahrain*	*Oman*	*Total*
Total	35 (26.3%)	49 (36.8%)	18 (13.5)	13 (9.8)	8 (7%)	10 (7.5%)	133 (100%)
Variable/statements	*Level*			*Respondents in numbers* (N = *133)*			*Data in %*
Domicile (Districts of Bihar)	Siwan			57			42.8
	Gopalganj			41			30.8
	Patna			10			7.5
	Champaran			17			12.7
	Others			8			6
Education	Not Educated			29			21.8
	Primary school			37			27.8
	High School/ Intermediate			32			24
	Diploma/Professional Certificate/ Graduation/Post-Graduation			35			26.3
Married	Yes			107			80.5
	No			26			19.5
Number of Dependents	between 2 and 4			57			43
	5 or more			76			57
Emigrated to GCC through RA	Yes			125			94
	No			8			6

Source Authors calculation from the interview questionnaire (RA: Recruit Agent)

37.4% earned between \$500 and \$2000. Only 3.7% earned more than \$2000 (Table 2).

Most Bihar labourers (80.4%) reported having no other source of income in their home country; however, 19.6% reported having other sources of income from small shops, income from another person in the family, and income from agriculture. More than half of the emigrant workers (58.6%) remit below \$400 (US dollars), 20.1% remit more than \$400 but less than \$800, and 17.2% remit between \$800 and \$1,000. Only 3.8% of remittances of more than \$1000 per month were recorded (supplementary material Table 33). These emigrant workers took care of the needs of their family members by sending remittances home. Around 57% reported having a family of five or more, while 43% reported having a

Table 2 Employment structure and remittances

Variables	*Levels*	*Frequency*	*Percentage (%)*
Occupation	Constructions and Maintenance	96	72.1
	Sales workers at Cafes/ Restaurants	2	1.5
	Drivers	2	1.5
	Small/big business owners	1	0.7
	Professionals	13	9.7
	Managers/HR	8	6.0
	Medical Staff	2	1.5
	Foreman/Safety Manager	9	6.7
Employed during COVID-19 lockdown	Yes	97	73
	Yes- waiting for the work permit to renew	9	6.7
	NO—Employment visa not renewed/contract-over/ resigned/terminated	27	20.3
Monthly earning (in \$)	Below \$500	78	58.6
	500–1000	25	18.7
	1000–1500	13	9.7
	1500–2000	12	9.0
	Above \$2000	5	3.7
Remittance sent before lockdown (in \$)	Below 400	78	58.6
	400–800	27	20.1
	800–1000	23	17.2
	Above 1000	5	3.8

Source Calculated by the author from the interview questionnaire

family of four or fewer (Supplementary Table 32). Loss of income due to the COVID-19 shutdown has an additional negative effect on emigrant workers: fewer remittances were sent home to their families. There was a rise in the percentage of respondent emigrants who reported sending less than $400 during the lockdown (77.4%). This figure shows an increment of 18.8%.

5.3 *Working Status and Conditions During COVID-19 Lockdown*

Table 34 describes the working conditions of emigrant workers during the COVID-19 lockdown. COVID-19 dramatically changes the lives and work patterns of emigrant workers. These changes were likely to have significant effects on the incomes and well-being of these migrant workers. Many migrant workers employed as low-skilled workers were recorded at 54.8% visiting their construction sites or workplaces, and 12.7% were working WFH (work from home). However, 30.8% of employees were recorded as not working during the lockdown in the GCC, and on the other hand, few (1.5%) visited their offices. These workers on the construction site continue to work the same number of hours (45.1%), some worked more than 8 hours (18%), and a few (6%) were recorded working less than 5 hours. This is because, many construction projects were racing against the clock to meet their goals, and constructing an adequate quarantine facility was also under tight deadline pressure (Table 3).

As a result of the COVID-19 slowdown, emigrant workers who were working fewer hours spent most of their time talking to their left-behind families in their home countries, using social networking sites like Facebook, IMO, WhatsApp, etc.; many agreed to watch TV during their free time after work. Since many of them recorded not working or working fewer hours, it is evident that this lockdown had a severe impact on the earnings of the migrant workers. A majority of workers (65.4%) recorded a loss of wages below $200 (US dollars) per month, however, 15.0% recorded a wage loss between $200 and $400, and 14.9% recorded a wage loss between $400 and $500 per month (see supplementary material Table 34).

Table 3 Working status and conditions during COVID-19 lockdown (LD)

Statements	*Levels*	*Data in numbers*	*Data in %*
Working during LD	Work from home,	17	12.7
	Visiting the office/ Hospital etc.	2	1.5
	Visiting construction site/ workplace	73	54.8
	Not working	41	30.8
Number of hours working during LD (in hours)	Not Worked	41	30.8
	1–5	8	6.0
	5–7	60	45.1
	Above 8	24	18.0
Loss of wages during LD (in $)	Below 200	87	65.4
	200–400	20	15.0
	400–500	15	11.2
	Above 500	5	3.7
Remittances sent during LD (in $)	Below 400	103	77.4
	400–800	25	18.8
	800–1000	5	3.8

Source Calculated by the author from the interview questionnaire

5.4 *Issue of Wage Theft with Migrant Workers in GCC Countries*

Based on the collected data (Table 35), it is revealed that only 13.5% of respondents have been working in the GCC for more than one year but less than three years; this group reflects the new and young population of respondents who relocated to the GCC before the current pandemic began. Only 21.8% have worked in the GCC for less than six years, whereas 36.1% have worked there for less than a decade, and 28.6% have worked there for more than a decade. The findings show that these emigrant workers face wage issues, such as delayed salaries or loss of wages, when their companies are not able to pay their salaries during their work contracts. Approximately 37.5% of migrant employees agreed that they had wage-related concerns during their time in the GCC. The numbers are higher in Saudi Arabia and the United Arab Emirates, followed by Kuwait, Bahrain, Oman, and finally Qatar. The coronavirus pandemic has made the economic situation even more dire for these workers. During a lockdown, these numbers increase (54.1%).

Many respondents recorded issues related to their wages during COVID-19. Saudi Arabia and the UAE continued to be the most responsive GCC countries for wage issues, followed by Qatar, Oman, Kuwait, and Bahrain.

Most of these respondent employees come from lower-income families. In the GCC, their earrings are typically worn to raise funds for family members back home. During the time of lockdown, the majority of respondents either promised to get paid later (51.3%) by their employer or did not receive their salaries. The financial hardship led many of the low-skilled, low-income workers to borrow money (30%) in order to make their monthly remittances at home (see the supplementary material, Table 35) (Table 4).

5.5 *Changing Remittance and Wage Loss*

Figure 6 in Chapter 12 represents the changes in the distribution of remittances and the issue of wages due to the pandemic. Due to the issue of wage loss or salary cuts during the pandemic, this change in remittances has received a lot of attention (Figure 28 and Table 30). The majority of migrants remitted less than $400 before and after the pandemic; however, before the pandemic, 58.6% of migrants remitted this amount; the majority of them were low-skilled workers, but during the pandemic's lockdown period, that figure rose to 77.4%. This means that more migrants were remitting a lesser amount. Remittances from the GCC countries were reduced by 20.1% and 17.2%, respectively, before the pandemic, and by 18.8% and 3.8%, respectively, during the pandemic (see supplementary material, Tables 33 and 34). It was also found that the remittances of skilled workers fell exceedingly during the lockdown period of the pandemic. Prior to the pandemic, those who sent (3.8%) more than US$1000 were recorded as sending less than US$1000 (3.8%). This shows that not just low-skilled workers, but skilled or highly skilled workers were also economically affected by the pandemic (Tables 33 and 34) (Figs. 1 and 2).

5.6 *Dependent Sample* t-*Test*

A dependent or paired sample *t*-test is used to compare the differences in the value of the same sample at two different times. A *t*-test is applied to test whether the comparison of remittances shown in Figs. 27 i.e 1 and 28 i.e. 2 is statistically significant. The null hypothesis was 'there is

Table 4 Issue of wage theft with Migrant workers in GCC Countries

Statement	*Range*		*Frequency*		*Data in %*	
Years Spent working in the GCC (in years)	More than 1, but less than 3		18		13.5	
	3–6		29		21.8	
	6–10		48		36.1	
	More than 10		38		28.6	
Ever experienced wage issues during working in the GCC (%)	UAE	KSA	Kuwait	Qatar	Bahrain	Oman
Yes = 50 (37.5%)	14	23	7	1	3	2
No = 83 (62.4%)	21	26	11	12	5	8
Wage issues during COVID-19 LD (%)	UAE	KSA	Kuwait	Qatar	Bahrain	Oman
Yes = 72 (54.1%)	24	31	3	6	2	6
No = 61 (45.8%)	11	18	15	7	6	4
Manage to Receive all the salary dues during the lockdown	Scale		Data in Numbers (out of 72)		In %	
	Yes		23		31.9	
	No		37		51.3	
	Promise to receive later		12		16.6	
Money Borrowed to send remittances home	Yes		39		29.3	
	No		94		70.6	

Source Calculated by the author from the interview questionnaire

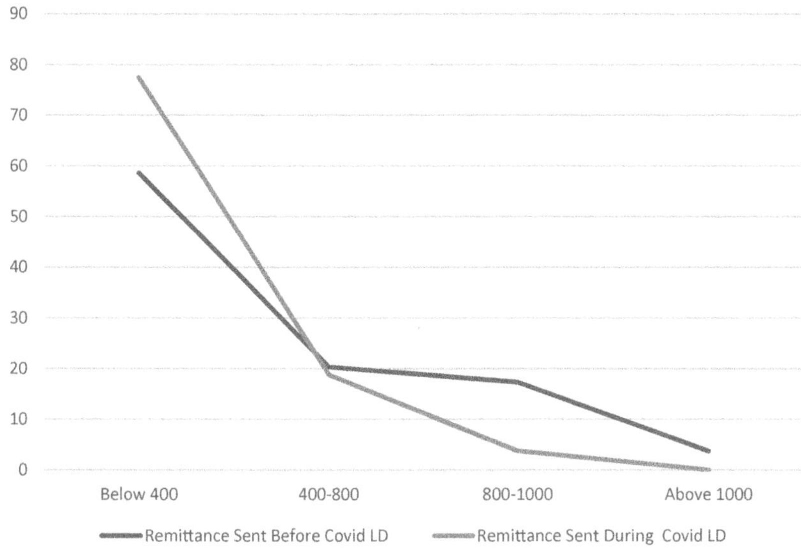

Fig. 1 Remittance sent before and during COVID-19 (in $) (*Source* Calculated by the author from the interview questionnaire)

no statistical difference in remittances and wage loss before and during the lockdown of the pandemic'. The mean and standard deviation of remittances before lockdown were estimated to be 1.66 and 0.895, respectively, and during lockdown, the mean = 1.26 and Std. Deviation = 0.520. The mean and standard deviation of wage issues during lockdown were estimated to be 1.62 and 0.486, respectively, and during lockdown, the mean = 1.45 and 0.500. Table S5 describes the results of the paired t-test for remittance and wage of loss. We reject the null hypothesis because the statistics of 9.351 and 5.115 with 132 degrees of freedom corresponded to a p-value of = 0.000, which is less than 0.05. It indicates that there is a statistically significant difference in remittances and wage loss before and after the lockdown. (Supplemental Table 36) (Table 5).

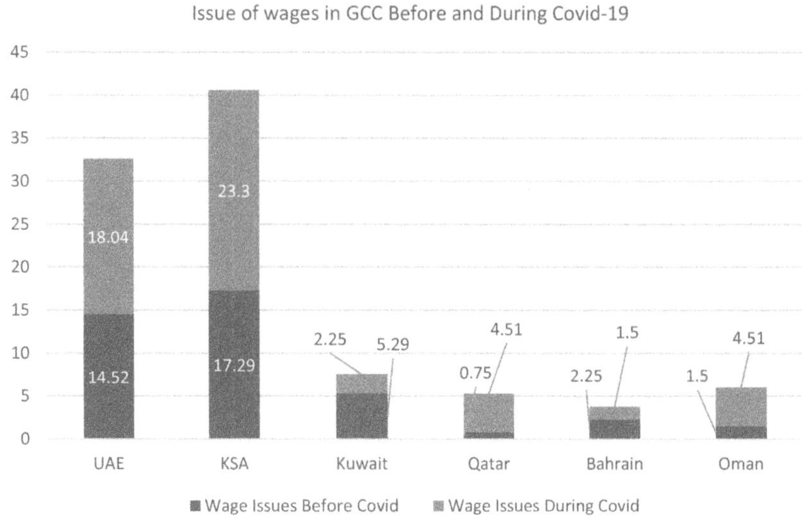

Fig. 2 Issue of wages in the GCC before and during COVID-19 (*Source* Calculated by the author from the interview questionnaire)

5.7 Emigrants' Perception Towards COVID-19 Management by the GCC

The author used six questions to assess low-skilled and skilled emigrants' perceptions towards COVID-19 management by the GCC (Table 37). The responses were registered on a three-point Likert scale varying from "dissatisfied, 'neither dissatisfied nor satisfied (neutral)' and 'satisfied', as presented in Table 37". The low-skilled (27.8%) and skilled (12.7%) emigrants were found to be satisfied with the COVID-19 protection-related information provided by the government of the GCC. Together, both low-skilled and skilled workers (45.1%) responded and were found to be satisfied with the improved living conditions during the lockdown. The majority of 28.5% of low-skilled workers were recorded as dissatisfied with living conditions, and 17.2% remained neutral towards living conditions. This shift in emigrants' perceptions during COVID-19 shows that GCC nations have been on the radar since Qatar was chosen to host the FIFA World Cup in 2022 back in 2010. Since then, numerous non-governmental organisations have criticised the working and living

Table 5 Paired sample *t*-test

Paired samples t-*test*

95% Confidence Interval of the Difference

	Mean	Std. Deviation	Std. Error Mean	Lower	Upper	t	df	p-value
Remittance Before LD – Remittance During LD	0.398	0.491	0.426	0.314	0.482	9.351	132	0.000
Issue of Wage cut/delay before COVID-19 – after COVID-19	0.165	0.372	0.323	0.101	0.229	5.115	132	0.000

Source Calculated by the author from the interview questionnaire

conditions of emigrants in the Persian Gulf. Furthermore, 24.0% of low-skilled and 9.0% of skilled emigrant respondents agreed on satisfactory arrangements for quarantine facilities during the lockdown by the GCC government, 36.8% of low-skilled and 4.5% of skilled respondents were recorded as not satisfied due to proper or no quarantine facilities, and the rest remained neutral. Although only 24.0% of low-skilled emigrant workers and 6.7% of skilled emigrant workers reported having access to adequate medical care, nearly 22.5% were neutral, and more than 45% were dissatisfied with the GCC government's medical care. The majority of dissatisfied respondents are high among low-skilled workers, i.e., 40.6%. This is most likely due to the fact that many public hospitals and health care facilities prioritised treating local residents. In response to protective measures taken during lockdown at a place of living or working, like the provision of PPE kits, sanitisers, masks and gloves, etc., around 38.3% of low-skilled and 15.75% of skilled respondents reported being satisfied, 24.8% of low-skilled respondents were dissatisfied, and 23.3% reported being neutral. Moreover, almost 38.3% of the low-skilled expressed dissatisfaction upon asking about the food and other facilities provided during the lockdown, 24.8% of the low-skilled were reported as satisfied, and some (18.7%) stayed neutral. On the other hand, only 1.5% of skilled workers reported being dissatisfied, while 10.5% reported being satisfied (Table 6).

A chi-square test was applied to discover the association between perceptions of COVID-19 management by the government across the different occupations. The sample data on occupational structure were low-skilled and skilled (see Table 33). The null hypothesis was "There is no significant difference in the perception of the emigrant workers towards the COVID-19 management by the GCC government between low-skilled and skilled occupation workers", and the alternative hypothesis was "There is a significant difference in the perception of the migrant workers towards the COVID-19 management by the GCC government between low-skilled and skilled occupation workers". The relationship between these variables was found to be significant as calculated by the chi-square value and p-value is < 0.05 (5% level of significance) as presented in Supplementary Table S6. Therefore, the author rejects the null hypothesis. It means that there was a significant difference in the perception of the emigrant workers towards COVID-19 management in the GCC countries. During the lockdown, low-skilled workers were found to have a low negative opinion of COVID-19 management.

Table 6 Emigrants' perception towards COVID-19 management by the GCC—Age, Gulf countries and occupation ($n = 133$, %)

N = *133*			*Age*				
Statements		*Total*	*Below 30*	*31–40*	*41–50*	*Above 51*	p-*value*
The post-COVID-19 time has increased the employment opportunities in GCC for Migrant Workers	D	75 (56.3%)	21 (15.7%)	18 (13.5%)	15 (11.2%)	21 (15.7%)	0.093
	N	13 (9.7%)	2 (1.5%)	4 (3.0%)	2 (1.5%)	5 (4.5%)	
	A	45 (33.8%)	14 (10.5%)	15 (11.2%)	13 (9.7%)	3 (2.2%)	
Living condition for emigrants in GCC has changed in post-COVID-19 time	D	38 (28.5%)	13 (9.7%)	8 (6.0%)	7 (5.2%)	10 (7.5%)	0.400
	N	40 (30.0%)	12 (9.0%)	14 (10.5%)	6 (4.5%)	8 (6.0%)	
	A	55 (41.3%)	12 (9.0%)	15 (11.2%)	17 (12.7%)	11 (8.2%)	
Workload increased in post-COVID-19 time	D	13 (9.7%)	7 (5.2%)	1 (0.7%)	4 (3.0%)	1 (0.7%)	0.143
	N	55 (41.3%)	13 (9.7%)	14 (10.5%)	15 (11.2%)	13 (9.7%)	
	A	65 (48.8%)	17 (12.7%)	22 (16.5%)	11 (8.2%)	15 (11.2%)	
More hygiene at the workplace/accommodation	D	23 (17.2%)	7 (5.2%)	4 (3.0%)	6 (4.5%)	6 (4.5%)	0.089
	N	54 (40.6%)	21 (15.7%)	10 (7.5%)	12 (9.0%)	11 (8.2%)	
	A	55 (41.3%)	9 (6.7%)	22 (16.5%)	12 (9.0%)	12 (9.0%)	
Safety and security in the workplace have increased	D	14 (10.5%)	2 (1.5%)	1 (0.7%)	7 (5.2%)	4 (3.0%)	0.004
	N	70 (52.6%)	21 (15.7%)	16 (12.0%)	12 (9.0%)	21 (15.7%)	
	A	49 (36.8%)	14 (10.5%)	20 (15.0%)	11 (8.2%)	4 (3.0%)	

(continued)

Table 6 (continued)

N = *133*			*Age*				
Statements		*Total*	*Below 30*	*31–40*	*41–50*	*Above 51*	p-*value*
The post-COVID-19 has resulted in a reduction of salary for emigrants in the GCC	D	24 (18.0%)	15 (11.2%)	3 (2.2%)	0 (0.0%)	6 (4.5%)	< 0.001
	N	24 (18.0%)	10 (7.5%)	6 (4.5%)	1 (0.7%)	7 (5.2%)	
	A	85 (63.9%)	12 (9.0%)	28 (21.0%)	29 (21.8%)	16 (12.0%)	
Do you believe that domestic policy changes vis a vis migrant in certain, Gulf nations have put your job at risk?	D	19 (14.2%)	4 (3.0%)	8 (6.0%)	3 (2.2%)	4 (3.0%)	0.452
	N	34 (25.5%)	10 (7.5%)	11 (8.2%)	9 (6.7%)	4 (3.0%)	
	A	80 (60.1%)	23 (17.2%)	18 (13.5%)	18 (13.5%)	21 (15.7%)	
Given the fact that India is at the highest level of unemployment in the last 45 years, do you think that getting a chance to work in GCC is a kind of boon in the post-COVID-19 period?	D	6 (4.5%)	2 (1.5%)	0 (0.0%)	1 (0.7%)	3 (2.2%)	0.058
	N	20 (15.0%)	10 (7.5%)	3 (2.2%)	2 (1.5%)	5 (4.5%)	
	A	107 (80.4%)	25 (18.7%)	34 (25.5%)	27 (20.35)	21 (15.7%)	
Want to continue working in GCC	D	56 (42.1%)	15 (11.2%)	19 (14.2%)	13 (9.7%)	9 (6.7%)	0.422
	N	0 (0.0%)	0 (0.0%)	0 (0.0%)	0 (0.0%)	0 (0.0%)	
	A	77 (57.8%)	22 (16.5%)	18 (13.5%)	17 (12.7%)	20 (15.0%)	

N = *133*			*Countries*						
Statements		*Total*	*UAE*	*KSA*	*Kuwait*	*Qatar*	*Bahrain*	*Oman*	p-*value*
The post-COVID-19 time has increased the employment opportunities in GCC for Migrant Workers	D	75 (56.3%)	21 (15.7%)	27 (20.0%)	9 (6.7%)	9 (6.7%)	4 (3.0%)	5 (4.5%)	0.256
	N	13 (9.7%)	7 (5.2%)	5 (4.5%)	0 (0.0%)	0 (0.0%)	0 (0.0%)	1 (0.7%)	
	A	45 (33.8%)	7 (5.2%)	7 (5.2%)	9 (6.7%)	4 (3.0%)	4 (3.0%)	4 (3.0%)	
Living condition for emigrants in GCC has changed in post-COVID-19 time	D	38 (28.5%)	9 (6.7%)	18 (13.5%)	2 (1.5%)	5 (4.5%)	2 (1.5%)	2 (1.5%)	0.330
	N	40 (30.0%)	13 (9.7%)	13 (9.7%)	9 (6.7%)	2 (1.5%)	1 (0.7%)	2 (1.5%)	
	A	55 (41.3%)	13 (9.7%)	18 (13.5%)	7 (5.2%)	16 (12.0%)	5 (4.5%)	6 (4.5%)	
Workload increased in post-COVID-19 time	D	13 (9.7%)	4 (3.0%)	6 (4.5%)	1 (0.7%)	1 (0.7%)	1 (0.7%)	0 (0.0%)	0.941
	N	55 (41.3%)	14 (10.5%)	18 (13.5%)	7 (5.2%)	7 (5.2%)	3 (2.2%)	6 (4.5%)	
	A	65 (48.8%)	17 (12.7%)	25 (18.7%)	10 (7.5%)	5 (4.5%)	4 (3.0%)	4 (3.0%)	
More hygiene at the workplace/ accommodation	D	23 (17.2%)	7 (5.2%)	9 (6.7%)	3 (2.2%)	2 (1.5%)	1 (0.7%)	1 (0.7%)	0.999
	N	54 (40.6%)	13 (9.7%)	21 (15.7%)	7 (5.2%)	6 (4.5%)	3 (2.2%)	4 (3.0%)	
	A	55 (41.3%)	15 (11.2%)	19 (14.2%)	7 (5.2%)	5 (4.5%)	4 (3.0%)	5 (4.5%)	
Safety and security in the workplace have increased	D	14 (10.5%)	6 (4.5%)	4 (3.0%)	2 (1.5%)	1 (0.7%)	1 (0.7%)	0 (0.0%)	0.694
	N	70 (52.6%)	18 (13.5%)	26 (19.5%)	12 (9.0%)	5 (4.5%)	3 (2.2%)	6 (4.5%)	
	A	49 (36.8%)	11 (8.2%)	19 (14.2%)	4 (3.0%)	7 (5.2%)	4 (3.0%)	4 (3.0%)	
The post-COVID-19 has resulted in a reduction of salary for emigrants in the GCC	D	24 (18.0%)	2 (1.5%)	12 (9.0%)	2 (1.5%)	5 (4.5%)	2 (1.5%)	1 (0.7%)	0.212
	N	24 (18.0%)	8 (6.0%)	11 (8.2%)	2 (1.5%)	1 (0.7%)	1 (0.7%)	1 (0.7%)	

(continued)

Table 6 (continued)

N = *133*			*Countries*						
Statements		*Total*	*UAE*	*KSA*	*Kuwait*	*Qatar*	*Bahrain*	*Oman*	p-*value*
	A	85 (63.9%)	25 (18.7%)	26 (19.5%)	14 (10.5%)	7 (5.2%)	5 (4.5%)	8 (6.0%)	
Do you believe that domestic policy changes vis a vis migrant in certain, Gulf nations have put your job at risk?	D	19 (14.2%)	5 (4.5%)	8 (6.0%)	0 (0.0%)	1 (0.7%)	3 (2.2%)	2 (1.5%)	0.501
	N	34 (25.5%)	7 (5.2%)	13 (9.7%)	6 (4.5%)	5 (4.5%)	1 (0.7%)	1 (0.7%)	
	A	80 (60.1%)	23 (17.2%)	28 (21.0%)	12 (9.0%)	7 (5.2%)	4 (3.0%)	6 (4.5%)	
Given the fact that India is at the highest level of unemployment in the last 45 years, do you think that getting a chance to work in GCC is a kind of boon in the post-COVID-19 period?	D	6 (4.5%)	3 (2.2%)	1 (0.7%)	2 (1.5%)	0 (0.0%)	0 (0.0%)	0 (0.0%)	0.623
	N	20 (15.0%)	3 (2.2%)	8 (6.0%)	3 (2.2%)	2 (1.5%)	1 (0.7%)	3 (2.2%)	
	A	107 (80.4%)	29 (21.8%)	40 (30.0%)	13 (9.7%)	11 (8.2%)	7 (5.2%)	7 (5.2%)	
Want to continue working in GCC	D	56 (42.1%)	13 (9.7%)	15 (11.2%)	9 (6.7%)	8 (6.0%)	5 (4.5%)	6 (4.5%)	0.148
	N	0 (0.0%)	0 (0.0%)	0 (0.0%)	0 (0.0%)	0 (0.0%)	0 (0.0%)	0 (0.0%)	
	A	77 (57.8%)	22 (16.5%)	34 (25.5%)	9 (6.7%)	5 (4.5%)	3 (2.2%)	4 (3.0%)	

N = *133*			*Occupation*		
Statements		*Total*	*Low skilled worker*	*Skilled worker*	p-*value*
The post-COVID-19 time has increased the employment opportunities in GCC for Migrant Workers	D	75 (56.3%)	59 (44.3%)	16 (12.0%)	0.001
	N	13 (9.7%)	7 (5.2%)	6 (4.5%)	
	A	45 (33.8%)	43 (32.3%)	2 (1.5%)	
Living condition for emigrants in GCC has changed in post-COVID-19 time	D	38 (28.5%)	36 (27.0%)	2 (1.5%)	0.042
	N	40 (30.0%)	30 (22.5%)	10 (7.5%)	
	A	55 (41.3%)	43 (32.3%)	12 (9.0%)	
Workload increased in post-COVID-19 time	D	13 (9.7%)	12 (9.0%)	1 (0.7%)	0.285
	N	55 (41.3%)	47 (35.3%)	8 (6.0%)	
	A	65 (48.8%)	50 37.5%)	15 (11.2%)	
More hygiene at the workplace/ accommodation	D	23 (17.2%)	22 (16.5%)	1 (0.7%)	0.001
	N	54 (40.6%)	49 (36.8%)	5 (4.5%)	
	A	55 (41.3%)	37 (27.8%)	18 (13.5%)	
Safety and security in the workplace have increased	D	14 (10.5%)	10 (7.5%)	4 (3.0%)	0.163
	N	70 (52.6%)	55 (41.3%)	15 (11.2%)	
	A	49 (36.8%)	44 (33.0%)	5 (4.5%)	
The post-COVID-19 has resulted in a reduction of salary for emigrants in the GCC	D	24 (18.0%)	24 (18.0%)	0 (0.0%)	0.039
	N	24 (18.0%)	19 (14.2%)	5 (4.5%)	
	A	85 (63.9%)	66 (49.6%)	19 (14.2%)	

(continued)

Table 6 (continued)

N = *133*			*Occupation*		
Statements		*Total*	*Low skilled worker*	*Skilled worker*	p-*value*
Do you believe that domestic policy changes vis a vis migrant in certain, Gulf nations have put your job at risk?	D	19 (14.2%)	18 (13.5%)	1 (0.7%)	0.092
	N	34 (25.5%)	30 (22.5%)	4 (3.0%)	
	A	80 (60.1%)	61 (45.8%)	19 (14.2%)	
Given the fact that India is at the highest level of unemployment in the last 45 years, do you think that getting a chance to work in GCC is a kind of boon in the post-COVID-19 period?	D	6 (4.5%)	4 (3.0%)	2 (1.5%)	0.379
	N	20 (15.0%)	15 (11.2%)	5 (4.5%)	
	A	107 (80.4%)	90 (67.6%)	17 (12.7%)	
Want to continue working in GCC	D	56 (42.1%)	48 (36.0%)	8 (6.0%)	0.336
	N	0 (0.0%)	0 (0.0%)	0 (0.0%)	
	A	77 (57.8%)	61 (45.8%)	16 (12.0%)	

The figure is particularly high among young emigrants. However, skilled workers had a highly positive perception of COVID-19 management during the lockdown.

5.8 *Emigrant's Perception of the Future Prospects of Employment in the GCC in the Post-COVID-19*

The author used nine questions to assess the emigrants' perceptions of their own employability in the post-COVID-19 situation in the GCC. The responses were registered on a three-point Likert scale varying from "disagree", "neither disagree nor agree" (neutral), and "agree", as presented in Table 38 (see Supplementary Table 38). These perceptions are based on how emigrants from Bihar perceive their future employment based on the various other ongoing events in the GCC in the post-COVID-19 period. A majority of 44.3% of low-skilled workers disagreed with increasing employment opportunities in post-COVID-19 times, and 12.0% of skilled workers believe the same. This is since many construction projects remain on hold even in the post-COVID-19 period, and many companies were hiring nationals as a part of the nationalisation drive in the GCC during COVID-19 times. When asked about their decreased perception of employment opportunities, many respondents stated that salaries have not increased since they arrived, no overtime work is permitted, there is no skill gain, there is a wage loss, there is a new labour policy in the post-COVID-19 era, the cost of living in the GCC has increased, and many are willing to return home. Many respondents (29.2%) below the age of 30 and between the ages of 31 and 40 (representing the young emigrants) believe work-related opportunities are not increasing as compared to respondents (26.9%) between the ages of 41 and above 51. Roughly 33.8% of respondents expect to see increased emigration in the future due to various lined-up infrastructure projects in the GCC countries. On the other hand, 9.7% stayed neutral (Table 38).

As living conditions remained the same during lockdown (e.g., number of emigrants living in per room, ventilation in the room, proper living facilities, social distancing among labours, etc.), around 28.5% of emigrants disagreed with perception in the GCC, 41.3% of emigrants agreed that the situation has improved, and 30.0% of respondents reported as neutral, with no difference in working and living conditions in post-COVID-19 times. Around 48.8% of emigrant (both low-skilled and skilled) respondents agree that post-COVID-19 time resulted in increased workload; this is because many labours were repatriated to their home countries during COVID-19 and many were not working. Around 41.3% of respondents reported that their workload remained the same as before COVID-19, and 9.7% had disagreements with an increased workload (Table 38) (Table 7).

Around 17.2% disagree on more hygiene at the place of living and working, like more cleanliness in the place of living, the use of masks and sanitisers, and proper distancing. More than 40% of respondents agreed on following proper hygiene in their living and working places, while 40.6% stayed neutral. In response to the increase in safety and security, following safety-related instructions during work, and taking safety and security measures while working, 36.8% agreed, 52.6% stayed neutral, and some (10.5%) disagreed. Perception six was about whether emigrants believe that post-COVID-19 has resulted in a reduction of salaries for emigrants in the GCC. In response to this, 63.9% of emigrants experienced a reduction in salary or delay in their wages in post-COVID-19, and the majority of low-skilled respondents were 49.6% and skilled workers were 14.2%. In total, 18.0% disagreed, and 18.0% were reported to be neutral. The author asked for the perception of the emigrants on "Do you believe that policy changes vis-à-vis migrants in certain Gulf nations have put your job at risk?" Around 60.1% of emigrants believe that their employment in the post-COVID-19 period is jeopardised because so many emigrants have left jobs and returned home. Many emigrants in the GCC, voluntarily or involuntarily resigned or been removed from their jobs. Only 14.2% were reported as disagreeing, and 25.5% were neutral. These emigrants see their emigration to the GCC as a boon. Many respondent emigrants (80.4%) agreed that many respondents are low-skilled workers who have stayed for a longer period in the GCC. While very few (4.5%) disagreed and 15.0% stayed neutral, on asking how emigrants see their employability in the coming years in the GCC, most emigrants were positive (57.8%) and willing to continue their employment despite the ongoing crisis in the GCC, which means a silver lining. while some (42.1%) respondents reported quitting work when their contract expired (Table 38).

For this, a chi-square test was applied to discover the association between emigrants' perceptions of their own employability in the post-COVID-19 situation in the GCC among low-skilled and skilled occupations/workers. The null hypothesis was "There is no significant difference

Table 7 Emigrant's Perception of the Future Prospects of Employment in the GCC in the Post-COVID-19—Age and Gulf Countries and Occupation ($n = 133$, %)

N = *133*			*Age*				
Statements		*Total*	*Below 30*	*31–40*	*41–50*	*Above 51*	p-*value*
The post-COVID-19 time has increased the employment opportunities in GCC for Migrant Workers	D	75 (56.3%)	21 (15.7%)	18 (13.5%)	15 (11.2%)	21 (15.7%)	0.093
	N	13 (9.7%)	2 (1.5%)	4 (3.0%)	2 (1.5%)	5 (4.5%)	
	A	45 (33.8%)	14 (10.5%)	15 (11.2%)	13 (9.7%)	3 (2.2%)	
Living condition for emigrants in GCC has changed in post-COVID-19 time	D	38 (28.5%)	13 (9.7%)	8 (6.0%)	7 (5.2%)	10 (7.5%)	0.400
	N	40 (30.0%)	12 (9.0%)	14 (10.5%)	6 (4.5%)	8 (6.0%)	
	A	55 (41.3%)	12 (9.0%)	15 (11.2%)	17 (12.7%)	11 (8.2%)	
Workload increased in post-COVID-19 time	D	13 (9.7%)	7 (5.2%)	1 (0.7%)	4 (3.0%)	1 (0.7%)	0.143
	N	55 (41.3%)	13 (9.7%)	14 (10.5%)	15 (11.2%)	13 (9.7%)	
	A	65 (48.8%)	17 (12.7%)	22 (16.5%)	11 (8.2%)	15 (11.2%)	
More hygiene at the workplace/ accommodation	D	23 (17.2%)	7 (5.2%)	4 (3.0%)	6 (4.5%)	6 (4.5%)	0.089
	N	54 (40.6%)	21 (15.7%)	10 (7.5%)	12 (9.0%)	11 (8.2%)	
	A	55 (41.3%)	9 (6.7%)	22 (16.5%)	12 (9.0%)	12 (9.0%)	
Safety and security in the workplace have increased	D	14 (10.5%)	2 (1.5%)	1 (0.7%)	7 (5.2%)	4 (3.0%)	0.004
	N	70 (52.6%)	21 (15.7%)	16 (12.0%)	12 (9.0%)	21 (15.7%)	
	A	49 (36.8%)	14 (10.5%)	20 (15.0%)	11 (8.2%)	4 (3.0%)	
The post-COVID-19 has resulted in a reduction of salary for emigrants in the GCC	D	24 (18.0%)	15 (11.2%)	3 (2.2%)	0 (0.0%)	6 (4.5%)	< 0.001
	N	24 (18.0%)	10 (7.5%)	6 (4.5%)	1 (0.7%)	7 (5.2%)	

(continued)

Table 7 (continued)

N = *133*			*Age*				
Statements		*Total*	*Below 30*	*31–40*	*41–50*	*Above 51*	p-*value*
	A	85 (63.9%)	12 (9.0%)	28 (21.0%)	29 (21.8%)	16 (12.0%)	
Do you believe that domestic policy changes vis a vis migrant in certain, Gulf nations have put your job at risk?	D	19 (14.2%)	4 (3.0%)	8 (6.0%)	3 (2.2%)	4 (3.0%)	0.452
	N	34 (25.5%)	10 (7.5%)	11 (8.2%)	9 (6.7%)	4 (3.0%)	
	A	80 (60.1%)	23 (17.2%)	18 (13.5%)	18 (13.5%)	21 (15.7%)	
Given the fact that India is at the highest level of unemployment in the last 45 years, do you think that getting a chance to work in GCC is a kind of boon in the post-COVID-19 period?	D	6 (4.5%)	2 (1.5%)	0 (0.0%)	1 (0.7%)	3 (2.2%)	0.058
	N	20 (15.0%)	10 (7.5%)	3 (2.2%)	2 (1.5%)	5 (4.5%)	
	A	107 (80.4%)	25 (18.7%)	34 (25.5%)	27 (20.35)	21 (15.7%)	
Want to continue working in GCC	D	56 (42.1%)	15 (11.2%)	19 (14.2%)	13 (9.7%)	9 (6.7%)	0.422
	N	0 (0.0%)	0 (0.0%)	0 (0.0%)	0 (0.0%)	0 (0.0%)	
	A	77 (57.8%)	22 (16.5%)	18 (13.5%)	17 (12.7%)	20 (15.0%)	

N = *133*			*Countries*						
Statements		*Total*	*UAE*	*KSA*	*Kuwait*	*Qatar*	*Bahrain*	*Oman*	p-*value ara>*
The post-COVID-19 time has increased the employment opportunities in GCC for Migrant Workers	D	75 (56.3%)	21 (15.7%)	27 (20.0%)	9 (6.7%)	9 (6.7%)	4 (3.0%)	5 (4.5%)	0.256
	N	13 (9.7%)	7 (5.2%)	5 (4.5%)	0 (0.0%)	0 (0.0%)	0 (0.0%)	1 (0.7%)	
	A	45 (33.8%)	7 (5.2%)	7 (5.2%)	9 (6.7%)	4 (3.0%)	4 (3.0%)	4 (3.0%)	
Living condition for emigrants in GCC has changed in post-COVID-19 time	D	38 (28.5%)	9 (6.7%)	18 (13.5%)	2 (1.5%)	5 (4.5%)	2 (1.5%)	2 (1.5%)	0.330
	N	40 (30.0%)	13 (9.7%)	13 (9.7%)	9 (6.7%)	2 (1.5%)	1 (0.7%)	2 (1.5%)	
	A	55 (41.3%)	13 (9.7%)	18 (13.5%)	7 (5.2%)	16 (12.0%)	5 (4.5%)	6 (4.5%)	
Workload increased in post-COVID-19 time	D	13 (9.7%)	4 (3.0%)	6 (4.5%)	1 (0.7%)	1 (0.7%)	1 (0.7%)	0 (0.0%)	0.941
	N	55 (41.3%)	14 (10.5%)	18 (13.5%)	7 (5.2%)	7 (5.2%)	3 (2.2%)	6 (4.5%)	
	A	65 (48.8%)	17 (12.7%)	25 (18.7%)	10 (7.5%)	5 (4.5%)	4 (3.0%)	4 (3.0%)	
More hygiene at the workplace/ accommodation	D	23 (17.2%)	7 (5.2%)	9 (6.7%)	3 (2.2%)	2 (1.5%)	1 (0.7%)	1 (0.7%)	0.999
	N	54 (40.6%)	13 (9.7%)	21 (15.7%)	7 (5.2%)	6 (4.5%)	3 (2.2%)	4 (3.0%)	
	A	55 (41.3%)	15 (11.2%)	19 (14.2%)	7 (5.2%)	5 (4.5%)	4 (3.0%)	5 (4.5%)	
Safety and security in the workplace have increased	D	14 (10.5%)	6 (4.5%)	4 (3.0%)	2 (1.5%)	1 (0.7%)	1 (0.7%)	0 (0.0%)	0.694
	N	70 (52.6%)	18 (13.5%)	26 (19.5%)	12 (9.0%)	5 (4.5%)	3 (2.2%)	6 (4.5%)	
	A	49 (36.8%)	11 (8.2%)	19 (14.2%)	4 (3.0%)	7 (5.2%)	4 (3.0%)	4 (3.0%)	

(continued)

Table 7 (continued)

N = *133*			*Countries*						
Statements		*Total*	*UAE*	*KSA*	*Kuwait*	*Qatar*	*Bahrain*	*Oman*	p-*value ara>*
The post-COVID-19 has resulted in a reduction of salary for emigrants in the GCC	D	24 (18.0%)	2 (1.5%)	12 (9.0%)	2 (1.5%)	5 (4.5%)	2 (1.5%)	1 (0.7%)	0.212
	N	24 (18.0%)	8 (6.0%)	11 (8.2%)	2 (1.5%)	1 (0.7%)	1 (0.7%)	1 (0.7%)	
	A	85 (63.9%)	25 (18.7%)	26 (19.5%)	14 (10.5%)	7 (5.2%)	5 (4.5%)	8 (6.0%)	
Do you believe that domestic policy changes vis a vis migrant in certain, Gulf nations have put your job at risk?	D	19 (14.2%)	5 (4.5%)	8 (6.0%)	0 (0.0%)	1 (0.7%)	3 (2.2%)	2 (1.5%)	0.501
	N	34 (25.5%)	7 (5.2%)	13 (9.7%)	6 (4.5%)	5 (4.5%)	1 (0.7%)	1 (0.7%)	
	A	80 (60.1%)	23 (17.2%)	28 (21.0%)	12 (9.0%)	7 (5.2%)	4 (3.0%)	6 (4.5%)	
Given the fact that India is at the highest level of unemployment in the last 45 years, do you think that getting a chance to work in GCC is a kind of boon in the post-COVID-19 period?	D	6 (4.5%)	3 (2.2%)	1 (0.7%)	2 (1.5%)	0 (0.0%)	0 (0.0%)	0 (0.0%)	0.623
	N	20 (15.0%)	3 (2.2%)	8 (6.0%)	3 (2.2%)	2 (1.5%)	1 (0.7%)	3 (2.2%)	
	A	107 (80.4%)	29 (21.8%)	40 (30.0%)	13 (9.7%)	11 (8.2%)	7 (5.2%)	7 (5.2%)	
Want to continue working in GCC	D	56 (42.1%)	13 (9.7%)	15 (11.2%)	9 (6.7%)	8 (6.0%)	5 (4.5%)	6 (4.5%)	0.148
	N	0 (0.0%)	0 (0.0%)	0 (0.0%)	0 (0.0%)	0 (0.0%)	0 (0.0%)	0 (0.0%)	
	A	77 (57.8%)	22 (16.5%)	34 (25.5%)	9 (6.7%)	5 (4.5%)	3 (2.2%)	4 (3.0%)	

N = 133			*Occupation*		
Statements		*Total*	*Low skilled worker*	*Skilled worker*	*p-value*
The post-COVID-19 time has increased the employment opportunities in GCC for Migrant Workers	D	75 (56.3%)	59 (44.3%)	16 (12.0%)	0.001
	N	13 (9.7%)	7 (5.2%)	6 (4.5%)	
	A	45 (33.8%)	43 (32.3%)	2 (1.5%)	
Living condition for emigrants in GCC has changed in post-COVID-19 time	D	38 (28.5%)	36 (27.0%)	2 (1.5%)	0.042
	N	40 (30.0%)	30 (22.5%)	10 (7.5%)	
	A	55 (41.3%)	43 (32.3%)	12 (9.0%)	
Workload increased in post-COVID-19 time	D	13 (9.7%)	12 (9.0%)	1 (0.7%)	0.285
	N	55 (41.3%)	47 (35.3%)	8 (6.0%)	
	A	65 (48.8%)	50 37.5%)	15 (11.2%)	
More hygiene at the workplace/ accommodation	D	23 (17.2%)	22 (16.5%)	1 (0.7%)	0.001
	N	54 (40.6%)	49 (36.8%)	5 (4.5%)	
	A	55 (41.3%)	37 (27.8%)	18 (13.5%)	
Safety and security in the workplace have increased	D	14 (10.5%)	10 (7.5%)	4 (3.0%)	0.163
	N	70 (52.6%)	55 (41.3%)	15 (11.2%)	
	A	49 (36.8%)	44 (33.0%)	5 (4.5%)	
The post-COVID-19 has resulted in a reduction of salary for emigrants in the GCC	D	24 (18.0%)	24 (18.0%)	0 (0.0%)	0.039
	N	24 (18.0%)	19 (14.2%)	5 (4.5%)	
	A	85 (63.9%)	66 (49.6%)	19 (14.2%)	
Do you believe that domestic policy changes vis a vis migrant in certain, Gulf nations have put your job at risk?	D	19 (14.2%)	18 (13.5%)	1 (0.7%)	0.092

(continued)

Table 7 (continued)

N = *133*			*Occupation*		
Statements		*Total*	*Low skilled worker*	*Skilled worker*	p-*value*
	N	34 (25.5%)	30 (22.5%)	4 (3.0%)	
	A	80 (60.1%)	61 (45.8%)	19 (14.2%)	
Given the fact that India is at the highest level of unemployment in the last 45 years, do you think that getting a chance to work in GCC is a kind of boon in the post-COVID-19 period?	D	6 (4.5%)	4 (3.0%)	2 (1.5%)	0.379
	N	20 (15.0%)	15 (11.2%)	5 (4.5%)	
	A	107 (80.4%)	90 (67.6%)	17 (12.7%)	
Want to continue working in GCC	D	56 (42.1%)	48 (36.0%)	8 (6.0%)	0.336
	N	0 (0.0%)	0 (0.0%)	0 (0.0%)	
	A	77 (57.8%)	61 (45.8%)	16 (12.0%)	

in the perception of the emigrant workers towards their future employability in post-COVID-19 times between low-skilled and skilled workers", and the alternative hypothesis was "there is a significant difference in the perception of the emigrant workers towards their future employability in post-COVID-19 times between low-skilled and skilled workers". The relationship between these variables was generally found to be significant as calculated by the chi-square value and *p*-value of < 0.05 (5% level of significance) as presented in Supplementary Table 38. Therefore, the author rejects the null hypothesis. It means that there was a significant difference in the perception of the emigrant workers towards their future employability in post-COVID-19 times between low-skilled and skilled workers.

6 Conclusion

Emigrants in the GCC have long been facing problems like living in unhealthy conditions, exploitation under the Kafala regime, repatriation in times of economic slowdown, mistrust, or maltreatment from local people, and delayed or reduced wages at the discretion of employers. The pandemic entrenched the economic deterioration of migrant workers, which has implications for their workability and prospects in the region. The deteriorating economic condition can be assessed from the fact that during the pandemic, migrants remitted less than $400 (77.4%) compared to a figure of 58.6% prior to the pandemic. This has equally impacted the well-being of left-behind families in home communities who solely rely on these remittances. This is because many emigrants were rendered unemployed (30.8%), forced to work fewer hours (12.7%), on slashed wages, or had their wages arbitrarily cut. The pandemic period has cost heavily on expatriate workers, especially in terms of health care facilities and financial loss. The stigma associated with them, treating them as 'social other' and a threat to health security by the host populations, has altered the perception of migrants about living and employability in the Gulf in the future. The expatriates faced innumerable restrictions on their movement, accessing facilities, and being lodged in filthy quarantine facilities if they contracted a virus.

Besides being repatriated for an indefinite period along with imposition of age restriction on the travel ban left many workers dwindling between certainty and uncertainty about their future job prospect in the GCC countries. This plight of Indian emigrant in the GCC highlights the unwarranted catastrophes may encounter, especially those workers who fall outside the purview of social safety nets. The absence of concrete policy measures to safeguard such workers during the COVID-19 pandemic and potential future crises exacerbates their vulnerability. This underscores the profound impact of the pandemic, adding an additional layer of complexity to the already challenging lives of Indian emigrant workers. It serves as a poignant reminder that urgent and comprehensive reforms are imperative in Gulf migration regimes. Such reforms are crucial not only to minimise the vulnerabilities faced by migrant workers but also to address issues of social othering and enhance their future job prospects. The COVID-19 crisis has accentuated the critical need for proactive measures and systemic changes to ensure the well-being and protection of these essential contributors to the GCC economies.

Conflict of Interest The author declares that I have no conflict of interest.

Note

1. Numerous expatriate workers had been laid off and sent back to their home countries without receiving the full pay, compensations, or benefits to which they are legally entitled. Under the Vande Bharat Mission, a repatriation mission under which more than nine lakhs expatriates returned to India in September 20202 due to COVID-19 crisis were from the UAE (457596), followed by Saudi Arabia (163851), Qatar (104444), Kuwait (97802), and Oman (85498) & Bahrain (24704) (MEA, 2020).

References

Abdul-Aziz, A.-R., et al. (2018). South Asian migrants and the construction sector of the Gulf. In M. Chowdhury & S. Irudaya Rajan (Eds.), *South Asian Migration in the Gulf* (pp. 165–189). https://doi.org/10.1007/978-3-319-71821-7_9

Beck, M., & Richter, T. (2021). Oil and the political economy in the Middle East: Overcoming rentierism?. In *Oil and the political economy in the Middle East* (pp. 237–268). Manchester University Press.

Bloomer, P. (2017, July 6). Migrant workers bear the brunt of Qatar rift. *Thomas Reuter Foundation News*. https://news.trust.org/item/20170706110123-itx2e/

Business and Human Rights Resource Centre. (n.d.). *Gulf construction trends in 2018 & 2019. Migrant workers at risk: Trends in Gulf construction 2018–2019*. https://media.business-humanrights.org/media/documents/files/FINAL_Gulf_Construction_trends_in_2018__2019.pdf

Diop, A., Johnston, T., & Le, K. T. (2018). Migration policies across the GCC: Challenges in reforming the Kafala. In P. Fargues & N. M. Shah (Eds.), *Migration to the Gulf: Policies in sending and receiving countries* (pp. 33–60). GLMM.

E-Migrate. (2021). *Indian emigration reports on various years*. https://emigrate.gov.in/ext/

Fasano, U., & Iqbal, Z. (2003). *GCC countries: From oil dependence to diversification*. International Monetary Fund. https://www.imf.org/external/pubs/ft/med/2003/eng/fasano/

International Monetary Fund (IMF). (2015, November 10). GCC countries: From oil dependence to diversification GCC countries: From oil dependence to diversification GCC countries: From oil dependence to diversification Annual Meeting of Ministers of Finance and Central Bank Governors, Doha, Qatar. www.imf.org/external/np/pp/eng/2015/111015.pdf

Khan, A., & Harroff-Tavel, H. (2011). Reforming the Kafala: Challenges and opportunities in moving forward. *Asian and Pacific Migration Journal, 20*(3–4), 293–313. https://doi.org/10.1177/011719681102000303

Khan, M. A., Khan, M. I., Illiyan, A., & Khojah, M. (2021, September). The economic and psychological impacts of COVID-19 pandemic on Indian migrant workers in the Kingdom of Saudi Arabia. In *Healthcare* (Vol. 9, No. 9, p. 1152). MDPI.

Linesight. (n.d). *Volatile oil prices and the impact on the GCC construction sector*. https://www.linesight.com/en-us/insights/volatile-oil-prices-and-the-impact-on-the-gcc-construction-sector/

Malit, F., Jr., & Naufal, G. (2016). Taxing remittances: Consequences for migrant labour populations in the GCC countries. Gulf Labour Markets and Migration (GLMM), GLMM - EN - No. 1/2016. https://gulfmigration.grc.net/media/pubs/exno/GLMM_EN_2016_01.pdf

McGinley, J. (2008). Expatriate adjustment within a social context: Examination of a sample in Russia. *The Journal of Social, Evolutionary, and Cultural Psychology, 2*, 56–68.

Migrant Forum in Asia (MFA). (2013, September). *Social protection for low-skilled migrant workers and their families* (Policy Brief No. 7). www.ilo.org/dyn/migpractice/docs/137/PB7.pdf

Migrant-Rights.Org. (2015, August 27). *Oil companies leave migrant workers stranded in Oman without pay*. https://www.migrant-rights.org/2015/08/oil-companies-leaves-migrants-stranded-in-oman-without-pay/

Migrant-Rights.Org. (2017, August 6). *Qatari companies send workers on unpaid extended leave as gulf crisis continues*. Business & Human Resource Centre. https://www.business-humanrights.org/en/latest-news/qatari-companies-send-workers-on-unpaid-extended-leave-as-gulf-crisis-continues/

Migration Forum Asia. (2012). Policy Brief No. 2 | Reform of the Kafala (Sponsorship) System. https://mfasia.org/policy-brief-no-2-reform-of-the-kafala-sponsorship-system/

Ministry of External Affairs. (2020, September 22). Question No. 1369 Evacuations under Vande Bharat Mission.

Mishrif, A. (2018). Introduction to economic diversification in the GCC Region. In A. Mishrif & Y. Al Balushi (Eds.), *Economic diversification in the Gulf Region, Volume I, The political economy of the Middle East* (pp. 1–26). Gulf Research Centre Cambridge. https://doi.org/10.1007/978-981-10-5783-0_1

Obeid, J. (2020, April 3). *The GCC construction sector: The oil price war hits home*. Italian Institute for International Political Studies. https://www.ispionline.it/en/pubblicazione/gcc-construction-sector-oil-price-war-hits-home-25664

Randeree, K. (2009). Strategy, policy and practice in the nationalisation of human capital: 'Project Emiratisation'. *Research and Practice in Human Resource Management, 17*(1), 71–91.

Rashad, M. (2016, May 2). Saudi builder Binladin cuts 77,000 jobs, to lay off Saudis—report. *Reuters News*. https://www.zawya.com/en/business/saudi-builder-binladin-cuts-77-000-jobs-to-lay-off-saudis-report-tcawo7av

Ratha, D., De, S., & Schuettler, K. (2017, March 24). Why taxing remittances is a bad idea. *World Bank Blog*. https://blogs.worldbank.org/peoplemove/why-taxing-remittances-bad-idea#:~:text=Estimates%20suggest%20that%20the%20revenue%20raised%20from%20a,of%20GDP%20of%20the%20GCC%20countries%20%28IMF%202016%29

Richardson, J., & McKenna, S. (2003). International experience and academic careers: What do academics have to say? *Personnel Review, 32*(6), 774–795.

Robinson, K. (2021). *What is Kafala System? Council on foreign relation*. https://www.cfr.org/backgrounder/what-kafala-system

Shah, N. M. (2012). Socio-demographic transitions among nationals of GCC countries: Implications for migration and labour force trends. *Migration and Development, 1*(1), 138–148.

Snudden, S. (2018). International remittances, migration and primary commodities. *The World Economy, 41*(11), 2934–2953.

Stark, O., & Budzinski, W. (2018, July 13). *On the taxing of migrants' earnings while retaining a migrant workforce*. Center for Development Research (ZEF)—Discussion Papers on Development Policy No. 263. https://ssrn.com/abstract=3213248 or http://doi.org/10.2139/ssrn.3213248

Ulrichsen, K. C. (2014, October 14). Gulf States Gamble on Ambitious but Risky Mega-Projects. *World Politics Review*. http://www.worldpoliticsreview.com/articles/14195/gulf-states-gamble-on-ambitious-but-risky-mega-projects

Vohra, R. (2017). The impact of oil prices on GCC economies. *International Journal of Business and Social Science, 8*(2), 7–14.

Ward, C., Bochner, S., & Furnham, A. (2001). The psychology of culture shock (2nd ed.). Routledge (As cited by Mcginley, J. (2008). Expatriate adjustment within a social context: Examination of a sample in Russia. *The Journal of Social, Evolutionary, and Cultural Psychology, 2*, 56–68).

CHAPTER 12

Implications of COVID-19 for Workforce in Oman

Ashraf Mishrif and Wejdan Al-Subeihi

1 Introduction

The Covid-19 caused many negative impacts on the labor market, especially on the workforce policies. The lockdown measures had a substantial influence on three-quarters of all informal employment worldwide. The disparities in the workplace worsened during Covid-19 (ILO, 2020). The global extreme poverty rate increased from 8.4% in 2019 to over 9.5% in 2020. Since 1998, the level of extreme poverty worldwide has risen for the first time in more than 20 years in 2020 (United Nations, 2021).

The Covid-19 health crisis quickly developed into a labor market crisis, which had an impact on both the availability and demand of labor. Public health measures, such as travel bans, quarantines, and other mobility restrictions, became necessary due to the rate of contagion, illness, and mortality. The measures prevented many workers from going to work. Global and local supply networks shattered due to the scarcity of labor,

---

A. Mishrif (✉) · W. Al-Subeihi
Humanities Research Centre, Sultan Qaboos University, Al-Khoud, Oman
e-mail: amishrif@squ.edu.om

A. Mishrif (ed.), *Business Resilience and Market Adaptability*, The Political Economy of the Middle East,
https://doi.org/10.1007/978-981-97-2962-3_12

part-time industrial operation, and decreased consumer demand. Even after the worst of the health crisis has passed, the lingering issue and the uncertainty around its scope and long-term effects discourage investments and new hires. The loss of livelihoods, increased unemployment, and permanent business closures were major worries (Carranza et al., 2020).

If quick and thorough remedies are not given, employment repercussions are significant and run the risk of having long-lasting implications. This chapter discusses workforce policies that help people and businesses during a job crisis, that is, what governments did when the strictest public health measures are still necessary. The interval between decline and recovery, which is controlled by the duration of social distancing measures, determines how governments should respond (Gourinchas, 2020). Since the start of the pandemic in 2020, about 10 million people lost their insurance. This was because of cancellation by employer or expiration of insurance coverage (Planalp et al., 2020). The enrollment in Medicaid and the Marketplace has quickened (Karpman et al., 2020a, 2020b).

In the Sultanate of Oman, the Supreme Committee directed private companies to employ the fewest number of people possible and set up remote work arrangements for their employees. However, many companies, including those in the construction industry, were unable to implement any work-from-home systems (Al Harthy & Wigley, 2020). Therefore, this chapter's aim is to investigate the changes in policies of the workforce in Oman including leave policies, incentives, working hours, health insurance, benefits, and training programs. Unexpected events such as Covid-19 forces the companies and institutions' decision makers to change policies in terms of employees' incentives, benefits, and training programs.

This research chapter has used a quantitative approach to demonstrate Covid-19 impacts in the workforce policies. It analyzes the data collected by a survey that was conducted offline and online for participants from different private and public companies operating in the Sultanate of Oman. This chapter's findings will help the employees, employers, and government to readjust their crisis management policies. This might be in case those policy makers can see the chapter outcomes and based on that many policies can be changed and re-aligned with workforce needs. Several companies did not provide their workers' health insurance and flexible leave; the government might force companies to provide it in future to avoid high treatment costs when a similar crisis might take place in the future. Furthermore, employers and decision makers can be in harmony with uncertain situations, companies' abilities and employees' benefits can adjust incentives and benefits.

The study is divided into six sections. The literature review is described in Sect. 2. The research method is presented in Sect. 3. The results are discussed in Sect. 4. Section 5 illustrates the discussion. The last section summarizes the findings.

2 Literature Review

The Covid-19 pandemic had affected employment and the economy in addition to healthcare. Around the world, the Covid-19 pandemic has had a disastrous impact on workforce, livelihoods, and economy.

2.1 Covid-19 Impact on Leave Policies

In the Organization for Economic Cooperation and Development members, the workers in the United States of America do not get the paid leaves in contrast to the European Union member states (Vanhercke et al., 2017). As a result, it's the states, cities, and employer who decides whether to offer paid sick leave (Susser & Ziebarth, 2016; Spasova et al., 2016). The Covid-19 pandemic has brought attention of this issue to the policy makers. These people include the "important" and front-line employees who have worked in hospitals and clinics, carried out takeaway orders, and delivered essentials all during the health crisis. In 2019, only 58% of service workers had paid sick leave in contrast to the management, business, and finance who got 90% (Pizzella, & Beach, 2019). DeSilver (2020) discovered in his study that more high-income employees had paid sick leaves as compared to low-income and part-time workers.

The US federal government in response to Covid-19 enacted the Families First Coronavirus Reaction Act. It established a temporary nationwide paid sick leave program. According to this law, an employee can have paid sick leave in the event of Covid-19 infection to him/her, his/her family members or even to take care of child at home. The law was in effect from April 1, 2020, through December 31, 2020 (Williamson & Maye, 2022). This legislation successfully decreased Covid-19 transmission (Pichler et al., 2020). Nonetheless, the regulation did not apply to firms who employed 500 or fewer than 50 people (Schneider et al., 2021).

These unpaid sick leave coverage gaps have a substantial impact on employee and public health (Garrow, 2016; Kinman, 2019). According to quasi-experimental studies, coverage rates rise in the cities and states with greater paid sick leave requirements (Callison & Pesko, 2022; Maclean et al., 2020). The findings related to the relationship between these laws and leave taking have varied because of the expansion of paid sick leave. While some researchers found decrease in leave taking, perhaps because the need for leave is lessened by decreased disease transmission (Stearns & White, 2018), others have reported the way around (Callison & Pesko, 2022; Maclean et al., 2020). There is some evidence that presentism considerably decreases as paid sick leave is expanded, mainly the service sector employees with low wages (Callison & Pesko, 2022; Schneider, 2020). According to Smith and Kim (2010) employees without paid sick time are more likely to come to work sick. The transmission of communicable disease declines once workers have access to paid sick leave (Pichler & Ziebarth, 2017; Pichler et al., 2020).

The Labor Law (RD 35/2003) enacted by Omani government, allows every year paid leaves of 30 days. Both employees and employers need to agree on the timing of the leave. In the time of Covid-19 several companies in Oman allowed annual leaves with full pay (Ministry of Labor, 2022). The conditions of any leave policies in place, together with other considerations, determine the business's capacity to enforce any annual leave. This includes any effort to implement pay reductions while on leave. Any modification to the annual leave policy must be agreed in advance with the Ministry of Labor. It was necessary to give the Ministry justifications for amending the policy as well as information on how to do so which supported the company's operations and its employees. The length of time it took to receive such clearances was anticipated to grow due to the decreased personnel levels across all government agencies. As it stands, companies cannot compel workers to take unpaid vacation under Oman's labor rules (Al Harthy & Wigley, 2020).

2.2 *Covid-19 Impact on Health Insurance*

The US economy lost over 22 million jobs between February–April and 7.5 million jobs between April–June in 2020 as a result of social isolation measures taken to slow the spread of the Covid-19 (Bureau of Labor Statistics, 2020). The layoff of workers caused health insurance panic, since they and their family might no longer have insurance coverage

(Banthin et al., 2020; Blumberg et al., 2020; Garrett & Gangopadhyaya, 2020). The statistical observations offered conflicting indications regarding how coverage has evolved since the start of the Covid-19. The uninsured rate for persons aged 18 to 64 remained largely unchanged between April 23–May 5 (12.6%) where? worldwide, according to the Census Bureau's latest Household Pulse Survey (12.8%) (Bureau of Labor Statistics, 2020). Also nearly constant were the proportions of non-elderly adults reporting private and public coverage. However, the Household Pulse Survey wasn't released until more than a month after the epidemic had already cost millions of people their employment and there is possibility that a section of people might have lost the insurance even before the survey was conducted.

The discrepancy in the federal surveys on unemployment and the Household Pulse Survey on health insurance is explained by two additional data sources. First, many people who lost their employment did not have insurance via those employers, and second those who had ESI coverage might be able to keep it even if they were temporarily laid off (Karpman et al., 2020a, 2020b). Workers with low salaries have been hit harder by the crisis than those with higher incomes since in most cases they do not have ESI access (Johnston et al., 2020). According to Banthin et al (2020) the employees who had lost their jobs had ESI coverage in one to five employees' proportion. Furthermore, in many cases the laid-off employees were not covered by their companies instead some of them were not insured while others had coverage from Medicaid, Medicare, etc. (Collins et al., 2020). In the early phases of the pandemic the employees were on temporary layoffs, however during Feb–June 2020 their number increased from 801,000 to 10.6 million and permanent layoffs increased from 1.3 to 2.9 million (Bureau of Labor Statistics, 2020). In some cases, the employees had less hours to work, while in other cases although employees were on temporary layoff, they were kept under the insurance coverage (Lucia et al., 2020).

2.3 *Covid-19 Impact on Working Hours*

With the worsening of the coronavirus outbreak in the Sultanate, the Omani government released a circular limiting the number of personnel who could conduct their work from government headquarters while following the necessary health procedures to a maximum of 30% of the total number of employees. This was put into effect on July 3, 2020.

Many people who worked from their homes affirmed that working online gave them flexibility in scheduling their time, interdependence of location, and saved money, all of which contributed to improved productivity (Oman News Agency, 2021).

On March 15, 2020, the Omani government undertook a nationwide closure of educational institutions switching to distance mode. At first, the educational system was closed for one month but as the number of cases increased, the duration of this intervention was extended. Although online classes were in operation, many students and teachers missed their lessons after having been infected, suffering from post-Covid-19 effects. As a result, students and instructors' performance was impacted negatively, meaning less contribution to the future national income. Although the education sector's contribution to GDP is expected to increase from 4.9% to 6.2% by the end of the 10th Five-Year Development Plan (2021–2025), the Covid-19 may force the opposite to occur (Abushammala et al., 2021).

The construction industry could not switch to remote work and as such it faced a very tough situation during Covid-19. While decisions on a comprehensive construction embargo were not taken at the same time (Alandijany et al., 2020), rigorous quarantine led to the almost total suspension of construction in the USA, Italy, and Spain (KHL, 2020). Only non-critical construction sites were suspended in other viral spreading hubs. In Oman, like the other parts of the world, the sales in the construction industry decreased and also the delivery of projects got delayed (Al Amri & Marey-Pérez, 2020). Oman's construction industry has suffered greatly because of restrictions and a change in firm focus away from the building sector. During the Covid-19 people were spending on the basic needs such as food and healthcare, and this caused revenue losses to Oman's construction industry. Construction activity in Oman decreased dramatically as the Middle East contract rate fell to approximately 75% in March 2020 (Mordor Intelligence, 2020).

2.4 *Covid-19 Impact on Incentives and Benefits*

Abston and Bryant (2021) claimed that the pandemic influenced the compensation and benefits sector due to higher expenses and lost revenue. Naturally, one of the main topics of conversation has been the ability to work remotely, and employees are also searching for more alternatives for paid time off (PTO). (2020 Hampton). However, the epidemic made things difficult for pension plans, particularly for those that were already having trouble. The opportunity to identify intervention opportunities for HRM experts about the typical workweek, worker classification, employee benefits, and workplace safety has been examined by Lester et al. (2021).

Ferneini (2020) experienced the short- and long-term financial effects of Covid-19. Due to the outbreak, many doctors and dentists had to close their doors, which created a severe scarcity of these professionals. Although the US government temporarily covered the costs of laid-off employees, most doctors' overall expenses were far higher (Ferneini, 2019). The second wave of the Covid-19 created an already dire financial situation. Many Boston hospitals have already cut physician compensation and stopped awarding bonuses for completed work. The government reduced the incentives and reimbursements.

2.5 *Covid-19 and Training Programs*

In organizations and companies, training and collaboration forms one of the core components. The environment such as Covid-19 motivated the Human Resource Development (HRD) to look for new technologies and devices for the virtual/remote environments (Hughes, 2021). The employees and the HRD professionals require collaboration to successfully implement and use the technology for the training programs (Bennett, 2010). Such an activity would call for different developmental approaches from what was typically done before the disturbance at work. To prepare employees, firms must plan for continued digital change and consider how to use virtual human resource development (VHRD) (Bennett & McWhorter, 2021). The digital platforms for remote training and learning bring ease to the employees and employers (Bennett & McWhorter, 2021; Boyd & Jackson, 2004).

However, according to social learning theory (Bandura, 1977a), social interaction is critical for employee development. It also explores how the work environment and emotional support can influence one's professional development and advancement (Bandura, 1977b). The Bandura's social learning theory emphasizes social contacts and interactions (Bond & Blevins, 2020), however such contacts are not possible in the remote or virtual environment (Yarberry & Sims, 2021). Several private companies and government institutions did not provide their workers training programs during the pandemic, although that would have enhanced their abilities and capabilities.

3 Research Method

This study has used quantitative research method. Quantitative research focuses on measurements based on the statistical analysis of data collected through surveys. Quantitative research helps in determining the association between dependent and independent variables within a certain population. The primary goal of a quantitative research chapter is to identify features and develop statistical models to explain the results (USC Libraries, 2022; Pichler & Ziebarth, 2017). The quantitative method is a well-known technique and has been used by several researchers in conducting similar kinds of chapters. For instance, (Collins et al., 2020; Karpman et al., 2020a, 2020b).

3.1 Survey Questionnaire Design

The questionnaire survey was designed in both Arabic and English after identifying relevant workforce factors from literature review. The specific factors selected are relevant to Oman's workforce. The key variables used are leave policies, health insurance, working hours, incentives and benefits, and training programs. The questions designed were put in a google form to be distributed among SMEs employees from Muscat, Sohar, and Dhofar. The survey question was refined in terms of language, questions clarity, and time taken to complete the questions before the actual distribution. Based on participant input and comments, the research team was able to apply certain changes as a result of the pilot study.

3.2 Data Collection and Cleaning

The online and offline mode was used to distribute the survey between March 1, 2021, and April 30, 2021. Google form used in the online distribution. In the offline mode companies' visits were planned, and the employees were briefed about the survey objectives. A number of companies lies in the special economic zones and industrial zones of Oman. The companies were found to be operating in different domains including food and beverage, hospitality and tourism, agriculture, education, healthcare, manufacturing, information and communication technology, and logistics and supply chain. A total of 160 survey responses were collected. The collected data was cleaned, and any incomplete response and duplicated information were removed and discarded from analysis. Further, the responses were coded before feeding to SPSS software for analysis. Out of 160 survey responses, 128 valid responses were used in the final analysis.

4 Analysis and Results

The survey analysis is based on 128 authentic responses from employees. Most respondents participated in the survey were male represented 64.8% and the remaining are female with 35.2%. 79.7% of the respondents are Omanis and the rest are non-Omanis. The job seekers were with only 7.03%, while the employed participants were 93%. The main applicants were responded to the survey are from Muscat (48.4%), and Al Batinah (25%), whereas the governorates of Al Dakhliyah, Al Dhahira, Al Buraimi, Al Sharqiya, Dhofar, and Al Wusta were underrepresented with just 7.03%, 6.25%, 6.25%, 4.7%, 2.3%, and 1.5% responses, sequentially. The profile of respondents is represented by 50% employees having a bachelor's degree, while employees having PhD, Masters, High Diploma, and less than High Diploma were 7.8%, 14.1%, 16.4%, and 11.7%, respectively. Table 1 shows the demographic characteristics of the respondents.

Table 1 Demographic characteristics of the respondents

	PhD (%)	*Masters (%)*	*Bachelor (%)*	*High Diploma (%)*	*Less than High Diploma (%)*	*Total (%)*
Female	3.5	3.9	22.7	2.3	1.6	35.2
Male	3.1	10.2	27.3	14.1	10.2	64.8
Total	7.8	14.1	50	16.4	11.7	100

Source survey conducted by authors in 2021

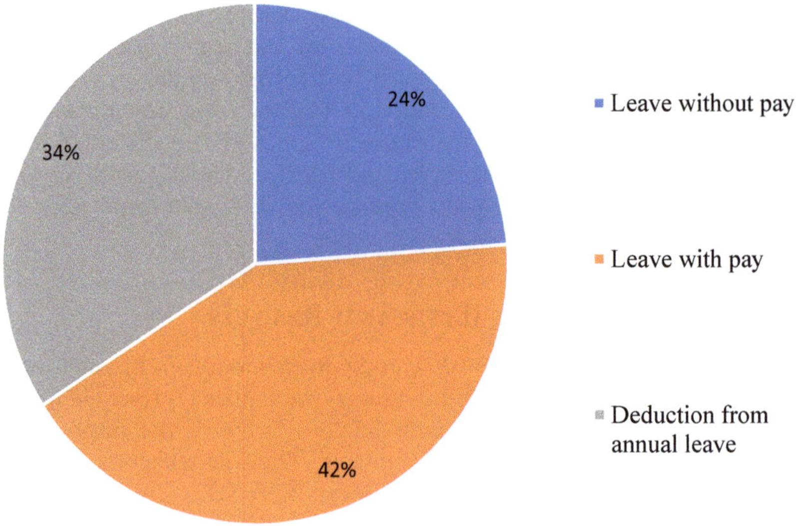

Fig. 1 Leave policies in the companies during Covid-19 (*Source* Survey conducted by authors in 2021)

4.1 Covid-19 and Leave Policies

About 42% of the employees said that they got leave with pay, while 34% said that they got leave from their annual pay, and the remaining 24% got leave without payment. Figure 1 shows the leave policies in the companies during Covid-19 for quarantine.

About 27% of respondents got leave with payment, 13% of the respondents admitted that the leave policy was leave without pay and 7% confirmed that they did not get the leave at all. The leave policies changed because of Covid-19, more than 50% of respondents observed no change in their organizations as shown in Fig. 2.

4.2 Covid-19 and Health Insurance

The employees and staff in the companies were asked about the health insurance policies. 44% of participants reported that all staff were insured before Covid-19, while 40% of participants confirmed that none of the staff were insured before Covid-19. Only 8% of participants informed

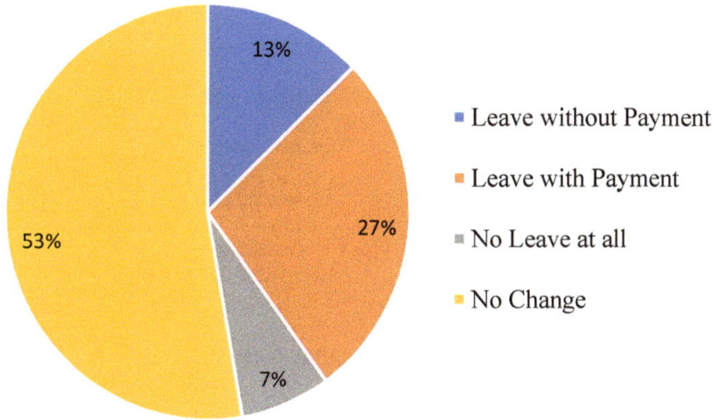

Fig. 2 Change in the leave policies during Covid-19 (*Source* Survey authors own)

us that some of the staff were insured before Covid-19. Around 5% of respondents agreed that some of the staff was insured during Covid-19, while 3% respondents replied that all the staff got insured during Covid-19. This implies that companies have many differences in terms of health insurance which might be because of the nature of the business itself and the revenues earned by the firm. Figure 3 shows the health insurance policies in the companies during Covid-19.

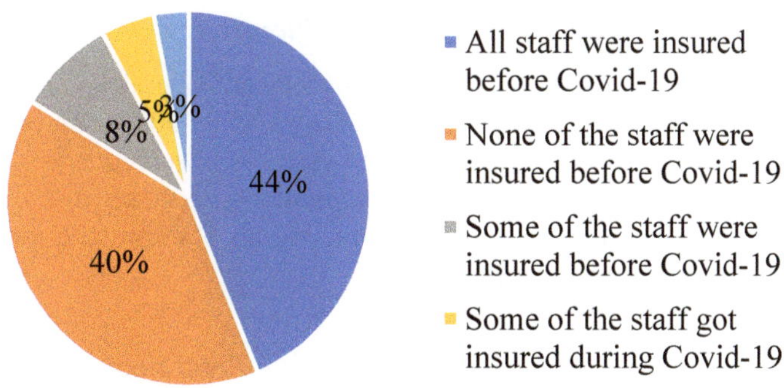

Fig. 3 Health insurance policies during Covid-19 (*Source* Survey authors own)

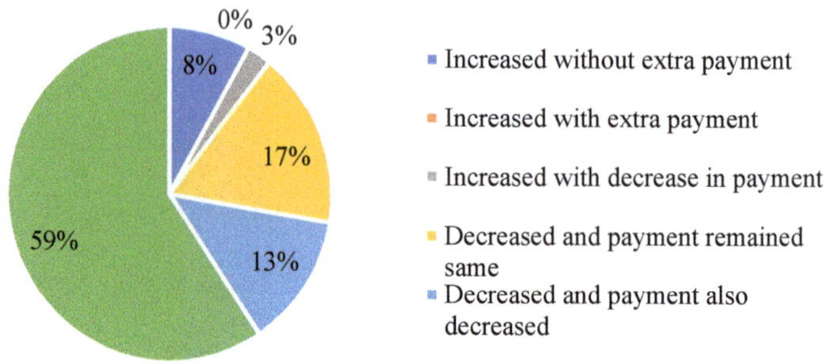

Fig. 4 Payment and working hours in companies during the Covid-19 (*Source* Authors' own work)

4.3 *Covid-19 and Working Hours*

More than 55% of participants confirmed that their organizations did not change their working hours, 17% agreed that their organizations decreased working hours and payment remained the same, 13% said that working hours decreased and payment decreased. Some companies increased working hours without extra payment that was started by 8% of respondents, while 3% agreed that their working hours were increased with decrease in payment. Moreover, it was found that no companies increased the working hours and paid extra payment. Figure 4 shows the payment and working hours in companies during the Covid-19.

4.4 *Covid-19 and Incentives*

Moreover, Covid-19 affected the company's incentive policies. The incentive policies were discontinued in 21% of cases while 20% got a reduction in the incentives. About 31% of the respondents observed no change in the incentive policy while 28% of the respondents reported that they had no incentive policy in their organization. Figure 5 shows the incentives policies in companies during Covid-19.

4.5 *Covid-19 and Training Programs*

When enquired about the Covid-19 effect on training programs, in-house training through seniors emerged as the most popular method was taken by the companies operating in Oman to provide training to

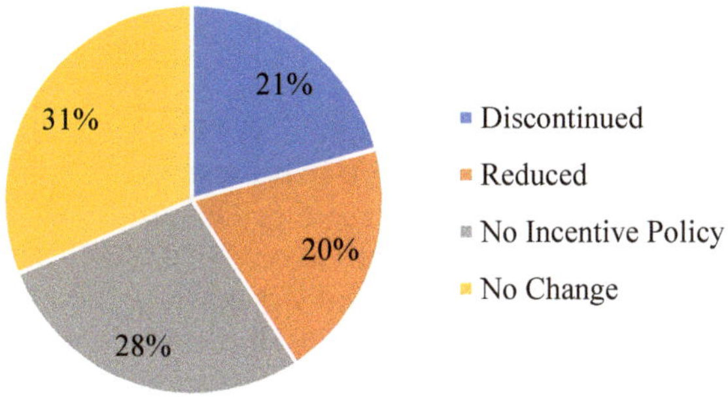

Fig. 5 The incentives policies in companies during Covid-19 (*Source* Authors' own work)

their employees as indicated by 39% of respondents and this was followed by workshops through experts' invitations (with 26%). The international exchange programs were also provided during Covid-19 with 13% responses. This was applied since companies did not leave any room for benefiting their workers even in hard situations. On the other hand, around 22% said that they had no training programs at all since their employer's care about the diffusion of coronaviruses. Figure 6 shows the training programs in companies during Covid-19.

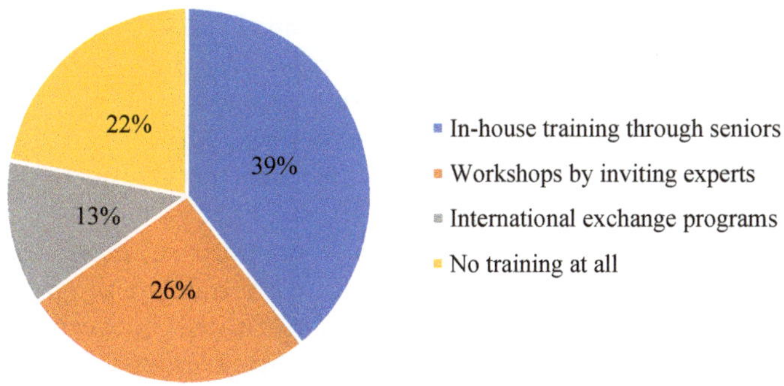

Fig. 6 Impact of Covid-19 on the companies training programs (*Source* Authors' own work)

5 Discussion

The survey analysis showed that many organizations provide leave with payment for employees leaving quarantine and more than half of organizations did not change their leave policy because of Covid-19. This is in harmony with labor law in the Sultanate of Oman, which provides paid sick leave for employees (Ministry of Labor, 2022). On the other hand, there was a variability in providing paid sick leave in the USA according to each state or city (DeSilver, 2020). This disparity might come since our chapter is a localized one and the economic situation in Oman is different from the USA.

This chapter also examined the impact of Covid-19 on health insurance, concluding that most businesses and organizations provided health insurance to all their employees prior to the outbreak. Several of them offered health insurance to all their employees throughout the pandemic. However, those who lost their jobs could not have insurance, the researchers including (Banthin et al., 2020; Blumberg et al., 2020; Garrett & Gangopadhyaya, 2020) found. The difference between our results and other studies is because of using different data sources and methods in analyzing data.

Furthermore, our survey results indicated that many companies did not change their incentive policy because of the pandemic. However, some of them reduced their incentives, especially in the private sector. This is in correspondence with the closure policy that most countries followed which hit many businesses from creating profits (Ferneini, 2020). On the other hand, the closure policy did not affect working hours in Oman since most organizations used online platforms to work from home (Oman News Agency, 2021) as the chapter results show. Moreover, schools and high educational institutions followed the same mechanism to continue the learning process (Abushammala et al., 2021).

In addition, the closure policy did not obstruct more than half of companies from providing their staff with training programs who participated in the chapter. The programs varied between in-house training through seniors, workshops by inviting experts, and international exchange programs. This is emphasized that better technology has made it possible for trainers to demonstrate that learning technologies aid employee development rather than being a detriment. Employing modern technologies for professional growth and other organizationally linked training gives all employees the help they need to build their skill sets (Hughes, 2021). Furthermore, understanding how individuals take control of their professional performance during unexpected changes in the workplace is heavily reliant on their ability to overcome feelings of isolation, persevere in staying engaged, and gain empowerment (Yarberry & Sims, 2021).

5.1 *Theoretical Implications*

Our findings are stated to be important since they help to improve our understanding of impacts of Covid-19 pandemic in the field of workforce in terms of leave policies, working hours, health insurance, incentives, and training programs. Furthermore, our results.

5.2 *Practical Implications for Policy Makers and Companies*

Based on our findings, the policy makers can reform policies that are related to the workforce market to eliminate any issues that could happen because of uncertain situations. This might be on developing a unified policy for all companies to provide health insurance to all their staff. This comes since some of them did not provide health insurance, which resulted in many employees struggling with paying healthcare costs during Covid-19. Moreover, leave policies were affected during Covid-19 which enforce some employees to have sick leave without pay or from their vacations balance. As a result, the government should enforce companies to have a flexible leave policy in case employees do not lose their salary or their leave balance in undetermined situations.

Our results emphasized that companies witnessed different changes in their workforce policies because of the pandemic. According to that, they might work on modifying the working hours policy to make it more flexible since that workers' productivity depends on their ability to finish work efficiently and effectively, not in coming to the workplace at a strict time. This will help in reducing workers' expenses in fuels. Also, the gas emission from cars and environmental pollution will be reduced as well. Moreover, during corona time, training programs allowed many institutions to collaborate with inside and outside experts to provide the initial training to their staff by using diverse online platforms.

6 Conclusion

This study examined the effects of the Covid-19 pandemic on Oman's employment policies, particularly in terms of leave restrictions, incentives, working hours, benefits, health insurance, and training. For many of the organizations who participated in the chapter, the epidemic had little effect on their leave or incentive policies. Furthermore, Oman's existing infrastructure and culture of incorporating technology into the curriculum has enabled institutions to collectively embrace various types of remote working methods, hence facilitating continuous working hours and training programs. As a result, most employees have the technological tools they need to operate remotely. However, Covid-19 created economic issues for many employees, hurting their families' ability to pay fees. Some institutions have implemented measures to assist employees with fee payment; nonetheless, the chapter recommends that flexible fee payment methods be utilized on a larger scale. This chapter's scope is limited to the Sultanate of Oman. However, it is recommended that a comparative chapter be conducted to compare Oman to other countries with similar economic situations.

Acknowledgements The Ministry of Higher Education, Scientific Research and Innovation, Sultanate of Oman supported this work. Grant number: RC/Covid-19/DVC/HURC/20/01.

References

Abston, K. A., & Bryant, P. C. (2021). Compensation and benefits in a pandemic and post pandemic world: Introduction to compensation & benefits review. *Compensation & Benefits Review, 53*(1), 3–7. https://doi.org/10.1177/0886368720953347

Abushammala, M., Qazi, W., & Manchiryal, R. K. (2021). The impact of COVID-19 on the private higher education system and students in Oman. *Journal of University Teaching and Learning Practice, 18*(3). https://doi.org/10.53761/1.18.3.13

Al Amri, T., & Marey-Pérez, M. (2020). Impact of Covid-19 on Oman's Construction Industry. *Technium Social Sciences Journal, 9*(July), 661–670. https://doi.org/10.47577/tssj.v9i1.1021

Alandijany, T. A., Faizo, A. A., & Azhar, E. I. (2020). Coronavirus disease of 2019 (COVID-19) in the Gulf Cooperation Council (GCC) countries: Status and management practices. *Journal of Infection and Public Health, 13*(6), 839–842. https://doi.org/10.1016/j.jiph.2020.05.020

Al Harthy, R., & Wigley, T. (2020, April 1). Covid-19: Employment update – issues to consider in Oman. Covid-19: Employment update – Issues to consider in Oman -Trowers & Hamlins. Retrieved July 18, 2022, from https://www.trowers.com/insights/2020/april/covid-19---employment-update---issues-to-consider-in-oman

Bandura, A. (1977a). *Social learning theory*. Prentice-Hall.

Bandura, A. (1977b). Self-efficacy: Toward a unifying theory of behavioral change. *Psychological Review, 84*(2), 191–215.

Banthin, J., Simpson, M., Buettgens, M., & ... (2020). Changes in health insurance coverage due to the COVID-19 recession: Preliminary estimates using microsimulation (pp. 1–9). Urban Institute. https://www.alreporter.com/wp-content/uploads/2020/09/RWJStudy.pdf

Bennett, E. E. (2010). The coming paradigm shift: Synthesis and future directions for virtual HRD. *Advances in Developing Human Resources, 12*(6), 728–741. https://doi.org/10.1177/1523422310394796

Bennett, E. E., & McWhorter, R. R. (2021). Virtual HRD's role in crisis and the post Covid-19 professional lifeworld: Accelerating skills for digital transformation. *Advances in Developing Human Resources, 23*(1), 5–25. https://doi.org/10.1177/1523422320973288

Blumberg, L. J., Simpson, M., Buettgens, M., Holahan, J., & Banthin, J. (2020). COVID-19, unemployment compensation, and state medicaid expansion decisions: Some workers losing jobs and health insurance remain ineligible for subsidized coverage (pp. 1–8). Urban Institute. https://www.urban.org/sites/default/files/publication/102259/covid-19-unemployment-compensation-and-state-medicaid-expansion-decisions_1.pdf

Bond, M. A., & Blevins, S. J. (2020). Using faculty professional development to foster organizational change: A social learning framework. *TechTrends, 64*(2), 229–237. https://doi.org/10.1007/s11528-019-00459-2

Boyd, A. M., & Jackson, M. L. (2004). An effective model for rapid skills acquisition through a simulation-based integrated learning environment. *Journal of Educational Computing Research, 30*(1–2), 1–21. https://doi.org/10.2190/E8CN-91GX-R6WA-Y05N

Bureau of Labor Statistics. (2020, July 2). "The Employment Situation," news release. https://www.bls.gov/news.release/archives/empsit_07022020.pdf

Callison, K., & Pesko, M. F. (2022). The effect of paid sick leave mandates on coverage, work absences, and presenteeism. *Journal of Human Resources, 57*(4), 1178–1208.

Carranza, E., Farole, T., Gentilini, U., Morgandi, M., Packard, T., Santos, I., & Weber, M. (2020). Managing the employment impacts of the COVID-19 crisis: Policy options for relief and restructuring the COVID-19 crisis.

World Bank, 49. https://openknowledge.worldbank.org/bitstream/handle/10986/34263/Managing-the-Employment-Impacts-of-the-COVID-19-Crisis-Policy-Options-for-Relief-and-Restructuring.pdf?sequence=4&isAllowed=y

Collins, S. R., Gunja, M. Z., Aboulafia, G. N., Czyzewicz, E., Kline, C. H., Rapoport, R., & Glancey, S. (2020). An early look at the potential implications of the COVID-19 pandemic for health insurance coverage (pp. 1–14).

DeSilver, D. (2020, July 27). As coronavirus spreads, which U.S. workers have paid sick leave – and which don't? Pew Research Center. Retrieved July 19, 2022, from https://www.pewresearch.org/fact-tank/2020/03/12/as-coronavirus-spreads-which-u-s-workers-have-paid-sick-leave-and-which-dont/

Ferneini, E. M. (2019). Corporate America's impact on our daily clinical practice. *Journal of Oral and Maxillofacial Surgery, 77*(10), 1955–1957.

Ferneini, E. M. (2020). The financial impact of COVID-19 on our practice. *Journal of Oral and Maxillofacial Surgery, 78*(7), 1047–1048. https://doi.org/10.1016/j.joms.2020.03.045

Garrett, A. B., & Gangopadhyaya, A. (2020). How the COVID-19 recession could affect health insurance coverage. Available at SSRN 3598558.

Garrow, V. (2016, February). Presenteeism: A review of current thinking. In Institute for Employment Studies. https://www.employment-studies.co.uk/system/files/resources/files/507_0.pdf

Gourinchas, P.-O. (2020). Flattening the pandemic and recesion curves. In *Mitigating the COVID economic crisis: Act fast and do whatever it takes* (pp. 31–39). CEPR Press. https://cepr.org/voxeu/columns/flattening-pandemic-and-recession-curves

Hughes, C. (2021). The changing learning technological landscape for trainers in the wake of COVID-19. *Advances in Developing Human Resources, 23*(1), 66–74. https://doi.org/10.1177/1523422320972108

International Labor Organization (ILO). (2020). Covid-19 and the world of work. International Labor Organization. Retrieved July 19, 2022, from https://www.ilo.org/global/topics/coronavirus/lang--en/index.htm

Johnston, E. M., Kenney, G. M., Gonzalez, D., & Wengle, E. (2020). Employer-sponsored insurance access, affordability, and enrollment in 2018: State and national estimates and implications for low-income working families.

Karpman, M., Zuckerman, S., & Peterson, G. (2020). Adults in Families Losing Jobs During the Pandemic Also Lost Employer-sponsored Health Insurance. Brief (Urban Institute). https://search.bvsalud.org/global-literature-on-novel-coronavirus-2019-ncov/resource/en/grc-740395

Karpman, M., Zuckerman, S., Gonzalez, D., & Kenney, G. M. (2020b). *The COVID-19 pandemic is straining families' abilities to afford basic needs* (p. 500). Urban Institute.

KHL. (2020, May 21). Europe's Construction Industry. KHL Group. Retrieved July 28, 2022, from https://www.khl.com/1144207.article

Kinman, G. (2019). Sickness presenteeism at work: Prevalence, costs and management.

Lester, G. V., Brock Baskin, M. E., & Clinton, M. S. (2021). Employer-sponsored benefits in the United States: The past, present, and future. *Compensation and Benefits Review, 53*(1), 24–42. https://doi.org/10.1177/0886368720947609

Lucia, K., Blumberg, L. J., Curran, E., Holahan, J., Wengle, E., Hoppe, O., & Corlette, S. (2020, June). The COVID-19 Pandemic–Insurer Insights Into Challenges, Implications, and Lessons Learned. Urban Institute. https://www.urban.org/sites/default/files/publication/102483/the-covid-19-pandemic-insurer-insights-into-challenges-implications-and-lessons-learned_0.pdf

Maclean, J. C., Pichler, S., & Ziebarth, N. R. (2020). Mandated sick pay: Coverage, utilization, and welfare effects (No. w26832). National Bureau of Economic Research.

Ministry of labor. (2022). Labor Law. https://www.mol.gov.om/Laborlaw

Mordor Intelligence. (2020). Oman construction market - Growth, trends, covid-19 impact, and forecasts (2022–2027). Retrieved July 28, 2022, from https://www.mordorintelligence.com/industry-reports/oman-construction-market

Oman News Agency (ONA). (2021). Oman Vision 2040 Unit Publishes Report on Progress of Economic Diversification in 2020. https://omannews.gov.om/NewsDescription/ArtMID/392/ArticleID/37304/Oman-Vision-2040-Unit-Publishes-Report-on-Progress-of-Economic-Diversification-in-2020

Pichler, S., Wen, K., & Ziebarth, N. R. (2020). COVID-19 emergency sick leave has helped flatten the curve in the United States. *Health Affairs, 39*(12), 2197–2204. https://doi.org/10.1377/hlthaff.2020.00863

Pizzella, P., & Beach, W. (2019). National compensation survey: Employee benefits in the United States. U.S. Bureau of Labor Statistics. *Bulletin*. 2791, September 2019. https://www.bls.gov/ebs/publications/pdf/bulletin-2791-september-2019-employee-benefits-in-the-united-states-march-2019.pdf

Pichler, S., & Ziebarth, N. R. (2017). The pros and cons of sick pay schemes: Testing for contagious presenteeism and noncontagious absenteeism behavior. *Journal of Public Economics, 156*, 14–33. https://doi.org/10.1016/j.jpubeco.2017.07.003

Planalp, C., Alarcon, G., & Blewett, L. A. (2020). Coronavirus pandemic caused more than 10 million US adults to lose health insurance. State Health Access Data Assistance Center.

Schneider, D. (2020). Paid sick leave in Washington State: Evidence on employee outcomes, 2016–2018. *American Journal of Public Health, 110*(4), 499–504. https://doi.org/10.2105/AJPH.2019.305481

Schneider, D., Harknett, K., & Vivas-Portillo, E. (2021). Olive garden's expansion of paid sick leave during covid-19 reduced the share of employees working while sick. *Health Affairs, 40*(8), 1328–1336. https://doi.org/10.1377/HLTHAFF.2020.02320

Smith, T. W., & Kim, J. (2010). *Paid sick days: Attitudes and experiences*. Public Welfare Foundation.

Spasova, S., Bouget, D., & Vanhercke, B. (2016, October). Sick pay and sickness benefit schemes in the European Union. In European Commission. Directorate-General for Employment, Social Affairs and Inclusion.

Stearns, J., & White, C. (2018). Can paid sick leave mandates reduce leave-taking? *Labour Economics, 51*(C), 227–246.

Susser, P., & Ziebarth, N. (2016). Profiling the US sick leave landscape, No 9709. IZA Discussion Papers, Institute of Labor Economics (IZA).

United Nations. (2021). - SDG indicators. United Nations. Retrieved July 19, 2022, from https://unstats.un.org/sdgs/report/2021/goal-01/

USC Libraries. (2022, July 22). Organizing your Social Sciences Research Paper: Quantitative Methods. Research Guides. Retrieved August 4, 2022, from https://libguides.usc.edu/writingguide/quantitative#:~:text=Quantitative%20methods%20emphasize%20objective%20measurements,statistical%20data%20using%20computational%20techniques.

Vanhercke, B., Bouget, D., & Spasova, S. (2017, April 18). Sick pay and Sickness Benefit Schemes in the European Union. Photo of Publications Office of the European Union. Retrieved July 19, 2022, from https://op.europa.eu/en/publication-detail/-/publication/fc7a58b4-2599-11e7-ab65-01aa75ed71a1

Yarberry, S., & Sims, C. (2021). The impact of COVID-19-prompted virtual/Remote work environments on employees' career development: Social learning theory, belongingness, and self-empowerment. *Advances in Developing Human Resources, 23*(3), 237–252. https://doi.org/10.1177/15234223211017850

Williamson, E., & Maye, A. (2022, April 1). Amended and new state and local laws and guidance on paid sick days in response to covid-19. CLASP. Retrieved July 19, 2022, from https://www.clasp.org/publications/fact-sheet/amended-and-new-state-and-local-laws-and-guidance-paid-sick-days-response/

CHAPTER 13

The Prospect of the Business Sector in Post-pandemic

Ashraf Mishrif

1 Introduction

The COVID-19 pandemic has left us with an unprecedented experience that all people, companies, organizations, and countries cannot forget or ignore. In 2020, most economic and commercial activities decreased significantly due to borders closure, lockdown, and social distance measures that brought life to near standstill. The pandemic also presented an unparalleled test of business resilience, where managerial competence, leadership skills, organizational structure, operational capacity, technological capacity of all small and large companies were tested. Undoubtedly, most companies struggled to cope with the economic impact of the pandemic as the precautionary measures taken to control the virus disrupted the productive sectors and global supply chain. One can hardly comprehend the difficulties in decision-making, where company executives must choose between ceasing operations to protect the workforce

A. Mishrif (✉)
Humanities Research Centre, Sultan Qaboos University, Al-Khoud, Oman
e-mail: amishrif@squ.edu.om

A. Mishrif (ed.), *Business Resilience and Market Adaptability*, The Political Economy of the Middle East,
https://doi.org/10.1007/978-981-97-2962-3_13

and respond to decreased demand of goods and services and operating as usual and taking the risk of increasing human and financial losses. Some companies took the ease route by downsizing or suspending operations. Others stood up to the challenge, strategically prioritized their needs, and sought innovative means to overcome the consequences of the pandemic.

What remains critical in this discussion is how governments, markets, and enterprises are well-equipped to deal with a similar crisis. The pandemic experience shows that the world was unprepared to deal with COVID-19. The global healthcare system was near collapse, many large and small companies went into administration due to financial difficulties, debts increased due to excessive borrowing, factories closed due to lack of raw materials and spare parts, food insecurity intensified because of disruption to the supply chains, to mention but a few. The complexity of the international order and acceleration of globalization have increased the levels of threats to business and markets that are highly sensitive to geopolitical tension, instability of the energy markets, public health crises, global or regional financial crises, or possibly any types of biological wars.

Thus, this chapter aims to identify the strategic areas where government officials and company executives must work on to put in place and develop more sophisticated strategies that ensure resilience and adaptability at the time of crises. It also aims to analyze the causes, responses, and consequences of the pandemic to extract lessons and identify key strategic areas for the future. The ability to realize these aims requires the employment of a descriptive analytical approach that digs deep into the causes of the pandemic and the efforts made by governments, enterprises, and individuals to survive during the pandemic. My approach here is not to show understanding but to identify practical means and steps that focus on preparedness in readiness and response to future challenges. I would also like to stress here that success and failure in withstanding future crises does not only depend on the ability of the respected stakeholders to foresee changes but on their ability to act adaptably to the changing business environment.

2 Integration of Technology in Business

Undoubtedly, the prospect of business depends on the ability of governments and companies to integrate technology into the business domain. Technology has been an effective mediating tool during the pandemic that heightened uncertainties in the global economy. Of course, understanding these uncertainties helps in analyzing the pandemic effects on the economy, evaluating the policy effectiveness in controlling the pandemic, and putting together effective measures for economic recovery. Song and Zhou (2020) argue that the development of new technology, together with structural reforms and re-integration, is a fundamental factor in economic recovery. With broadly examining the need for a new global social contract supported by strong public policy at the national levels to ease the socio-economic impact of the pandemic, they also stressed the importance of innovation and technology in helping the government to communicate with its people and companies to connect with their staff, suppliers, and consumers.

In fact, COVID-19 has accelerated the integration of technology in the business sector, which, in turn, helped entrepreneurs launch online platforms to provide services, make their products, and enhance their access to customers. This required extensive investment by the government to create a solid digital infrastructure such as online services, online payment, e-commerce, and e-marketing to support enterprises during the pandemic. Technology facilitates all these electronic activities and transactions, many of them are conducted and developed by SMEs. This is indicated in chapter two, where the authors claimed that the Public Authority of the Small and Medium Enterprises Development (Riyada) in the Sultanate of Oman offered entrepreneurial training programs for young people, technical support to entrepreneurs, promoted entrepreneurship, and launched online platforms for business owners to marketing and selling their products and services. The impact of these efforts materialized in an increase in the number of Entrepreneurship Card holders by 62.6% in 2021. The integration of technology in business also helped the government to focus more on vaccination and treatment rather than lockdown and social distance.

To ease pressure on the business sector and keep companies competitive in the market, the government extended its financial support to SMEs to cover areas such as banking facilities support, tax facilities and exemptions, license fee exemptions, postponement of payment of monthly subscriptions in the social insurance system, reduction licensing fees, exemption from delay fines, emergency funding programs, and postponement of payment of and bank loans. The government also established electronic link for receiving complaints and suggestions during the pandemic. The reported challenges were mainly related to low demand due to the lockdown, delay in the arrival of expatriate workers, delay of goods and resources delivery, increased transportation fees, and an increase in inventory cost. Most SMEs enjoyed a range of services and privileges, including the exemption from the Omanization rate in the first of two years as well as giving priority in the entitlement of 10% of government tenders and purchases, resulting in more companies being created after 2020.

Analysis also reveals that integrating technology in business serves the interests of all stakeholders in society. For example, the use of technology such as Tarassud application allowed the Omani government to monitor and control the spread of COVID-19, while providing users with accurate data on the presence of the virus and levels of risk of infection in the surrounding areas. The case study of Tarassud indicates the usability and simplicity of technology and the readiness of society for its utilization, while illustrating the capacity of public health professionals, healthcare workers, and the public to adapt to the new technology. Using online telehealth as a response to the pandemic also confirms that the pandemic created an opportunity to develop technology-based solutions.

3 Building Digital Infrastructure

The experience of the pandemic underlines the need for building a strong digital infrastructure that supports business activities and stimulates economic growth. Building digital infrastructure can be done at two levels. At the national level, the government must make significant public investments in developing the public communication and internet infrastructure that includes the solutions and systems that facilitate essential society functions and services. This type of infrastructure covers areas such as information technology, smart grid, communication network, emerging wireless communication technologies for smart grid applications, and installation of the advanced networks using fiber optic and 5G networks. At the company level, digital infrastructure is the applications and technology used by the company to conduct its operations. Main components of digital infrastructure include email and instant message applications, marketing automation platforms, company website, accounting applications and payroll, software applications, and machinery programs. Digital infrastructure also covers data centers, data integration, cloud computing, computer networks, virtualization software, digital communication suites, and mobile telecom and broadband.

The experience of COVID-19 illustrates the important of the investment and development of digital infrastructure in the time of crisis (Bryce et al., 2022). Our analysis in this book shows that digital technology was not only useful for the survival of enterprises, but it was also the enabler that fostered e-business and e-commerce during the pandemic. Literature reveals that the upsurge in access to online shopping website during COVID-19 caused Chinese and American companies to capture the largest market shares in electronic commerce. Asia topped the first rank in terms of the volume of income generated from electronic commerce followed by America and Europe, and the largest rise in online sales was in the food sector, especially in China, Italy, and the USA. Our analysis also confirms that COVID-19 accelerated e-commerce growth and digital transform, which, in turn, created more business opportunities as people started to shift toward online payment methods due to the fear of disease transfer during the pandemic. Moreover, e-commerce also created opportunities for business whose activities were suspended during the imposition of lockdown and social distance precautions. Consumers shift to online shopping was also due to the lower prices. Data shows that global e-retail business recorded 22 billion monthly visits due to COVID-19. As a result, E-commerce increased by 57% in global electronic transactions during the first quarter of 2020, and Amazon profits shares doubled in the second quarter of the same year.

Our analysis also highlights some of the challenges and risks of electronic commerce, mainly the disruption in delivery and supply during the pandemic and fear of using online shopping methods in remote and rural areas in many developing countries. Concerns about the lack of protective and secure policy for electronic accounts caused many consumers to refuse using their cards for online payment. In some developing countries, e-commerce was out of reach due to inappropriate regulations and the lack of technology and infrastructure. Thus, the prospect of e-commerce depends on building a strong digital infrastructure, enhance internet quality, develop effective, rapid, and tested solutions to activate trade; link the merchant's account with local banks, which will facilitate payment through websites, and to develop awareness programs on the importance of e-commerce.

Another important sector where digital transformation was essential is logistics and supply chain. In fact, the pandemic caused unprecedented decline of international trade, supply chain, consumption, and demand, which, in turn, severely affected transport, logistics, and supply chain.

Many ports witnessed a decline in ship arrivals because of cancelation of cruise routes due to the pandemic, while oil tankers experienced the largest drop among cargo vessel types. In areas where digital infrastructure was underdeveloped, the recovery in trade flow was slow due to the inability of ports to balance between rising demand and limited cargo capacity supplies, resulting in a decrease in service reliability and an increase in freight costs. For the post-pandemic phase, our analysis stresses the importance of acceleration in the automation of production systems as well as having more efficient and less complex supply chain with new levels of resilience to business volatility in the face of crises and external shocks. It also reveals that the resilience of the global supply chain to shocks can be enhanced by increasing the diversification of inputs across countries and increasing the substitution of inputs among different countries. This study recommends utilizing technology, digitalization to enhance logistic, transportation sustainability, and resilience, addressing the high freight rates and set emergency response mechanism to mitigate the impact of high transportation cost to maintain food security.

Moreover, the pandemic triggered the worst crisis in the labor market, where a significant acceleration of automation changed the job market landscape. The use of technology forced many companies to reduce their workforce, causing serious ramification in the economy because of workers' layoff, wage reduction, labor income uncertainty, and reduced bargaining power that affected the demand side of the economy. Another change brought about by the pandemic was remote work and online learning that became a new norm. Digital transformation encouraged both the government and companies to introduce provisions of online learning opportunities for employees and encourage employees to seek online learning opportunities and develop skills that are essential for their operations. This endeavor has contributed directly and indirectly to increasing digital literacy among individuals and accelerated technological integration into life.

4 Fostering Creativity in the Business Environment

The analysis of this publication underlines the significance of creation and innovation in the business environment. The overarching argument in the discussion here is that the opportunity evaluation decisions and self-perceived creativity are related to e-entrepreneurial intentions. A study by Abdel Fattah et al. (see Chapter 4) finds that opportunity evaluation decisions and e-entrepreneurial intentions relationship is mediated by self-perceived creativity. It was found that opportunity evaluation decisions positively affect the e-entrepreneurial intention and self-perceived creativity, which, in turn, have positively affected e-entrepreneurial intention and meditate opportunity evaluation decisions and e-entrepreneurial intention relationship.

This study also highlights the critical role of creativity in formulating entrepreneurial goals, with opportunity evaluation decisions functioning as a stimulus for improved e-entrepreneurial intention. It indicates an association between opportunity evaluation decisions and e-entrepreneurial intentions, which is mediated by self-perceived creativity. For future research, the study suggests focusing of active entrepreneurs in other industries who started as hobbyists, adding elements to the current model like performance and profit development following business setup. Government is recommended to prioritize cultivating entrepreneurship's innovative spirit and cultural value to boost the number of students ready and able to start their enterprises.

Moreover, this study finds that creativity and entrepreneurial alertness are associated with crisis management. It also shows the importance of strategic vigilance system in achieving competitive advantage for institution by keeping pace with the accelerated changes and development, making the maximum use of opportunities, and avoiding negative results attendant. It points to the importance of supplying truthful information, continuous auditing, and maintaining complete archival information while considering accuracy as a factor for planning and responding to the crisis's events. In the context of the pandemic, developing risk management strategies proved to be a vital tool for institutions and companies to minimize the risk and avoid being trapped in a vicious circle of human and financial losses, economic damage, or the fear of crowding out.

Thus, this examination confirms that strategic vigilance can help support the planning process of SMEs, contribute to strategies formation and crystallization, and evaluating resulting objectives. The pandemic has affected some forerunner qualities in crisis management, in which the main qualities of initiative in crisis management is the capacity to restrain. Other forerunner qualities include supporting the component of positive reaction to the occasion, supporting creativity and innovation methodologies, and problem-solving and decision support.

5 Protection the Rights of Workforce

The pandemic experience provides a clear test case for the negative effects of COVID-19 on the workforce. When examining the effect of the pandemic on labor policy in Oman, Mishrif and Al Subaihi (see Chapter 11) found a negative effect of the pandemic on leave policies, health insurance, working hours, incentives and benefits, and training programs. They found that leave policy and incentive policy were not significantly affected by the pandemic, while the impact on health insurance was not significantly high, as, unlike before the pandemic, only few organizations and companies provided their staff with health insurance during the pandemic. Also, their results show that over 50% of participants reported that there were no changes in working hours, and 17% reported decreasing working hours without decreasing payment, while 13% reported a reduction in both working hours and payment. Lastly, the study found that COIVD-19 did not obstruct more than half of companies from providing their staff with training programs.

The study recommends that policymakers should work toward reforming the labor market, particularly those policies related to the welfare of the national workforce. Also, the government should enforce companies to have a flexible leave policy in case employees do not lose their salary or their leaves balance in undetermined situations. Finally, companies are recommended to modify the working hours policy to make it more flexible.

As for the expatriates in the Gulf countries, Indian workers experienced a dramatic change in their lives and work patterns. During lockdown, many Indian workers were recorded as not working or were forced to work for less than the slandered. This has severely affected their earnings; many migrant workers recorded a loss of wages that ranged between less than US$200 and US$500 per month, and some did not receive any salary and had to borrow money to make their monthly remittances at home. Employment opportunities for low-skilled and skilled employees in the GCC have been negatively impacted due to COIVD-19 restrictions, both high- and low-skilled emigrant employees strongly agree that recent and ongoing changes in domestic policy have jeopardized their employment prospects. Since emigrant workers make important contribution to economic development in the Gulf region, new policy measured should be formulated to minimize any negative effects on similar crises on the living, working, and earning patterns of expatriates working in the region.

6 Conclusion

The chapter provided some interesting remarks on the prospect of the business sector in post-pandemic. While stressing the huge negative effects of the pandemic on enterprises and institutions, this chapter also underlines the need to put in place a more sophisticated strategies and policy measure that could support the business sector in time of crises like the pandemic. It also identified four key factors and milestones that the business sector must seriously consider if enterprises are able to adapt to the changing dynamics of the markets, particularly in the time of crises. The resilience of the business sector depends on the ability of enterprises to integrate technology in business, building digital infrastructure, prompting digital transformation, and fostering creativity and innovation in the business environment. Finally, the prospect of business cannot be guaranteed by protecting the rights of workers, who are key factor in the production process and a critical component in the social fabric of society.

References

Bryce, C., Ring, P., Ashby, S., & Wardman, J. (2022). Resilience in the face of uncertainty: Early lessons from the COVID-19 pandemic. In J. Wardman & R. Lofstedt (Eds.), *COVID-19 Confronting a New World Risk*. Routledge. https://doi.org/10.4324/9781003316169

Song, L., & Zhou, Y. (2020). The COVID-19 pandemic and its impact on the global economy: What does it take to turn crisis into opportunity? *China and World Economy, 28*(4), 1–25. https://doi.org/10.1111/cwe.12349

Index

A. Mishrif (ed.), *Business Resilience and Market Adaptability*, The Political Economy of the Middle East,
https://doi.org/10.1007/978-981-97-2962-3

D

E

www.ingramcontent.com/pod-product-compliance
Ingram Content Group UK Ltd.
Pitfield, Milton Keynes, MK11 3LW, UK
UKHW021420091026
15624UKWH00010B/277
* 9 7 8 9 8 1 9 7 2 9 6 1 6 *